THE NEW

HUMAN

REVOLUTION

VOLUME 4

THE NEW HUMAN REVOLUTION VOLUME 4

DAISAKU IKEDA

ILLUSTRATIONS BY KENICHIRO UCHIDA

SGI-USA

Published by SGI-USA
525 Wilshire Boulevard,
Santa Monica, California 90401-1427

Complete Set   ISBN 0-915678-32-2
Volume 4   ISBN 0-915678-36-5

First edition: December 1996

Cover Design: Richard Turtletaub

Contents

Chapter 1: Spring Storm 7

Chapter 2: Triumph 67

Chapter 3: Fresh Leaves 131

Chapter 4: Rissho Ankoku 199

Chapter 5: Great Light 251

July - 1999

Dedicated To
you "young Lions"
    Susan & Dale

W-love
    Eelna & Mother.

Spring Storm

T O go among the people — from the human solidarity arising from this impassioned and enduring spirit unfolds a new page in history.

There is no greater force than the people, no foundation more solid. Nor is anything more fearsome than the people's cries for justice. When compared with the people, authority, riches and fame are as insubstantial as smoke.

Shin'ichi Yamamoto returned to Japan from his tour of Asian countries on February 14, 1961. Two days later, on February 16, he attended the inaugural meeting of Hojo Chapter held in Toyohashi City in Aichi Prefecture. The local members had thought that President Yamamoto might not attend the meeting, scheduled as it was so soon after his trip; so when Shin'ichi appeared at the Toyohashi Civic Hall, there was a storm of cheers and thunderous applause.

That night, Shin'ichi stressed the importance of conducting oneself with sound common sense.

"Buddhism constitutes the highest form of reason. Those of us who believe in this Buddhism should always strive to be courteous and circumspect in our behavior. When attending discussion meetings at someone's house, take care not to inconvenience the owners, who have so generously opened their homes. You mustn't take liberties or act as if you own the place.

"And when introducing others to Buddhism or giving guidance in faith, you must absolutely refrain from using coarse and abusive language or adopting a patronizing attitude. Rude and thoughtless words or actions can create great misunderstanding toward the Soka Gakkai. Unless we gain the reputation that Gakkai members are decent, well-mannered people, I don't think we can say that we are setting a proper example in faith."

Shin'ichi stated that the Gohonzon exists within the life of each individual and closed his speech, expressing the hope that all would unlock their inner "treasure towers" through faith and lead supremely happy lives.

His emphasis on common sense arose from his belief that by deepening their faith, people could perfect their character and develop outstanding wisdom and judgment — qualities that would win the trust and confidence of those around them. Another reason was that members in many parts of Japan were increasingly subject to incidents of ostracism and discrimination in their communities. Not a few of these could be traced to some small instance of careless speech or unseemly conduct by one or a few members, which had resulted in misunderstanding.

The real underlying cause of such ostracism and discrimination, however, was an emotional reaction arising from misunderstanding and prejudice toward the Soka Gakkai itself. Many of these incidents were incited by proponents of other religious groups who feared the Gakkai's dynamic efforts to awaken people to Nichiren Daishonin's Buddhism.

*S*INCE Shin'ichi's inauguration as president, the Gakkai's propagation efforts had surged ahead like a raging wave.

"Were it not for [devils arising], there would be no way of knowing that this is the true teaching" (MW-1, 145). Just as this Gosho passage states, it was natural that the Gakkai would encounter various kinds of persecution. Such trials were unavoidable; they would have to be endured.

Nevertheless, it would be extremely foolish if, through some thoughtless or unreasoned behavior, members were to cause misunderstanding toward the Gakkai and thus create needless friction within society. Buddhism, after all, is a teaching of the highest reason.

After the inaugural chapter meeting, Shin'ichi took time to chat with the local leaders. Congratulating them on the start of their new chapter, Shin'ichi said: "Your chapter's name, Hojo, means 'castle of abundance.' What a wonderful name it is! Please work together to build a castle that brims with abundant good fortune."

Shin'ichi then opened the floor to questions. Since he had just returned from overseas, many of the questions were about worldwide kosen-rufu. One youth, who appeared to be a student, asked: "If worldwide kosen-rufu is accomplished, then considering President Toda's advocacy of 'one-worldism,' will we see the formation of something like a global federation of nations?"

It was an exceedingly abstract question, but Shin'ichi replied with a warm smile: "I'll leave it to you to decide what's best in that regard! Please think about it long and hard. And please study diligently so that you will become accomplished enough even to take on the presidency of such a federation yourself!"

He added: "In striving for a great future, however, your daily struggles are crucial. You should consolidate your foundation where you are right now. Life is filled with changing circumstances. The Gakkai is also bound to encounter persecution in the future. But the important thing is never to retreat, never to run away, no matter what may happen. As long as you live, always take pride in being a Gakkai member. Be an active player committed to shouldering the responsibility for kosen-rufu, not just an idle spectator."

Shin'ichi was intent on establishing in Chubu a solid pillar for kosen-rufu rivaling that in Kansai. He therefore put his utmost energy into fostering the youth.

The following day, February 17, Shin'ichi went to the head temple. The purpose of his visit was twofold: to hold briefings with the priesthood on future construction plans at the head temple and to visit Toda's grave to report on his return from overseas.

Standing before his mentor's tomb, Shin'ichi silently related that the door to Asian kosen-rufu had been opened. He renewed his vow to continue upon the path of oneness of mentor and disciple.

*R*ETURNING to Tokyo after visiting the head temple, Shin'ichi was scheduled to depart almost immediately for the Tohoku region to attend inaugural meetings of six new chapters. However, the mound of paperwork that had piled up while he was away overseas now urgently required his attention. Unavoidably, he decided to ask the general director and some other top leaders to attend the joint inaugural meeting for Aizu and Taira chapters on the 18th, while he would attend a kickoff meeting for Semboku and Ishinomaki chapters on the 19th.

But it cut his heart like a knife to think how disappointed the members in Aizu and Taira, both cities in Fukushima Prefecture, would be when he did not attend.

More than those members he had the opportunity to meet, Shin'ichi was always thinking about those he could not meet; more than those who spoke joyfully about receiving benefit, he was concerned for those still burdened by suffering.

Shin'ichi left for Sendai in Miyagi Prefecture on the 19th according to schedule. As the train made its way through Fukushima Prefecture, he chanted daimoku silently to express his joy at the new start Fukushima had made the day before with the establishment of Aizu and Taira chapters.

The joint inaugural meeting of Semboku and Ishinomaki chapters got under way at the Sendai Civic Hall at 6:00 P.M. Miyagi Prefecture was home to Sendai Chapter, the first regional chapter to be established after Josei Toda's inauguration as second president. Now, two additional chapters would be formed.

The hall was awash with joy and excitement. Shin'ichi caught sight of the Ishinomaki chapter chief, Yasuji Yoshinari, among the leaders on the stage. Noticing that the chapter chief was moving his lips as if in a fervent whisper, Shin'ichi surmised he was chanting under his breath.

Yasuji, who had a sincere and honest character, was not very good at speaking in public. Whenever he had to speak in front of a group of people, he would become very nervous, and he was probably doubly nervous this evening because he was scheduled to deliver his determination as chapter chief. When Shin'ichi took his place on the stage, he caught Yoshinari's eye and smiled at him reassuringly. Yoshinari smiled back, some of the tension appearing to leave him.

Yasuji Yoshinari was a pioneer of kosen-rufu in Ishinomaki. Back in 1942, during the war, his eldest brother, Taizo, who was living in Tokyo at the time, had taken faith in Nichiren Daishonin's Buddhism after attending a discussion meeting where the first Soka Gakkai president, Tsunesaburo Makiguchi, was present. Yasuji, the third of six sons, had started to practice in 1943, the following year, at his brother's persuasion. Two of his younger brothers embraced the Daishonin's Buddhism a short time later.

Right after that, the militarist government began to persecute the Soka Gakkai in earnest. Starting with President Makiguchi and Josei Toda, who was then the general director, all of the organization's top leaders were rounded up and thrown into prison.

Even in such forbiddingly bleak times, the brothers' faith did not waver.

Though all were quiet, mild-mannered men, the Yoshinari brothers had squarely inherited the tenacious Tohoku spirit in that once they had decided on a course of action, they refused to retreat a single step.

After the war, the flames of their faith burned even brighter.

WHEN Sendai Chapter was formed after the war, the Yoshinari brothers devoted themselves earnestly on the forefront of kosen-rufu activities.

After seeking personal guidance from Josei Toda, Taizo, the eldest brother, decided to take vows as a priest;

he became the first Nichiren Shoshu priest to come from the Soka Gakkai membership.

In the fall of 1960, the year Shin'ichi became president, the third youngest brother, Nobumasa, joined the priesthood, too. Later, the youngest brother, who had joined the Gakkai after the war, also became a priest. In a rigidly authoritarian priesthood riddled with corruption, all three brothers devoted themselves to protecting the Gakkai and fighting courageously to uphold the integrity of the true teachings of Nichiren Daishonin.

The time had come for Ishinomaki Chapter Chief Yasuji Yoshinari to express his resolution at the inaugural chapter meeting.

"Everyone, I've made a determination. I will build this chapter into a king of propagation. I will work to serve you with all my might. Please fight together with me. And let's share both our tears and the joys of receiving great benefit!"

His words were very simple, but it was a determination that clearly revealed his warm character and great conviction. The participants responded with a loud burst of applause.

At this meeting, too, Shin'ichi spoke about the importance of having common sense, citing the principle that "faith manifests itself in daily life" and "Buddhism manifests itself in society."

"Ultimately, we practice Buddhism so that we can manifest our faith in daily life. It is not an empty theory, nor is it simply for cultivating our minds. Buddhism is a teaching for daily life — this was the profound perspective of Mr. Makiguchi and Mr. Toda. Buddhism is a fundamental teaching for creating the greatest value in living.

"Nichiren Daishonin teaches, 'All phenomena in the universe are manifestations of the Buddhist Law' (*Gosho*

Zenshu, p. 564). In contemporary terms, we express this as 'faith manifests itself in daily life.' That being so, our actions, as members of society and as human beings, have to be acceptable to others. Of vital importance here is common sense. If you behave in an irresponsible or unseemly manner and are criticized by others, if you operate under the delusion that you can do anything and behave any way you like just because you are practicing faith, then all you are doing is denigrating the Law.

"Just as birds and fish proceed along their own instinctive paths, human beings, too, follow a path. The supreme path for human beings is Buddhism. Nichiren Daishonin writes, 'The real meaning of the Lord Shakyamuni Buddha's appearance in this world lay in his behavior as a human being' (MW-2 [2ND ED.], 240). The Buddha's enlightenment, too, is ultimately manifested in his actions and behavior in the context of the realities of daily living. Another name by which the Buddha is known is 'hero of the world' (LS2, 24). Practitioners of the Buddhist Law must therefore strive to be individuals of outstanding character and unparalleled common sense in society."

SHIN'ICHI spoke further on the importance of common sense, using examples that were close to the members' lives: "In the event of the funeral of a friend or relative, some of you may not wish to attend if the services accord with another religion. But not to attend would be socially inappropriate.

"We attend a funeral not to practice another religion but to pay our respects, as human beings, to our deceased friend or relative and to pray for that person's eternal happiness. Irrespective of the kind of funeral service, our going there to chant daimoku in our hearts for the deceased is the greatest possible offering we can make. In all cases, if we have strong faith and are resolved to chant daimoku, then we can not only send our daimoku to the deceased but also cause all those around us to form a connection with the Daishonin's Buddhism by our presence.

"Similarly, let's not become so carried away in our enthusiasm to introduce others to this practice that we end up visiting their homes late at night, just when they might be ready to go to bed, and then keep them up until 11:00 or midnight engaged in discussion. That would be irresponsible and thoughtless. Even with the best of intentions, as far as the other person is concerned, you'd be nothing but a nuisance. Not realizing this, however, some people may wonder in bewilderment, 'Why can't that person sincerely try this practice?' It's unreasonable to expect others to embrace faith under such circumstances. Of course, I'm sure there's no one like that here tonight."

Laughter rang throughout the hall. His words obviously struck a chord among quite a few. Some looked embarrassed.

"As Buddhists, it's natural that we care about the happiness of those we wish to introduce to the practice, but our actions must always be based on common sense. We have to use wisdom. If we behave irrationally, then no matter how wonderful what we have to say may be, we won't truly touch or convince others. Though logic may tell them that what we are saying is right, their dislike for the Soka Gakkai will overshadow this. This is human nature.

"That's why it's so important that we each hone our wisdom and let our character shine, becoming people of rich common sense who will be respected by all."

With this, Shin'ichi concluded. There was much more he wanted to say, but, concerned for those who had traveled long distances to attend, he cut his speech short.

Besides those who filled the main hall, members had also gathered in three small conference rooms within the complex. Shin'ichi now went around to each room, wanting to meet and encourage them, too, even if only briefly.

THE people in the other meeting rooms had heard Shin'ichi speak only via speakers connected to the P.A. system in the main auditorium. Shin'ichi didn't want them to feel left out. When he arrived at each room, he greeted everyone with a smile: "Thank you for attending tonight despite the cold weather. Take care not to catch cold, and please have a safe trip home."

There was a stir of excitement at Shin'ichi's unexpected appearance.

"To the women's division members, I ask you all to shine beautifully with rich individuality in the radiant light of the Mystic Law, to always be gentle and warm to your husbands and children, and to always strive pureheartedly in faith. I ask, however, that you fight resolutely against erroneous teachings.

"But I want you to be absolutely sure not to get these two different stances confused. Because if you are hard on your husbands and children," Shin'ichi said humorously, "behaving like angry demons, or if you begin to practice faith in an arbitrary way, then not only you but those around you will become miserable as well!"

The audience roared with laughter.

"As for the men, please work hard so that you can give your wives lives of comfort. Strive to develop a state of life where you can sometimes give them a little extra money and say, 'Here, with this, why don't you go and spread this Buddhism in India for awhile' or 'Go ahead and encourage the members in America.'

"And one more thing for the men: please try to do gongyo of your own volition, without your wives having to tell you to do so."

There was another burst of laughter.

"In any event, please embrace the Gohonzon throughout your lives, dedicating yourselves to the cause of kosen-rufu along with the Gakkai. That's all I want to say. If you remember that, then you can forget the rest. The very best to you all!"

Some of the members from the northern part of the prefecture had traveled three or four hours by bus to attend the meeting. If time had permitted, Shin'ichi would have liked to shake the hands of all the members present and send them off with a personal word of encouragement.

Each participant was no doubt extremely heartened to be here surrounded by fellow members. Once back home, many were the sole Gakkai members in their villages. Some had to bear the full brunt of anti-Gakkai criticism alone in an atmosphere of deeply rooted attachments to old ways and local religious traditions.

When Shin'ichi thought of the harsh circumstances many of them faced, he wanted at the very least to give them warm and cheerful encouragement and to imbue them with confidence and hope.

He went out to the bus parking lot. Stars twinkled in the cold night sky as Shin'ichi silently cheered the members on: "Do your best! Don't give up!"

He waved goodbye, filled with a deep love for these children of the Buddha.

THE next day, February 20, Shin'ichi Yamamoto went to Hachinohe in Aomori Prefecture to attend an inaugural meeting for the newly formed Hachinohe Chapter.

The day was blessed with clear skies, sunlight dancing on the pristine snow. But for Shin'ichi, who had recently returned from the warm climes of Southeast Asia, the cold of this northern region seemed biting. His heart, however, was ablaze with happy anticipation at the thought of meeting many of his dear comrades in faith.

That day's venue, the Hachinohe Civic Hall, was located on what was once the site of Hachinohe Castle. When Shin'ichi arrived at the hall that evening, event staff from the youth division were cheerfully engaged in directing and ushering members into the hall.

"Thank you for coming. Please watch your step," he heard a voice say in slightly shaky Japanese.

Looking over, he saw several members who appeared to be Americans. Each wore a yellow event staff armband and, though large in build, moved with grace and agility.

Shin'ichi beamed with delight.

Hachinohe Chapter encompassed an area that included the city of Misawa, the site of a U.S. Air Force base. As a result, Americans had begun to join; the chapter now had about fifty American members.

"Oh! Thank you very much," Shin'ichi said in strained English, adding in Japanese, "I deeply appreciate your efforts."

He raised his hand to his forehead in a salute and then extended a firm handshake. As he shook each hand, the other party returned his grasp even more firmly.

These young men were precious treasures of the Soka Gakkai; after finishing their tour of military duty and returning to the United States, they would become pioneers of kosen-rufu in that country. Though it was but a momentary encounter, Shin'ichi wanted to plant something lasting in the life of each youth. His hand hurt a bit and was red and swollen after the series of powerful handshakes, but in each had flowed a warm exchange of the heart.

At the inaugural gathering attended by more than 4,000 members, Shin'ichi declared that the Gakkai was resolutely fighting for the happiness of ordinary individuals and for the peace of humankind and was thus the most respectable of organizations. He then expressed his hopes for the valiant efforts of his fellow Hachinohe members.

After the meeting, he chatted with the chapter leaders, asking how their families were doing. The new chapter women's division chief, Aiko Kasayama, offered apologetically, "My husband is away on business, so he couldn't attend today."

Since the chapter was centered in Hachinohe, and Kasayama lived in Towada, some distance away, it was quite probable that her new responsibility would impose a considerable burden. Shin'ichi felt he would like to meet her husband to explain the situation to him and gain his thorough understanding and support.

*T*HE next morning, Aiko Kasayama and some other chapter leaders came to visit Shin'ichi at the inn where he was staying. When Kasayama saw Shin'ichi, she said, "Actually, it's about my husband...."

Though her husband did gongyo and was supportive of his wife's activities, he almost never attended Gakkai meetings, mainly because of his busy work schedule.

Once, a local men's division leader had said to her: "Your husband does not participate in activities. We call that being a 'solitary bodhisattva.' That just won't do."

"Solitary bodhisattvas" refers to those bodhisattvas who come alone, without followers, when the Bodhisattvas of the Earth make their appearance in the "Emerging from the Earth" chapter of the Lotus Sutra (LS15, 212). Though they are "alone," they are still Bodhisattvas of the Earth. Nevertheless, the leader's words kept echoing in Kasayama's mind, leaving her with the lingering feeling that her husband could not become happy.

"Do you think it's wrong for my husband to be a 'solitary bodhisattva'?" Kasayama nervously asked Shin'ichi.

Shin'ichi smiled and replied: "There's no need to worry. Please put your mind at ease. Your husband is supporting you in your Gakkai activities and doing gongyo every day. He's a fine Bodhisattva of the Earth. He'll definitely participate in activities some day. Please convey my best regards to your husband and my apologies for the inconvenience he'll be caused by your taking on new leadership responsibilities."

Kasayama looked relieved, some color now returning to her face.

Sometimes, just a few words can cause a person worry or hurt. Similarly, just a few words can reassure or inspire courage. For this reason, the words we choose are important. To speak thoughtfully, attentive to the words we use, attests to the depth of our consideration.

The true emissaries of the Buddha are those who continue to lavish their friends with words of hope, words of encouragement, inspiration and truth, while leading them to develop profound faith.

Kasayama wanted to receive much more guidance from Shin'ichi on how to prepare herself for her new responsibility as chapter women's division chief.

"I have a request. Would you mind if we accompanied you to Akita?" Shin'ichi was to leave shortly for Odate City in neighboring Akita Prefecture to attend the inaugural meeting of Towada Chapter.

"I'd really like to share more guidance with you on a number of things, but your responsibilities to your families are important, too, so please go on home."

"It's all right, we've already gotten their consent. Please let us come with you."

"OK, then, everyone," Shin'ichi responded, "Let's go!"

Kasayama smiled brightly.

*S*HIN'ICHI made his way to Odate along with several leaders of Hachinohe Chapter. When they got off the train at Aomori Station to transfer to the Ou Main Line, members from the local Aomori Chapter were waiting to greet them.

Catching sight of Shin'ichi, Aomori Chapter Chief Tadashi Kaneki came rushing over. Hachinohe Chapter had been formed when Aomori Chapter divided.

"Congratulations on the formation of Hachinohe Chapter," Shin'ichi said. "Aomori Prefecture will be even stronger now, won't it?"

With one voice, Kaneki and the other members of Aomori Chapter cheerfully agreed.

Shin'ichi was delighted at their solidarity. He recalled the last time he had visited Aomori. That had been on November 3, 1958, when he was still Soka Gakkai general administrator. The purpose of his visit had been to prepare to establish a chapter there. He had first interviewed potential leaders for the young men's and young women's divisions. The interviews had been held at Mr. Kaneki's home.

At that time, Shin'ichi had said: "We will soon be establishing Aomori Chapter. I'd like you to open the door to a new phase of kosen-rufu through your efforts. The Chinese characters that make up the name *Aomori* also appear in the Japanese words for *youth* and *forest*. The youth are the heart of Aomori, which is a growing forest of outstanding capable people. I am convinced that Aomori is the place where youth with fighting spirit will stand up as front-runners for the rest of the world."

After the leadership interviews, Shin'ichi had attended a meeting to discuss details of the chapter's formation.

The establishment of Aomori Chapter brought together various Soka Gakkai groups in Aomori Prefecture that had belonged to many different chapters around

Japan. It was tentatively decided that Tadashi Kaneki would serve as chapter chief, and his wife, Kiyo, as chapter women's division chief. It was also agreed to divide the chapter into nine districts.

Diversity was the word that best described Aomori Prefecture. From feudal times, it had been divided between the two powerful domains of Tsugaru and Nambu, long regarded as rivals and archenemies. In the period of warlord Toyotomi Hideyoshi's rise to prominence, a military commander of Nambu lineage who owned a fief in the Tsugaru domain won his independence and established the Nambu domain. The inhabitants of the newly established Nambu domain nurtured a sense of rivalry with those in their old realm, traces of which had continued to the present.

Competition in a positive form can give impetus for growth. But emotional rivalry can only lead to the destruction of the organization for kosen-rufu. Consequently, the future development of activities in Aomori depended entirely on the success of the new Aomori Chapter in uniting members from different parts of Aomori into one cohesive force, and on whether they could inspire and challenge one another in a positive way.

After Shin'ichi unofficially announced the new leaders of the chapter, he said: "You all look as if you're tired from sitting so long in this meeting, so I'd like to ask Mr. Kaneki and the future district chiefs to stand up and come to the front."

TADASHI Kaneki and the nine other men filed down to the front of the room. Shin'ichi then said: "Okay. Now I'd like you to form a circle around Mr. Kaneki and put your arms on the shoulder of the person standing next to you."

Looking perplexed, they all moved to stand in a circle with Kaneki in the center.

The other members in the room watched expectantly, their eyes shining, wondering what was about to happen.

"Is this what you mean?" one of the men in the circle ventured, checking to see if they had followed his instructions correctly.

"Yes, that's fine. Please, everyone, I'd like you always to remember this picture. It's an example of the unity that Aomori Chapter should aim for. If the nine district leaders firmly unite around the chapter chief, no one can disrupt your solidarity. However, if this circle is broken and the nine district leaders become disconnected and out of sync with one another, confusion and disorder will soon result. Unity is strength."

Kaneki and the others at last began to understand Shin'ichi's intent in having them come up and stand together in a circle.

"Those of you who will become district leaders, please do your utmost to support and protect the chapter leader. And Mr. Kaneki, as chapter leader, please do everything in your power to assist the district leaders and work for the happiness of all the members in the chapter. If you protect the members, you in turn will be protected. This is the Buddhist law of cause and effect.

"The Soka Gakkai is an organization that embraces an objective that is the Buddha's will and mandate. If you let emotionalism cause you to quarrel and become divided, disrupting the harmonious unity of the organization as a result, your offense would be extremely grave. Therefore, no matter what may happen in the future, please never forget this circle and, by basing yourselves on faith and placing unity first, make Aomori the warmest and most harmonious chapter in all Japan."

The members expressed their hearty approval.

Intellectually, everyone present knew that unity was important, but Shin'ichi wanted them to engrave this truth deeply in their lives.

That same evening, a guidance meeting for leaders in Aomori Prefecture was held at the city's public hall. Here, too, Shin'ichi had called on the members to advance harmoniously, with unity as their number one priority, as disciples of the great leader of kosen-rufu, Josei Toda.

Aomori Chapter's establishment was announced officially a few days later at the Nineteenth Soka Gakkai General Meeting on November 9, 1958. But the real starting point of the chapter had been the leaders' guidance meeting with Shin'ichi on November 3.

The Aomori members' joy at forming their own chapter created an explosive surge in membership. After only one year, Aomori Chapter had doubled its original size — jumping from an initial membership of 7,500 households to 15,000 households. It was this phenomenal development that led to the creation of Hachinohe Chapter.

*A*FTER talking with Aomori Chapter members, Shin'ichi Yamamoto left for Odate in Akita Prefecture. The snow that had been falling as the train sped across the white-blanketed landscape stopped after awhile, and a ray of sunlight peeked through an opening in the clouds, resembling a silvery ladder reaching down from the heavens.

When Shin'ichi arrived at Odate Station, he was greeted by Tatsuo Shimazu, chapter chief of the new Towada Chapter, and a couple of other local leaders. They had come by car to drive him directly to the chapter inaugural meeting, where members from the northern part of Akita Prefecture were waiting to see him. But traffic along the way was extremely heavy. As the temperature rose, the snow on the road began to melt; ruts began to form and traffic slowed to a crawl.

Inside the car, Shin'ichi asked Shimazu, "How have you been feeling since the accident?"

"Oh, I've completely recovered. I'm fit as a fiddle, as you can see."

"I'm very glad to hear that."

Shimazu had joined the Soka Gakkai in 1951, after which he had exerted himself as a pioneer in the Akita area. Then, early one October morning in 1956, he suddenly passed out from anemia and fell headlong from the low veranda around his house into the garden outside. Hearing the noise, his family rushed out to find him lying on the ground, flat on his back. He was taken to the hospital, where his injuries were found to be serious — compressed fractures to the vertebrae in his neck, thorax and lower back. The surgeon shook his head and announced there was little hope for a complete recovery. When Shin'ichi heard this news, he was extremely concerned.

But Shimazu disproved the doctor's prognosis. Wanting to live to fulfill his mission for kosen-rufu, he was powerfully determined. He recovered enough to leave the hospital in just three months. Filled with joy at his progress and with deep appreciation for the Gohonzon, he devoted himself to sharing the Daishonin's Buddhism.

Forced to wear a rigid corset from the chin down, he would laugh and say, "It's just like wearing a suit of armor!" All the while, he poured his passion and energy into spreading the Law. Six months after the accident, he returned to work. Immediately after that, in May 1957, Shin'ichi, then youth division general chief of staff, visited him.

The morning after attending the general meeting of Akita Chapter, Shin'ichi had gone to see Lake Towada with Shimazu and several others. The bus they rode on wound its way up the mountain road, the sunlight shimmering brightly on the fresh green foliage all around them.

From the lookout at the top of Hakka Pass, Shin'ichi gazed down for the first time on Lake Towada. The fresh greenery of the surrounding mountain slopes was reflected vividly on the lake's pristine blue surface.

At that time, Shin'ichi had told the miraculously restored pioneer: "Mr. Shimazu, I'm glad to see you doing so well. You've triumphed over a major portion of negative karma."

"YES, even the doctor was surprised," Tatsuo Shimazu said proudly. "Through this experience, I've really come to feel from the bottom of my heart how great this faith is."

Shin'ichi nodded and said quietly: "That's because you've been sincerely striving to live for the cause of kosen-rufu. The power to transform negative karma comes from our strong inner resolve and practice to accomplish kosen-rufu. From such commitment and dedicated effort springs the pure, strong, majestic state of life of a Bodhisattva of the Earth." Shin'ichi looked down at the lake and then back at Shimazu.

"The water of this lake is crystal clear. But the world today is polluted. It is ruled by egoism and self-interest. To accomplish kosen-rufu means to purify this world. Mr. Shimazu, I hope you will continue to persevere with faith as pure as Lake Towada."

These words had touched Tatsuo Shimazu's heart. He was a stubborn man by nature, but his faith was pure. And since that exchange with Shin'ichi, he had striven with even greater purity. Today, he would leap once again to the forefront of the struggle to spread the Law as the new chief of Towada Chapter.

Looking at Shimazu — the man who had arisen from the brink of death like a phoenix — as they now headed for the Towada Chapter inaugural meeting, and seeing him in such vibrant good health, Shin'ichi was filled with a deep sense of joy.

Their car continued at a snail's pace. Finally, when they were almost there, the car's wheels wedged in a rut in the snowy road and could move no further. Frantic, the driver gunned the engine but to no avail; the wheels just spun in place. Shin'ichi and the others got out to push. A youth division event staff member saw them and came rushing over to help.

"Push!" They strained forward with all of their might.

Shin'ichi had not been wearing boots, so his trouser legs were soaked and his shoes were full of icy water. By the time they freed the car, it was almost time for the meeting to begin. Shin'ichi made a dash for the entrance.

The meeting began and soon it was time for Shin'ichi, as Soka Gakkai president, to speak. "Though I'm supposed to give a speech," he began, "I really can't say anything more than to ask all of you, Soka Gakkai members, to uphold the Gohonzon and become happy."

He continued in a frank and open way: "Your chapter chief, Mr. Shimazu, is a prime example of how to do this. He at one point faced death. Nevertheless, he has become as energetic and healthy as you see him here, and he has now taken on a position of responsibility to serve and care for all of you. This is an irrefutable fact. Please make him your model and persevere in faith, deeply confident of the Gohonzon's absolute beneficial power."

*A*S Shin'ichi spoke about Tatsuo Shimazu's experience, the chapter chief rose and bowed deeply to the audience, who responded with warm applause.

Those who have profoundly experienced the power of faith are strong. Their very presence is more convincing than a million words. Hardship, therefore, is a priceless treasure for human beings.

As Shin'ichi was about to continue, several hundred participants rose from their seats to leave, looking regretful that they could not stay. These were people from areas some distance away who had to leave early to make their trains. Mr. Shimazu had earlier informed Shin'ichi of their situation.

As they made their way from their seats, careful not to disturb those around them, Shin'ichi addressed them over the microphone: "I guess it's time for you to catch your train. Thank you very much for traveling so far to attend today's meeting. Please take care and return home safely. And please give my best regards to your families. I'm praying for your great success. Everyone, let's give them a big round of applause." Shin'ichi started clapping and the others joined in until the auditorium rang with applause. The departing members left the hall, waving cheerfully, bowing or shaking hands with their comrades remaining behind.

Shin'ichi knew how disappointing it could feel to have to leave an important meeting halfway through. He didn't want to let these people go home feeling that way.

Sending people off with a few encouraging words lightens their hearts and lets them start fresh, in high spirits. It may seem like a small thing, but such warm consideration is an important duty of leaders.

A genial camaraderie pervaded the hall as Shin'ichi resumed his speech, addressing the question of what was the most important philosophical foundation, or "backbone," a person could have. He went on to stress that Nichiren Daishonin's Buddhism is the greatest foundation for realizing world peace and human happiness.

"The stage for our activities is the entire world. As emissaries of the Buddha, let's proudly travel the globe to open the way to great human happiness."

Everyone felt hopeful. For those struggling quietly with earnest dedication in isolated, tradition-bound mountain villages, Shin'ichi's words swept away the heavy winter clouds and brought them rays of spring sunshine.

The inaugural chapter meeting ended in an atmosphere of great joy.

Shin'ichi's feet, still damp from their earlier soaking, now felt completely frozen. But there was no time to dry out his shoes. Immediately after the chapter meeting, he set off to meet with local district leaders. Here, too, he put all of his energy into encouraging the members.

*F*OLLOWING his guidance trip to the Tohoku region, Shin'ichi returned to Tokyo. There he spent a number of hectic days dealing with the work that had piled up in his absence.

The Soka Gakkai Headquarters Leaders Meeting for February was held on the 25th at the Tokyo Metropolitan Gymnasium. The hall surged with excitement as participants heard reports of President Yamamoto's guidance trip to neighboring Asian countries.

During that meeting, Shin'ichi talked about the study department examination scheduled for early March:

"With the exam not far off, I'm sure you are hard at work mentally and physically. What I'd like to stress today is that those who pass the exams should not act superior, and those who do not pass should not lose confidence or look down on themselves.

"Soka Gakkai study exams are held as a form of encouragement and as a way for us to mark our progress in our lifelong study of Nichiren Daishonin's great philosophy. So, even if you should pass the exam, if you let it go to your head and begin to look down on others, you will have failed as people of faith. On the other hand, if you do not pass, you can use that as a spur to challenge yourselves more earnestly in Buddhist study and thereby ultimately win a passing grade as people of faith, something far more important than simply passing the exam.

"In addition, I hope you will engrave the Gosho deeply in your hearts and develop faith that is truly firm and strong so that you will remain undaunted by any obstacle that might assail you."

Study exams were held on Sunday, March 5, at more than 180 sites in 125 cities nationwide. At 9:00 A.M., exams were held for study department teachers who wished to advance to the next level of assistant professor and for assistant instructors who wished to become teachers. Then at 2:00 P.M., the entrance exam was held for those seeking to become members of the study department for the first time.

That day, more than 110 thousand people took study department exams around Japan. It was roughly 3.3 times the number that had taken the last exams, in 1959, less than two years earlier.

This, too, showed the Soka Gakkai's phenomenal growth since Shin'ichi had become its president.

Among those taking the exams were housewives, company presidents, students and teachers. They were of all ages, from teenagers to senior citizens. Making use of the little spare time they had from their work commitments or school studies — not to mention Gakkai activities — all of them had earnestly studied the Gosho, striving to deepen their understanding of the profound teachings and philosophy of the Daishonin's Buddhism. From many parts of the country, there were even stories of people who had once been illiterate learning to read and write as a result of such tenacious efforts.

The building of a new era and society begins when people have a solid philosophy of life and a clear awareness of their personal mission. The Soka Gakkai's study program represented an unprecedented philosophical and educational movement among the common people.

*T*HE study exams were over. That evening at the Soka Gakkai Headquarters, Shin'ichi Yamamoto spotted Study Department Chief Chuhei Yamadaira and asked, "Is everything going smoothly with the grading of tests around the country?"

"Yes, very smoothly," Yamadaira affirmed.

Shin'ichi said softly: "Those who took the exams worked very hard. I'd like to give them all a passing grade."

"We can't do that!" Yamadaira shot back.

Shin'ichi couldn't help grinning at the study chief's emphatic response.

"I know that, of course; it's an exam, after all. I was just voicing my personal sentiment.

"But just think how difficult it is for, say, a women's division member who is busy as a mother and a homemaker. Just doing Gakkai activities is challenging enough, not to mention finding time to study the Gosho. With crying children and having to clean the house and prepare meals, it's almost impossible for her to find time to study quietly even if she wants to. It's like trying to open the Gosho on a battlefield!

"Though it may be natural to challenge ourselves in our Buddhist practice, I don't want people who've studied with all their might in far-from-favorable circumstances to be discouraged and disheartened because of their exam results. Those who pass are fine; we don't have to worry about them. My thoughts are constantly with those who don't pass and what we can do to encourage them, to fill them with hope."

Yamadaira was moved. He realized that while he had been wrapped up solely in collating the test results,

President Yamamoto was focused on the members, the individuals behind the statistics.

The exam grading began on the evening of March 5 and lasted through March 8. Those who passed the written exams to advance to a higher study level then had to undergo an oral exam.

Shin'ichi was at the Soka Gakkai Kansai Headquarters when he reviewed a March 8 report containing the written exam results. The average score had risen over that of previous exams. Since becoming president, he had consistently stressed the importance of Buddhist study. Now his appeals had come to bear substantial fruit.

At this time, incidentally, Shin'ichi was in the midst of an intense struggle to defend himself from the vicious attacks of authority. The trial arising from the Osaka Incident was now approaching a crucial stage.

The Osaka Incident began with two separate infringements of Japan's election law back in April 1957. The first was a vote-buying incident perpetrated by a small group of Gakkai members from Tokyo who had traveled to Osaka to assist the campaign of a Gakkai-sponsored candidate in the Osaka District by-election for the House of Councilors (Upper House of the Japanese Diet). The second was the arrest of several overzealous Gakkai members for door-to-door solicitation of votes.

Because Shin'ichi held overall responsibility for the election campaign, suspicion fell on him as the ringleader behind these incidents. He was arrested on July 3, 1957, and held in police custody for fifteen days. Takeo Konishi, then Soka Gakkai general director, had also been arrested after those directly responsible for the vote-buying made statements to the prosecutors while in custody implying that they had acted on Konishi's authorization.

*A*UTHORITIES viewed this incident, in which a few Gakkai members had been caught violating the election law, as an ideal opportunity to try to crush the growing influence of the Soka Gakkai, which had become a powerful new force in society.

During their interrogations, prosecutors apparently began to realize that Shin'ichi Yamamoto was not involved in the election law violations. Determined to present the incident as an organized violation carried out at Shin'ichi's directive, the prosecutors threatened to arrest President Josei Toda if Shin'ichi refused to admit to the crime.

Toda, who died nine months later in April, was already ailing physically. Shin'ichi feared that if his mentor was arrested, it would prove fatal. After much heart-wrenching deliberation, he decided to take all the blame himself for the time being, and then prove the truth in a court of law.

The trial began on October 18, 1957.

The indictment against Shin'ichi did not include charges of involvement in the vote-buying incident, only in the door-to-door vote soliciting.

At the end of February 1961, judgment had been handed down against the former general director, Konishi, and the Gakkai members implicated in the vote-buying. As was only fair, Konishi was acquitted.

The prosecutors did not appeal the decision, but they were now even more determined to secure a guilty verdict against the Soka Gakkai president, Shin'ichi Yamamoto, at all costs.

Further hearings in the case against Shin'ichi were held on March 6, 7 and 8, 1961, at the Osaka District Court. During this period, Shin'ichi met with the team of attorneys representing him. At that time, one of the lawyers said to him: "Mr. Yamamoto, the outlook is very grim. The other defendants' statements to both the police and the prosecution assert that they acted on your direction. In addition, you yourself made a statement to the prosecution confirming this. We'll do our best, but I think you should prepare yourself for a guilty verdict."

Looking indignant, Shin'ichi said: "Why must someone who is innocent be convicted of a crime? Isn't it the job of a lawyer to prove the truth and win exoneration for those wrongfully indicted?"

"Yes, that's so," one lawyer admitted. "But the prosecutors have very cleverly built a pile of testimony against us. It won't be easy to overturn it."

"I do not fear being declared guilty for myself. But I do fear that justice and human rights will be endangered if we permit government authorities, represented by the prosecution, to get away with such abuses of power. That's why I'll fight. I'm absolutely determined to win an acquittal."

The lawyers' comments had left Shin'ichi feeling deserted and alone.

*T*HE trial weighed heavily on Shin'ichi's mind. If worst came to worst, he — the Soka Gakkai's president — might be convicted and sent to prison for a crime he didn't commit. Even his lawyers had told him to be prepared for such an outcome. It pained him unbearably to think how grieved and saddened the members would be if this were to happen.

"Still," he thought, "when viewed in terms of the long journey we have yet to travel to accomplish kosen-rufu, these troubles are trifling. They are like a spring storm. The future is bound to hold unimaginably great persecutions."

The passionate life force arising from his unwavering determination to realize kosen-rufu brushed aside these hardships and stoked the flame of his fighting spirit to encourage his beloved fellow members.

While in Osaka, on the evening of March 7, Shin'ichi attended both the Kansai young men's division leaders meeting at the Chuo Civic Hall in Nakanoshima and the Kansai young women's division leaders meeting at the Otemae Civic Center. The following evening, he attended a joint leaders meeting of Kansai's three general chapters at the Osaka Metropolitan Central Gymnasium. At this meeting, the Kansai Soka Gakkai Brass Band and Fife and Drum Corps gave their first performances at an official gathering.

It was already quite late into the meeting, after a number of speeches by local leaders, when Shin'ichi finally rose to the microphone.

"Rather than talk on some difficult topic today, I'd like to lead you all in a song!"

These were his beloved Kansai members, who had fought alongside him and shared with him both joy and sorrow. It was a relationship that did not require many words. Sometimes a simple gesture could be more encouraging than all the words in the world.

"Since this year is the Year of Dynamic Advancement, let's sing the 'Song of Dynamic Advancement.'"

He brought out a Japanese folding fan, and in rhythm with the rousing strains of the Brass Band and Fife and Drum Corps, he led the song with the artistry of a powerfully choreographed dance; in their dignity and graceful fluidity, his movements resembled an eagle soaring with outstretched wings.

All the while, he called out in his heart, "Fight on, Kansai!"

The participants clapped in rhythm to the music as they sang at the top of their voices. When they had finished, the entire auditorium rocked with thunderous applause that seemed as if it would never stop.

Gazing at the members, Shin'ichi said, "OK, let's do it one more time, shall we?"

There was another burst of applause.

Shin'ichi began to lead the song again. It was even more powerful than the first time. The participants were deeply moved. Women had tears in their eyes. Youth sang until they were hoarse. Men, their faces filled with pride and emotion, clapped their hands vigorously in time with the beat.

As Shin'ichi led the song, his heart and the members' hearts became one, a chorus of joy and deep passion resounding through the hall.

*A*FTER leading the Gakkai song, Shin'ichi was deeply exhausted. Yet he said to the members from the microphone:

"Kansai is a castle of eternal victory, which I have put my heart and soul into building. It is the pride of my youth. I ask that all of you, my dear friends of Kansai, never be defeated no matter what may happen. Please be victorious come what may. And come what may, please join me in writing a golden history of kosen-rufu. I look forward to seeing you all again soon."

Except for a handful of top Kansai leaders, none of the participants realized the gravity of Shin'ichi's situation. The fervor with which he led the chorus and his impassioned words, arising from the innermost depths of his being, had made a profound impression upon them.

On March 16, Shin'ichi attended the youth division's first music festival. Three years had already gone by since March 16, 1958, when the youth division held its "dress rehearsal for kosen-rufu" at the head temple, in the presence of Josei Toda. On that occasion, in a monumental act of will given his desperate illness, Josei Toda appeared before the assembled youth, riding on a litter Shin'ichi had had

built out of his sincere concern for his mentor's well-being. Toda then entrusted the youth, led by Shin'ichi, with carrying out their mission as his successors of accomplishing kosen-rufu.

The music festival began at 6:00 P.M. at the Setagaya Civic Center in Tokyo's Setagaya Ward. In memory of Josei Toda, the Brass Band performed "The Mists of Kawanakajima," "Song of Courageous Departure," "Song of Comrades" and other favorites of their late mentor. Next, the Fife and Drum Corps performed a program that included the Russian folk song "Katyusha" (Kate). Then there were songs by the young men's division chorus, including the popular Hokkaido folk song "Soran-bushi," and the young women's division chorus, including the Italian folk song "Reginella Campagnola" (Village Maiden). This was followed by a program of combined performances by all four groups — the Brass Band, Fife and Drum Corps and the YMD and YWD choruses, including "Whale Song." Then participants and audience alike joined in singing "A Star Falls in the Autumn Wind on Wu-chang Plain."

The last song was a special favorite of Josei Toda. It also had been played at the funeral the Gakkai held for him at the Aoyama Funeral Home in Tokyo.

As Shin'ichi listened, memories of his mentor came flooding back vividly; waves of nostalgia engulfed him, at times accompanied by a surge of grief.

After the music program, color slides of Shin'ichi's visit to Asia were shown with the title, "Making the First Step for Kosen-rufu for All of Asia."

When the slides showed scenes of the burial of the granite plaque engraved with the Chinese characters "Kosen-rufu in Asia" and other items at Bodhgaya, a storm of applause resounded through the hall.

These images were also a living testimony to the mentor-disciple spirit — the commitment to fulfill the vow made on that first historic March 16.

*E*VENTUALLY it was Shin'ichi's turn to speak. After thanking the performers for their enthusiasm, he said that a great religion, a great philosophy of life, is an essential foundation for realizing true happiness and peace. He then spoke about the Gakkai's mission:

"Today, the world's leading nations talk of peace, loudly extolling the virtues of democracy and equality. Yet, while they should be setting an example for the rest of the world, they proudly flaunt their immense military might and political power. As long as this state of affairs prevails, no true peace will be possible. In this kind of environment, the Soka Gakkai alone has actualized, without brute force or government patronage, a commonwealth of humanity based on Nichiren Daishonin's philosophy of life, which teaches the equality of all human beings. Therefore, it is my conviction that individual happiness and world peace can be found in the ideals of this

Buddhism and within the Soka Gakkai's growing network of life-to-life ties."

Shin'ichi also shared some memories of his times with Josei Toda:

"March 16, 1958, was the day our mentor, President Toda, revealed for us the outline of kosen-rufu, letting us participate in a dress rehearsal for that time so that we would know in what direction to strive. A top government leader had promised to attend that day but in the end couldn't make it. President Toda declared that all of a nation's citizens, including its prime minister, are equal in front of the Gohonzon. He showed us a vision of kosen-rufu in which the light of the Mystic Law would shine equally on all people.

"After the ceremony and just before returning to his lodging, President Toda called out to us, 'Let us fight!' I think these words are profoundly meaningful. I feel certain he was referring to the whole spectrum of struggles we must grapple with: to help those suffering become happy, to challenge erroneous teachings, to fight against abuses and injustices committed by those in positions of power and our individual struggle against our own weaknesses.

"In any case, when I heard him call out, 'Let us fight!' — his eyes sharp and radiant, his voice strong and vibrant despite his terrible gauntness — I was electrified. At that time, I resolved anew to fight intrepidly for kosen-rufu. His cry came from the depths of his being; it was an appeal from his very life.

"Engraving our mentor's words deeply in our hearts, let's fight resolutely and unceasingly until the day we have finally achieved kosen-rufu."

Carried in the Soka Gakkai's newspaper, *Seikyo Shimbun*, Shin'ichi's remarks inspired members around the country. Soon, "Let us fight!" became their motto.

M EANWHILE, there was a sharp increase in the number of incidents where Gakkai members were unjustly ostracized in their communities.

One took place in a valley area in Aogaki-cho in Hyogo Prefecture. It was customary there for residents to rotate responsibility annually for maintaining the local Shinto shrine. Those whose turn it was were responsible for the shrine's daily upkeep, which involved cleaning and repairing the building as well as placing flowers on the Shinto altar and offering prayers to the Shinto gods.

The local community comprised about sixty families, a handful of whom had joined the Gakkai, including a unit chief named Haruo Tatsuta. That year, the Tatsuta family was in line for custodianship of the shrine. But Haruo Tatsuta could not agree to serving and worshipping at a Shinto shrine because it went against his religious beliefs. The other Gakkai members felt the same way.

At the community association meeting held in January, Tatsuta said: "We should be free to practice whatever religion we like. I will gladly cooperate when it comes to other community activities, but I will not participate in religious activities, such as serving as shrine custodian."

The Gakkai's membership was growing rapidly and so community officials, who had deep ties to the Shinto shrine, did not look favorably upon the Buddhist organization. A short time later, these officials called a special community meeting without informing the Gakkai families. They then proceeded to revise the local community's rules. They adopted a new rule that, to promote and maintain amity in the community, the head of each family had to take a turn at overseeing and organizing shrine events on a rotational basis. The rule even explicitly stated that those who failed to fulfill this duty would forfeit all rights as citizens of the community.

Shortly afterward, another community meeting was held. The residents who were Gakkai members were also present, the officials having made a point of notifying them this time. The head of the community association insisted that the Gakkai members participate in shrine activities and pressed them to quit the Soka Gakkai. But the Gakkai members' resolve was firm. With great pride and dignity, they declared their absolute refusal.

The following day, a member of the local water committee came to one Gakkai family's home. When they went out to see what he wanted, they saw him turn off the water main in front of their home and begin filling the box that housed the main valve with red earth.

"Hey, what are you doing!" they shouted indignantly.

"The association's rules state that those who fail to fulfill their communal duties are not entitled to tap the water supply. It's the community's water supply, you see."

As they looked on, the valve box was filled in with dirt. Tears of outrage and frustration welled up in their eyes.

The wireless system installed in each home to convey news and information about community events was also removed. In addition, the Gakkai members were deprived of their shared community rights to the surrounding forest.

With their water supply cut off, the Gakkai members had to draw water from a river some distance away, balancing two large earthenware jars in harnesses suspended from a pole across their shoulders.

Their neighbors also stopped greeting them and other children began to bully and tease their children.

THE ostracism of Gakkai members in Aogaki-cho clearly impinged on their religious freedom and fundamental civil rights guaranteed under the constitution. But having little knowledge of their legal rights, Haruo Tatsuta and the other Gakkai members were at a loss as to what to do. Their faith, however, wasn't shaken in the least. They encouraged one another, saying:

"Doesn't the Daishonin tell us, 'Those who embrace [the Lotus Sutra] should be prepared to meet difficulties' (MW-1, 127)? It proves that this practice is genuine."

Shin'ichi Yamamoto's emphasis on the importance of Buddhist study had resulted in the members' deepening conviction in faith.

When the Soka Gakkai Headquarters learned of this incident, it immediately assigned some senior leaders in Osaka to offer assistance to the affected members. In addition to encouraging and offering moral support, they called on the local Council of Civil Liberties commissioners to see if anything could be done.

The unlawfulness of the treatment received by the Gakkai members was plainly evident. When the commissioner who came to investigate the situation learned all the facts, he talked with the officers of the community association and asked them to promptly reconnect the water supply to the members' homes.

Judging that it might prove to their disadvantage if they continued to pressure the Gakkai members, the head of the association decided to reinstate the Gakkai members' community privileges.

It had taken almost two weeks to resolve the issue. Superficially, at least, a reconciliation was reached: The association's head and several other community leaders apologized to the Gakkai families at the Aogaki-cho Town Hall and acknowledged the restoration of their rights.

The harassment, however, continued. People stopped patronizing Haruo Tatsuta's small general store. Some neighbors told them confidentially, "We'd like to buy from you, but the local bigwigs will give us a hard time if we do."

Tatsuta had no choice but to take to the road to peddle his wares. Many locals did not even greet him when they met him on the street.

Despite being shunned, the Gakkai members remained in high spirits. Propagation in Aogaki-cho proceeded even more enthusiastically than before. The Gakkai members' assertions of unfair treatment were clearly valid in terms of the law and many began to admire these members' unflagging cheerfulness in the face of such trials.

A similar incident occurred in the city of Sanda, also in Hyogo Prefecture.

At the beginning of January that year, expenses for conducting memorial services at the local True Pure Land School (Jodo Shinshu) Buddhist temple, commemorating the anniversary of the death of Shinran (1173–1263), that school's founder, were to be split among each household in the community. This practice had long been a custom in the area. But Tamito Fukuda, a local youth who became a Gakkai member, refused to pay. Of the sixty-odd families in his community, only he belonged to the Soka Gakkai.

*T*AMITO Fukuda joined the Soka Gakkai in March 1959. He was living in the Toyonaka area of Osaka, but in April the following year, he moved back to his hometown, Sanda, aflame with a sense of mission for kosen-rufu.

With Shin'ichi Yamamoto's inauguration as Soka Gakkai president, Fukuda decided to stand up and take the lead in propagation activities in his community. But his zeal incurred the resentment of the local residents, due in no small part to the region's deeply ingrained traditions and religious practices. In this atmosphere, he refused demands to pay his share of the expenses for the temple event. He declared it unreasonable to be expected to put up money for the religious event of a temple whose faith he did not practice.

The townspeople's ill feeling toward the Fukuda family was already running high since the father, a former chief representative of the temple's parishioners, had decided to join the Soka Gakkai along with his son. The younger Fukuda's actions only added fuel to their smoldering displeasure.

Fukuda, however, hoped to use the issue of his temple donation as an opportunity to introduce the people in his community to the Daishonin's Buddhism and to show them the difference between a correct and an erroneous religion. When he asked the young men's division of the Gakkai organization in Osaka to support him, about twenty youth happily made their way to Sanda. They went around from house to house, calling on people they had never met and attempting to persuade them to embrace faith in the Mystic Law. Upon leaving each house, they would give a victory cheer and boisterously sing a Gakkai song as they went on to the next. This had taken place in mid-January 1961, that very year.

Though the youth had been in high spirits, their actions were lacking in common sense and smacked of egoism. That evening, a deluge of complaints from local residents descended on the Fukuda family. Some people even came roaring mad to lodge their protests in person.

This incident brought the violent criticism of Fukuda's refusal to pay his share of the temple expenses to a climax. The head of the community association tried one more time to persuade him to pay up, but Fukuda rejected this out of hand.

"I don't care what anyone says; I'm not going to give a penny to support the local Shinto shrine or Buddhist temple, not now or in the future."

The head of the community association then called a meeting of his fellow officers. In consultation with a lawyer, they drafted a set of community rules and regulations. One rule they set forth was that residents who acted counter to the articles adopted by the association would forfeit all civic rights in the community. A special community meeting was then slated for February 22, at which a resolution concerning the adoption of the rules would be formally passed.

The officers of the local community association visited each household to inform them of the meeting. In doing so, they said:

"We're going to throw Fukuda out at this meeting, you know. We'll be voting on a new set of rules for that purpose, so don't forget to bring your seal so you can register your agreement."

When Fukuda arrived at the hall at the meeting's starting time, the other residents were already gathered there waiting for him. All eyes were trained on him as he entered. Their gazes were cold and forbidding.

THE meeting began with the community association head addressing a separate piece of business, before warming up to his real subject in a quiet and deliberate way.

"As you are well aware, Mr. Fukuda's proselytizing of his new religion, ever since he returned from Osaka, threatens to shatter the peaceful tranquillity of our hitherto quiet community. It has long been a tradition here that each resident equally shares the burden of expenses for the annual temple memorial service for the anniversary of Shinran's death, and no one has ever complained or objected up to now. That is, until Mr. Fukuda came along; he now refuses to bear his share.

"In addition, a large group of his fellow Gakkai members came to our community and conducted an aggressive door-to-door proselytization campaign. This was truly frightening. When I contemplate this sort of thing continuing, I can't help being worried about what will happen in the future.

"That is why today, to set a certain standard of behavior for residents in this community, I propose that we adopt a set of rules that clearly says that any individuals committing acts that run counter to the traditions and customs of this community — acts, for instance, such as the refusal to cooperate in the activities and events held at our local temple — forfeit the right to use joint communal property. What do you all think?"

Cries of approval rang out around the room. A number of residents took turns getting up and voicing their grievances. Tamito Fukuda's impeachment by this kangaroo court of his fellow citizens had begun.

First, a middle-aged man rose to speak: "I have this to say to Mr. Fukuda: Do you really think this Soka Gakkai, or whatever it's called, will last? Organizations of this sort soon disappear. Where will that leave you? Who will conduct your funeral? That's why you have to value our local Buddhist temple. I think it's perfectly natural that a person who refuses to do so and disrupts the peace and order of our community deserves to lose his right to use joint communal property."

"Yeah, that's right!"

"Hear! Hear!"

The residents became increasingly enraged.

"Those who disrupt the community should have their communal water supply turned off!"

"If you don't quit the Gakkai, don't walk on our streets!"

"We won't let your kids play in the community playgrounds, either!"

The residents' remarks now bordered on threats. After everyone had said their piece, the community association head addressed Fukuda:

"Mr. Fukuda, if you have anything to say in your defense, please go ahead."

When Fukuda stood up, he was subjected to jeers and angry insults.

"What you're attempting to do is unconstitutional, an infringement on my civil rights," he said. "You won't get away with it! No matter what you do, I absolutely refuse to bear expenses for the temple. On this point I absolutely refuse to compromise!"

When Fukuda had finished speaking, the community association head said, "I will now announce the proposed set of rules that have been drawn up with the aim of protecting the peace of our community."

THE community association head read aloud the proposed new set of communal rules: "Based on the recognition that community peace and order cannot be maintained if resolutions deliberated and agreed upon by the residents of this community are disregarded at the arbitrary discretion of the individual, we herewith set forth the following mutually agreed-upon set of rules:

"Article 1: No persons shall be entitled to log an objection against the community's appropriation of communal property or funds for the purpose of community projects and events discussed and agreed upon by the local self-governing body of this community.

"Article 2: Persons who fail to perform the obligations pursuant to any of the articles set forth in this duly deliberated and agreed-upon set of rules shall [in principle] be deemed to have forfeited their right and qualification as members [householders] of this community.

"Article 3: Persons who commit a breach of the rules set forth herein shall be disqualified as members of this community, such disqualification becoming effective one year from the date on which the said breach is formally established."

It was now time to vote on the new rules.

Except for Tamito Fukuda and a middle-aged man who opposed the resolution, all present were in favor of the new community regulations. They signed their names and affixed their seals to the document.

The head of the community association then declared: "I hereby announce that the new rules are adopted by the decision of the majority. This set of rules will go into force from today."

Applause and cheers rang out through the room.

The community association had thoughtlessly approved an unconstitutional set of rules that stripped people of their religious freedoms and civil rights.

Jeers and snickers were directed at Fukuda as he turned and left the room. He shook with deep rage.

"Can such a thing be allowed to happen? It's wrong! Japan is a nation of laws. Do they think I'll stand by and watch my civil rights be trampled? I'll fight. I'll fight with everything I've got. I'm not going to let them win."

Staying in close communication with Gakkai leaders in Kansai, he lodged a complaint at the Sanda Police Station against the head of the community association for infringement of his civil rights and defamation of his character. He also contacted the local government Legal Affairs Bureau and reported the suspected unconstitutionality of this set of community rules and requested an investigation.

The Legal Affairs Bureau immediately began looking into the matter and then directed the community association head to revoke the rules. The local police, however, were sluggish in their efforts to enforce this order, owing to close ties with the officers of the community association. Even after receiving this local government directive, the community officials made no effort to revise their position. One was even heard to declare openly: "I don't care whether it's unconstitutional. The affairs of this community are governed by the community's set of rules."

Meanwhile, various pressures were brought to bear on the Fukuda family.

*T*HE area where Tamito Fukuda lived was renowned for its bamboo handicrafts. His family made bamboo baskets and other items. But the local wholesaler, who happened to be the chief representative of the temple parishioners, refused to buy their goods. Because Fukuda had an outside job, however, his family could make ends meet.

President Yamamoto's guidance on March 16, in which he had spoken of President Toda's final cry — "Let us fight!" — had been a great source of courage and strength for the young Fukuda. He did not become dejected about his circumstances, but instead told himself:

"Devilish functions are bound to arise in increasing number. My faith is being tested."

It would take some two years before the incident would be reconciled. In the end, they would reach an agreement in which the community association would revoke the discriminatory set of rules, and Fukuda would withdraw his lawsuit against them.

Such ostracism was not limited to Hyogo Prefecture. Around the same time, a similar incident occurred in the fishing district of Kumano City in Mie Prefecture. The refusal of thirteen Gakkai families to participate in an event celebrating a local "mountain god" led to them being stripped of certain property rights, following a community resolution, including their right to engage in the common use of the surrounding forest.

There were similar incidents in Ogunimachi in the Aso area of Kumamoto Prefecture and Annaka City in Gumma Prefecture. In these cases, Gakkai members, for their refusal to cooperate in events related to the local Shinto shrines, were ostracized by their communities and denied use of essential community-owned equipment needed for farming their land. There were even instances in which, each time a local festival was held, fellow residents carrying portable shrines through the streets would deliberately veer into stores owned by Gakkai members, causing varying degrees of damage and disarray in reprisal for their refusal to donate to the shrine. To these participants, festivals became opportunities for unrestrained collective violence.

Today, many local festivals in Japan have lost their original religious meaning; they now represent little more than cultural and social customs and an occasion for promoting good will in the community. Consequently, participating in such activities, so long as it is not an act of worship or faith, does not automatically constitute committing slander of the

Law. It is apparent that the cases of ostracism of Soka Gakkai families arose because they refused to be literally forced into participating in events that had strong religious overtones. This was clearly because their joining the Soka Gakkai had awakened them to their right to religious freedom.

People are introduced to the practice through dialogue. It stands to reason, then, that a person's decision to join the Soka Gakkai in itself represents human independence based on religious freedom — the freedom to choose or reject a religion as one pleases.

Each time Shin'ichi Yamamoto learned of discrimination against members, it pained him more than if it were happening to himself. He strove to encourage the members in any way he could — by sending messages, for example. He also instructed top Gakkai leaders and leaders of each region to warmly embrace and support each person being subjected to such discrimination.

*I*T deeply pained Shin'ichi that his fellow members, innocent of any crime, were subjected to grievous oppression. According to Buddhist teachings, however, such obstacles are inevitable. Since his inauguration as Soka Gakkai president, a fresh groundswell of propagation had unfolded. The kosen-rufu movement in Japan was growing rapidly. The reasons cited for ostracizing Gakkai members were invariably their failure to participate in ceremonies at a local temple or shrine or refusal to make donations. But these were merely pretexts. Fear of the Gakkai members' full-fledged propagation activities in each area was the real reason.

The Gakkai's efforts to spread the Daishonin's Buddhism first triggered panic and apprehension among the leaders of established temples and shrines, who were concerned about losing parishioners. Those in power in each area, and who were well connected to the local shrine or temple, then began to believe erroneously that an increase in Gakkai members would disrupt the community and threaten their own positions. As a result, these leaders tried to exclude Gakkai members from community life.

That other religious groups and some journalists promoted a distorted perception of the Soka Gakkai only worsened the situation.

As the Daishonin says, "Without tribulation there would be no votary of the Lotus Sutra" (MW-1, 9). Without obstacles, there can be no genuine faith. As kosen-rufu advances, storms of difficulty will arise without fail.

Though harsh winds had indeed begun to blow, Shin'ichi nevertheless sensed that these were still far from the real tempests that lay ahead. He recalled the Daishonin's words, "You should regard the appearance of obstacles as peace and comfort" (*Gosho Zenshu*, p. 750).

Shin'ichi realized that he must help each member become a person of strong faith who could face any adversity with courage and joy. He took the recent incidents of ostracism as an important step in that direction.

Also, from a social perspective, these incidents spoke of Japan's immaturity as a nation when it came to democracy and sensitivity to human rights. Since ancient times, the Japanese had believed in local guardian deities, and the indigenous religions and local communities had been tightly interwoven. In the Edo period (1600–1868), a temple parish system was developed to serve the military government's religious policy, and the general populace fell under the administration of the Buddhist temples. Over time, the belief that following the instructions of one's local temple constituted normal human behavior became deeply rooted in the people's consciousness. Moreover, when Shinto was instituted for all practical purposes as a state religion during the Meiji period (1868–1912), ordinary people's sense of subordination to religion and to Shinto in particular, grew even stronger.

JAPAN'S history of government and religion joining hands to control the populace had cultivated people's readiness to condemn those who ignored the demands of a local temple or shrine.

Even after religious freedom was guaranteed under the new postwar constitution, people's consciousness remained shackled to old traditions. Many still thought that every resident was obligated to worship at the local temple or shrine, to make donations to them and to participate in religious events, simply because doing so had been a community custom since olden times.

Why was it that people mouthing the virtues of democracy accepted uncritically the community's religion and could not break free from archaic traditions? Because they lacked the solid self-identity essential to democracy's success. Without a solid sense of self, individuals will remain spiritually enslaved to the group, even if the social system changes.

Another reason was the Japanese people's lack of a philosophical foundation for such independence. Such a role ordinarily falls to religion. But Japanese religion, provincially tied to a community or family group, could not foster spiritual independence.

For example, when the Japanese participate in religious events, they have little, if any, interest in the doctrines or teachings involved. This illustrates how they consider religion to be an inherent part of the community or family tradition but completely separate from their individual lives.

For individuals to embrace and believe in a religion of their own free will, they surely need to investigate that religion and confirm, among other things, whether its teachings are valid.

Because of their general apathy toward and ignorance of things religious, however, when Japanese are asked about their religion, in many cases they name their family religion or say they have no religion. They can't quite conceal a trace of embarrassment as they do so. By contrast, in Europe, America and many other parts of the world, it is commonplace for people to speak proudly and confidently of their religion.

Religion forms the basis of a person's character, values and way of life; it is at the very core of our convictions. The Japanese attitude appears peculiar indeed when compared to how the world at large views religion.

Despite this religious climate, Nichiren Daishonin's Buddhism worked its way deeply into individuals' hearts. Having been awakened to the dignity of the individual, Gakkai members clearly expressed their religious beliefs.

In these incidents of ostracism against Gakkai members, adherents of traditions that had long overshadowed the individual sought desperately to suppress the sprouts of democracy emerging from the soil of the masses.

HISAO Seki, a Soka Gakkai director and Upper House (House of Councilors) representative, viewed these incidents of ostracism against Gakkai members as extremely serious.

In terms of Buddhism, these were indisputably cases of persecution resulting from members' efforts to spread the True Law. Though Nichiren Daishonin's writings predicted such persecution, Seki's conscience as a politician would not let him turn a blind eye to discrimination in a country whose constitution guaranteed religious freedom. Moreover, the form and intensity of the ostracism made it conceivable that such persecution, if allowed to continue, might even threaten people's lives.

"If we allow this to go unchecked," Seki thought, "we may end up losing rights like religious freedom altogether. We cannot protect our basic civil liberties. Genuine politics must be committed to fighting for the rights of the individual. Actually, this is an issue that affects not only Soka Gakkai members but everyone with religious faith of any kind. More important, to ignore these incidents would be to condone discrimination against anyone, not just the religious; it would become a source of grave trouble for Japan in the future. It is a politician's job to rectify such wrongs."

Seki discussed the issue with the other Upper House members who had been elected with the Soka Gakkai's endorsement, and they agreed to bring the matter up before the Diet.

On March 23, at an Upper House Budget Committee meeting, Seki took the rostrum during the time allotted for general questions. After posing questions about emigration, infant day-care centers and youth welfare issues, he brought up the subject of ostracism against Gakkai members. He directed his question to the appropriate ministers and government officials:

"Recently, in different parts of the country, we have seen a spate of incidents in which individuals have been ostracized over disagreements concerning donations to local Shinto shrines and Buddhist temples. The communities in which these incidents have occurred make it mandatory for residents to contribute funds for festivals and other religious events. They declare it to be a sign of reverence for the local gods and respect for one's ancestors. Anyone refusing to pay, however, must endure ostracism and, not infrequently, wanton violence, for example, in the form of portable shrines being deliberately crashed into their property.

"I ask, first of all, whether you are aware of such incidents."

The home affairs minister was the first to rise and reply:

"Collecting donations from residents for community Shinto shrines, Buddhist temples, festivals and other events is a long-standing Japanese custom. If conducted with a spirit of harmony and good will, I don't think one can say there is anything wrong with it. But if, as you say, donations are compulsory, and violent incidents — like crashing portable shrines into the property of noncontributors — occur, then from here on we will take strict measures against those responsible, as we always have. At the same time, we will do our utmost to ensure that such incidents are not repeated."

H ISAO Seki continued his questioning: "Donations should be entirely up to the individual. Some may not wish to contribute funds for economic reasons or because they have different religious beliefs. Should donations to temples and shrines be made mandatory and people forced to comply, this would clearly be against the law. I think it would then be only natural for police to investigate and take measures against those responsible. But when the victims of such ostracism report it, the police are often very slow to respond. Sometimes, the police have even recommended that the donation be paid, saying that it merely represents a token of community good will. Is this an appropriate attitude for our police to take?"

The home affairs minister responded: "Such cases may have taken place, but I will see to it from now on that they are dealt with strictly and that this sort of thing will not happen again."

To illustrate the seriousness of the continuing incidents, Seki then related details of the ostracism in Aogaki-cho in Hyogo Prefecture, where Gakkai members had had their water supply cut off, and in Kumano City in Mie Prefecture, where members had been deprived of their rights to use communal property such as the surrounding forest.

"In Kumano City," he said, "when the victims reported the incident to the local police box, the officer there did nothing about it for a week. Finally, unable to endure the situation any longer, the plaintiffs went to the nearest police station. The police chief there was vaguely aware of their predicament, but told them: 'The authorities haven't filed a complaint yet, so we can't do anything about it. It's a matter for the Legal Affairs Bureau's civil liberties commissioners. We can't take any action unless we receive a request from them.'

"Such ostracism certainly violates Article 20 of the constitution, which reads: 'No person shall be compelled to take part in any religious act, celebration, rite or practice.' Indeed, it may even be regarded as 'intimidation' under Article 222 of the criminal code. I would like to have a clear answer as to how the related authorities view this question."

The home affairs minister rose again, looking weary of this line of questioning, and said, blinking tiredly: "If the kind of situations you describe exist, then I believe we must strictly deal with such incidents and prevent them from recurring. I will see to it that this matter is given urgent attention. Often, however, there are many complex reasons at the heart of this kind of issue. It may not always be appropriate to solve it using police powers. I would like to judge and deal with each situation separately, taking such points into consideration."

It was a vague, noncommittal response.

*H*ISAO Seki pressed the home affairs minister for a more specific answer: "Your reply might be interpreted as condoning ostracism when 'complex' issues are involved. But I think that, irrespective of the circumstances, ostracizing people for refusing to make a donation violates the constitution. As such, it is a criminal offense. What is your comment on this?"

This time the minister stated clearly that the examples of ostracism Seki had described were illegal and that he would ensure that they were dealt with strictly.

Seki further sought the opinion of the Safety Department chief of the National Police Agency.

The department chief chose his words carefully:

"Although I would have to examine the details of each case before coming to any concrete conclusion, the cases that Representative Seki just mentioned most probably correspond to intimidation under Article 222 of the criminal code."

Seki's questions now moved to the crux of the issue:

"May we consider, then, that when someone is ostracized for refusing to donate for a festival or for repairs to a Buddhist temple, and if the police fail to act against those responsible, then they are being negligent in performing their duty?"

"As far as I can assume from the information you have given me, the cases you have spoken of would constitute acts of intimidation under the law. Therefore, if the police, having received such a complaint, fail to look into the matter or conduct an investigation, then they would be somewhat at fault."

Seki keenly pressed on: "But as I just mentioned, such incidents are becoming all too frequent. Inquiry reveals that police often are acquaintances or drinking buddies of the town or village officials. And it is a fact that police show favoritism to these influential local leaders, making no attempt to intervene in the ostracism. How do you regard this?"

"It would be extremely regrettable if officers of the law allowed themselves to be swayed by personal considerations — such as their close relationships with community leaders — and refused to act on such a complaint. We need to give strict direction on this point."

This was the Safety Department chief's clear acknowledgment that the ostracism Gakkai members had encountered was illegal, and that the police were obliged to take immediate and decisive action once a complaint had been filed. Nevertheless, in areas where ancient traditions ran deep and community leaders and police were on intimate terms, the police had thus far failed to fulfill this natural responsibility and Gakkai members had been forced to endure unjust discrimination in silence.

A FTER Hisao Seki had posed his questions at the Upper House Budget Committee meeting, the police had begun to investigate Gakkai members' complaints of ostracism and seemed to be taking appropriate measures. But this did not mean an end to the tangible and intangible pressure and discrimination bearing down on Gakkai members. Harassment and more subtle forms of alienation continued in many areas.

The situation represented a struggle against what the Lotus Sutra calls "ignorant lay persons," the first of three powerful enemies the sutra states will vie to attack those who uphold the True Law. The members, however, bravely endured and tenaciously struggled against these onslaughts with faith.

Often in his travels, Shin'ichi would hear the stories of such members. He would invariably tell them:

"When viewed over the course of your entire life, this trial will last for but an instant. If anything, it will remain as a wonderful memory of your faith and practice. Buddhism is about winning. You will definitely win in the end. Never grow pessimistic. What matters is that you live with dignity, optimism and joy, whatever may happen.

"President Makiguchi died in prison. President Toda spent two years in prison during the war. The ostracism you've had to endure is no more than a mosquito bite in comparison. Some day, when your persecutors see the abundant benefit and happiness your family enjoys and the radiant virtue of your character, they will definitely feel deeply ashamed of what they did and will probably regret their actions for the rest of their lives."

Shin'ichi knew that sympathy alone would offer only temporary comfort. What these members needed far more, was the unyielding faith to stand firm before any storm. Only here could the path to eternal triumph be found.

The March Headquarters Leaders Meeting was held on the 27th at the Taito Gymnasium. New membership in March had increased by more than 44,800 households, lifting the Gakkai's total membership to more than 1.85

million households. Fifteen new chapters were established: Kiryu, Kita-Tama, Tachikawa, Kumagaya, Takasaki, Nagaoka, 'Atsuta, Aichi, Okazaki, Nara, Maizuru, Kobe, Hyogo, Fukuyama and Matsue. Next, results of the study department exams held earlier that month were formally announced: 571 people had become assistant professors; 2,790 had become teachers; and 22,874 had become assistant instructors. With this new influx, the size of the study department more than doubled, forming a great force of people well versed in the teachings of the Daishonin's Buddhism, some forty thousand strong.

The wave of the Gakkai's dynamic advancement gained further momentum, and the organization was poised to grow even further, aiming for May 3, the first anniversary of Shin'ichi's inauguration as president.

*A*PRIL 2, the third anniversary of second president Josei Toda's death, marked the first time Shin'ichi would observe the occasion since becoming president himself. The memorial service began at 1:00 P.M. at Jozai-ji, a temple in the Ikebukuro area of Tokyo.

The weather had been fine that morning, but around noon, as Shin'ichi arrived at the temple, the sky suddenly clouded over and big drops of rain began to fall. A strong wind blew and thunder rumbled. It was a spring storm.

Gazing at the rain pounding against the window, Shin'ichi could not help remembering Toda's guidance to "advance through the storm!"

He recalled the day, July 11, 1951, when the young men's division was formally established. It had rained heavily that day as well. During the meeting, Toda had stated serenely that the next Soka Gakkai president would come from among those present. He had also said that it was his own mission to achieve kosen-rufu without fail and had stressed how important it was to spread Nichiren Daishonin's Buddhism throughout Asia and the world.

Three years had already passed since Toda's death. Shin'ichi had not the slightest regret about the struggles he had waged over that time. As Toda's disciple, he was happy that he could proudly report this to his mentor.

The memorial service began. High Priest Nittatsu led the assembly in reciting gongyo and chanting daimoku, and then divisional representatives rose to speak. Finally, it was Shin'ichi's turn. Standing before the microphone, Shin'ichi spoke deliberately, as if deeply pondering each word:

"When Mr. Toda was inaugurated as president on May 3, 1951, a storm of criticism and slander swirled around him. He was berated because of the financial difficulties that had some time earlier plagued his business and the desperate efforts he had had to make to keep his head above water. On becoming president, Mr. Toda often said: 'I am now taking a stand and fighting, looking ahead 100 or 200 years into the future. But people don't understand this. Two centuries from now, my actions and my struggles will have been proven to be the only genuine struggle for truth and justice among all of humanity.'

"President Toda spoke of the future, 200 years from now, but today, only three years after his death, the real greatness of his struggle is already being proven."

The participants listened intently to Shin'ichi, their eyes bright with interest.

SHIN'ICHI'S voice reverberated powerfully throughout the room: "Today, throughout Japan, people who once suffered grave misery and misfortune are experiencing great benefit and showing how beautifully their lives have been revitalized by striving in faith, just as President Toda taught. No one before has succeeded in bringing such renewal to ordinary people's lives; it is a truly magnificent achievement. And it is not limited only to Japan, but has spread to North and South America and to our neighbors in Asia. This is indisputable proof of President Toda's integrity and the righteousness of his struggle.

"President Toda's spirit was to rid the world of misery through faith in the Gohonzon, to create a peaceful Japan and a peaceful planet. To achieve this, he stood alone to accomplish kosen-rufu, proudly declaring and spreading the Daishonin's teachings. We are his disciples. Our mentor was a great master of propagation; we must also be valiant champions of kosen-rufu. Let us realize great progress in spreading the Law, making each anniversary of our mentor's death an important milestone.

"As a representative of President Toda's disciples, I am determined to advance while looking forward with utmost joy to the day when I can report proudly before our mentor's tomb, 'We have accomplished kosen-rufu.' Should I not accomplish this during my lifetime, I fervently pray for you who will carry on after me to work for the realization of kosen-rufu with the same spirit. This concludes my speech."

After the memorial service, Shin'ichi looked out the window. Just as suddenly as it had come, the storm had passed. A cherry tree, its branches heavy with blossoms, swayed slightly in the now gentle breeze, soaking up the sunlight that streamed through a break in the clouds. The same tree had been in bloom on the day of Toda's funeral, its petals fluttering down as if grieving over his departure.

The storm that had blown so fiercely, as if enraged by the fragrant beauty of the cherry blossoms, had lasted no more than a moment.

Shin'ichi recalled a *waka* Toda composed:

Though assailed
by the three powerful enemies,
the lion cub proceeds
tall and undaunted
on the journey of kosen-rufu.

Toda had presented this poem to him to commemorate the Thirteenth Headquarters Leaders Meeting on November 3, 1955.

This lion cub had now begun to charge ahead resolutely, at full speed. When the lion charges, the earth will tremble and the wind will rise; clouds will move and storms will be stirred. Such signs were already evident. But Shin'ichi was prepared. A fresh resolve arose within him as he gazed at the branches of the cherry tree, which had so valiantly weathered the spring storm.

Triumph

*A*S May 3, the first anniversary of his inauguration as Soka Gakkai president approached, the pace of Shin'ichi Yamamoto's activities intensified all the more.

Advancing kosen-rufu means expanding the sphere of those who are happy. Such happiness is forged by establishing an indestructible treasure tower of life within each person's heart. Knowing this, Shin'ichi always regarded meeting with, encouraging and offering guidance to as many members as possible his foremost responsibility.

On April 3, the day after the memorial service for the third anniversary of Josei Toda's death, Shin'ichi set out on a guidance tour of the Joetsu region.[1] That evening, he was to attend the inaugural meeting for the new Takasaki[2] Chapter.

Arriving at Takasaki Station that afternoon, he and the leaders accompanying him went to the home of Nobuko Yanai, the newly appointed chapter women's division chief. Her husband, Koji, had operated a small foundry but had been killed in a traffic accident ten months earlier. Shin'ichi had come to visit Mrs. Yanai to conduct a memorial gongyo for her husband.

A year earlier, in March 1960, Shin'ichi had visited Takasaki to give a lecture to the members and to attend a meeting for group-level leaders. He fondly recalled talking with Koji Yanai and other local leaders at that time.

When he had learned that Koji and Nobuko Yanai had three sons and a daughter, Shin'ichi asked Koji, "How do you think you'd like to raise your children?"

"My oldest son is now in medical school, so I hope he'll become a doctor," Koji began. "My second son, I hope, will eventually take over the family business, and my youngest son I would like to see become a scholar. As for my daughter, I hope she will end up happily married."

Shin'ichi, smiling, then said: "That is a very human response. Usually when I ask people this, the reply that comes back is, 'I will raise my children to be capable people for kosen-rufu.' I am impressed by your honesty."

The Takasaki members placed great trust in Koji. He had made the earnest request that Shin'ichi come to their city. Then, three months after Shin'ichi's visit, Koji was gone. Nobuko now ran the foundry in her husband's stead.

After conducting the memorial gongyo for her husband, Shin'ichi said to Nobuko: "It must be a real struggle carrying out your responsibilities as chapter women's division chief while working full time to manage the foundry. But when leaders struggle valiantly amid difficult circumstances, not only does it elicit a sense of fellowship and empathy from the members, but those leaders can give guidance that is compelling and convincing. What's more, the dauntless spirit with which you live will encourage and inspire your fellow members. This is a crucial period in your human revolution."

*A*FTER her husband's death, Nobuko Yanai devoted herself energetically to managing the foundry, to taking care of her home and family, and to carrying out Gakkai activities. Because of this hectic lifestyle, however, she seemed to have grown somewhat careless about her clothing and general appearance.

Shin'ichi mildly admonished her:

"You may have to look after many things in your husband's place and be extremely busy, but as a woman it is important that you also attend to your personal appearance. When people see you struggling without giving a thought to how you look, they may think, 'She's really having a hard time.' But they certainly won't think, 'I'd like to be like her.' There's no need to be extravagant or overly stylish. But please don't forget to make an effort to ensure that you shine, not only spiritually but in your personal appearance as well.

"Your children will also be glad to see their mother always looking young and pretty; they'll be even prouder of you. Please become the kind of person of whom all will think in admiration, 'Despite her difficult situation, she's always so delightful and dresses with such good taste.'"

Mrs. Yanai had been completely oblivious to her appearance. She was warmly appreciative of Shin'ichi's attentive concern in bringing the matter to her attention.

Shin'ichi and the others drove to the site of the inaugural chapter meeting. When they got out of the car, they were greeted by a group of smiling, spirited youth. Among them were several he clearly remembered. They were the young men's division members who, as the core leaders of the area, had helped guide members into the meeting place during Shin'ichi's last visit to Takasaki a year earlier. At that time, he had spoken with them at the building's entrance, although only briefly.

Among these twenty or so youth, only a handful had worn suits. Most were clad in windbreakers, and among those who did wear suits some sported sneakers. Many of the young men worked at small local factories, and seemed to be struggling to make ends meet. But each, awakened to his mission for kosen-rufu, abounded with energy and enthusiasm and burned with pride in fighting for the Law, for the people and for society.

Shin'ichi had been impressed by their sincere attitude and told them: "At one time, not only was I very poor, but I also suffered from ill health. I worried and fretted over life's meaning. But by awakening to faith, I've overcome everything. Limitless glory is definitely in store for you. Please persevere in faith, calmly triumph over all difficulties and become trusted youth who can strive proudly as outstanding people in your places of work."

*T*HE young men earnestly listened to Shin'ichi's encouragement: "The most important thing for young people, no matter what your circumstances, is that you never demean yourselves. Faith lets us bring out our limitless potential and enjoy life to the fullest, come what may. The moment you think that you are no good, you stifle your own potential. The key to the future lies entirely in your determination at the present moment. Everything depends on whether you are living with enthusiasm right now.

"Today, as a tribute to your new start, I present you with a poem I composed in my youth, expressing my determination for the future."

Shin'ichi then proceeded to recite the poem:

Ablaze with hope,
I face the raging waves,
And though I may be destitute,
Though others may laugh at
Or ridicule me,
Watch me now
As I patiently endure.

I exhort myself:
"First work hard,
To the full extent of your youth.
Though some may scorn you,
Always wear a smile.
Heart aflame,
Advance strong and true
Along your chosen path."

Smiling brightly,
Serenely,
At the arduous road ahead,
Today, again,
I will advance —
Gazing up at the sky,
At the summit
Of a hope-filled future.

Shin'ichi looked into the eyes of these young men and said: "It's not much of a poem, but it expresses the spirit I cherished in my younger days. With that same spirit, please live with courage and dignity so that you may grow to be outstanding leaders, never defeated by any hardship or suffering you may encounter. I pray with all my heart that you will enjoy great victory in your youth."

Now, at the inaugural meeting of Takasaki Chapter, these young men he had encouraged a year earlier were gathered before him, each clearly having achieved splendid growth since he last saw them. The development of young people was Shin'ichi's greatest source of hope and joy.

In his speech, Shin'ichi explained that most of the criticism against the Gakkai arose from ignorance, and discussed the importance of telling people about the real Soka Gakkai with courage and persistence.

O N the 4th, the day after his visit to Takasaki, Shin'ichi traveled to Nagaoka in Niigata Prefecture where, at 2:00 P.M., he attended the inaugural meeting of Nagaoka Chapter.

Then, after completing his guidance tour of Joetsu, he went to the head temple on the 6th to attend the annual scroll-airing ceremony and a ground-breaking ceremony for the planned Dai-bo lodging complex. On the 8th, he attended a joint inaugural meeting of Tachikawa and Kita-Tama chapters, and on the 12th, he delivered a Gosho lecture at the Kansai Headquarters in Osaka. The following day, he went to the Chubu region, where he attended the inaugural meeting of Okazaki Chapter on the 14th and the joint inaugural meeting of the Aichi and Atsuta chapters on the 15th.

Everywhere he went, he channeled his energy into encouraging individuals.

While in the Chubu region, Shin'ichi also went to Mie and Gifu prefectures, and in Gifu visited the home of Chapter Chief Noboru Sawai. Several years earlier, the company Sawai operated fell victim to economic recession and went bankrupt. But he had successfully overcome this setback and had become chief of Gifu Chapter the previous year. He was a man of immense seeking spirit.

Gifu tended to be eclipsed by Nagoya, the major metropolis of the Chubu region. Even from an organizational standpoint, Gifu received relatively little attention. Leaders from Tokyo frequently went to Nagoya, but rarely did they go beyond there to visit Gifu, a smaller and slightly remote city. For that very reason, Shin'ichi wanted to encourage this valiant leader of the people who was flying the chapter flag and spearheading activities for kosen-rufu in Gifu.

Sawai's house was simple, located in a secluded lane. It served as the center of chapter activities. A scooter parked at the entrance was Sawai's vital means of transportation. No doubt he used this scooter to traverse ravines and steep mountain roads to encourage friends.

When he saw Shin'ichi, Sawai greeted him and his companions, saying with great humility: "I'm so sorry you have had to travel all this way. Thank you very much for coming."

"If I had the time," Shin'ichi replied, "I would visit each member's home. But unfortunately I cannot. I can only look to leaders such as yourself to visit and encourage these members in my stead. In that sense, I'm paying you a visit today to express my gratitude for your dedicated efforts."

These were Shin'ichi's honest sentiments.

Those who resolve to shoulder full responsibility for a given enterprise feel profound appreciation for those who lend their cooperation and assistance. Such people certainly will not behave arrogantly toward others.

On the other hand, if leaders take the support of those around them for granted, then it is inevitably a sign that they lack this unwavering commitment to take full responsibility for activities in their area.

SHIN'ICHI talked to Noboru Sawai about the importance of giving personal guidance in faith and visiting members at home to offer encouragement:

"To raise people, it is important to offer encouragement and guidance tailored to the individual. To illustrate, not all plants and trees will necessarily grow simply because the sun is shining. Some may be in the shade, shut off from the light, or be assailed by harmful insects. Some may be lacking in sufficient nutrients. Only when they are regularly given the appropriate care to address their specific circumstances and needs can plants grow.

"The same is true in the world of faith. If we compare the announcement of activity guidelines or the encouragement given to members at meetings to the light of the sun, then visiting members at their home or giving personal guidance can be likened to caring for the specific needs of each plant or tree.

"No matter how the organization might seem to be growing, unless leaders carry out such basic and steady activities, no capable people will emerge. The organization itself will eventually become deadlocked.

"Please continue, in your role as chapter chief, to reach out steadily to others by offering them guidance in faith with the determination: 'I cannot allow even one of my fellow members in Gifu to fall by the wayside.'"

Shin'ichi firmly shook Sawai's hand.

He also took time to speak with the other members who had gathered at Sawai's home.

After completing his guidance tour of the Chubu region, Shin'ichi attended the Third Student Division Speech Contest on April 18, held at Kyoritsu Auditorium in Kanda, Tokyo. And on the 19th, he went to Kumagaya in Saitama Prefecture to attend the inaugural meeting of Kumagaya Chapter.

As the train approached Omiya Station, Shin'ichi fondly recalled the day he and Josei Toda had visited the Omiya area. It was in 1950, as autumn was beginning to give way to winter. Together, they had called on a certain individual in hopes of finding a solution to the impasse Toda's business was facing, but to no avail. The prospect of an early way out of their dilemma, something they had pinned such high hopes on, had then vanished.

At the time, Toda stood almost literally on the line between survival and ruin. Toda's company continued to be in arrears in the payment of salaries and one by one his employees had deserted him until only a handful remained. At the same time, Shin'ichi, who had determined to faithfully support and protect Toda, was experiencing a steady deterioration of his health.

After their visit, he and Toda had taken a walk alongside a river. Stars twinkled down at them in the frosty stillness. The night sky was beautiful. But the cold bit into them. It was not just the cold of winter that numbed them, but the coldness of the world.

Toda and Shin'ichi continued to walk along the path by the river in silence.

*J*OSEI Toda was unruffled; his manner was no different than usual. But Shin'ichi felt deeply troubled, sorry that he could do nothing to help his mentor. Even though it concerned Toda's private business affairs, Shin'ichi could not stand seeing him struggling desperately to stay afloat and humbling himself by asking favors from others. Shin'ichi was bitterly frustrated and felt ashamed of his own powerlessness to adequately protect his mentor.

Shin'ichi himself was utterly exhausted. As they walked along, one of his shoes almost fell off. Looking down, he saw that the laces had come undone. The shoes were already worn down at the heels and had holes in them. Bending down to retie his laces, Shin'ichi casually sang to himself, "Who turned me into this kind of man?" parodying the line "Who turned me into this kind of woman?" from a then popular song.

Toda turned around and looked back at him, his eyeglasses sparkling. "I did!" he said, grinning broadly.

Shin'ichi felt something very warm in Toda's confident and smiling admission of responsibility in the midst of such uncertain and trying times.

He thought to himself: "The mentor's confidence always reveals the truth. So the disciple must respond in kind."

It was a period of bitter hardships, but the days that mentor and disciple spent struggling together were bathed in a warm, golden glow.

Now, more than ten years had passed.

At the inaugural meeting of Kumagaya Chapter, Shin'ichi shared some of his memories of those days he had spent with Toda. Victory in life, he said, is not something that is immediately apparent but may take ten or twenty years, or even an entire lifetime, to become clear. He also stressed the importance of having a strong life force:

"Life is filled with ups and downs. Those with strong life force can always traverse life's mountains and valleys with confidence and composure. They can make their way cheerfully, sometimes viewing cherry blossoms, sometimes pausing to enjoy a snack, sometimes relishing the challenge of climbing a steep incline. But if our life force is weak, then we will become exhausted; we cannot enjoy the surrounding scenery and instead feel only pain.

"We were born in this world to enjoy life to the fullest. To do so, we need strong vitality, and chanting daimoku is the wellspring of such vibrant life force. So please continue to exert yourselves courageously in faith. Determined to follow your chosen paths in life, always base yourselves on daimoku, regardless of what others may think or say. Those who do so will be happy. I also hope that you will develop your lives and your chapter organizations in such a way that you will be filled with an exhilarating sense of joy and delight."

*O*N the 20th, the day after visiting Kumagaya, Shin'ichi attended the opening and Gohonzon-enshrinement ceremony for a temple in Kiryu City, Gumma Prefecture, and the Kiryu Chapter inaugural meeting.

Kiryu had been the first area outside of Tokyo that Josei Toda visited to give guidance after the war, traveling there in September 1946. Several members who had joined under President Makiguchi were living in the area. They had evacuated to the countryside to escape the wartime air raids on major cities. For Toda's visit they had organized a discussion meeting, also inviting lay believers who belonged to the local Nichiren Shoshu temple.

Most temple parishioners could not do gongyo, yet some put on airs because their families had been affiliated with Nichiren Shoshu for generations. Toda sensed that they lacked a pure and vibrant seeking spirit.

"People's faith here is polluted," he remarked to the members accompanying him from Tokyo. "If we don't do something to refresh it, there'll be great misfortune later."

At the discussion meeting, one of the temple members, a man named Yajiro Miyata, sought guidance from Toda. Miyata, who ran a watch shop, suffered from spinal caries. He explained that he had been to one hospital after another but had not been cured.

Toda said that a crucial element in transforming one's destiny was introducing others to faith in Nichiren Daishonin's Buddhism. He urged the man to make a deep resolve to dedicate his life to the goal of kosen-rufu.

As the meeting drew to a close, Toda pronounced to all those present: "I, Toda, will accomplish kosen-rufu. I will never relinquish this mission to anyone. I hope all of you will lend me your solid support."

After hearing Toda's guidance, Miyata felt as though a blindfold had been lifted from his eyes. He had long been a lay follower of Nichiren Shoshu, but he had never carried out the essential practice of propagation. He freshly resolved to apply himself to introducing others to Nichiren Daishonin's Buddhism and promptly launched himself into action. He formed and became president of an organization called the Shoho-kai, comprising mainly parishioners of two temples — one in Ogo-machi, Gumma Prefecture, and the other in Toyoda-mura, Tochigi Prefecture — as well as a few local Soka Gakkai members.

In the years that followed, Toda frequently visited Kiryu to give guidance. While he never said anything about the Shoho-kai, he did on one occasion say to its members: "Can you declare, 'I will accomplish kosen-rufu'? I don't think so. I will be frank with you — this is something only I can do. Soon I will stand up in earnest. At that time, won't you join me in working to realize kosen-rufu?"

The membership in Kiryu steadily grew. By 1951, five years after Toda's first visit, it had reached around 300 households. Toward the end of March that year, a post-card from the Soka Gakkai Headquarters arrived at Miyata's home, announcing Josei Toda's upcoming inauguration as second Soka Gakkai president on May 3.

THE message on the postcard read: "Mr. Toda will now take his stand as Soka Gakkai president. This is something that you, the members of Kiryu, have no doubt been eagerly awaiting. Let us rally around Mr. Toda with a fresh new resolve."

Yajiro Miyata showed the postcard to the others at an informal meeting of Shoho-kai leaders.

"That's what it says, but what do you think?"

Someone replied: "We worship the same Gohonzon and carry out the same practice of propagation as they do. I think we should simply continue doing our best on our own."

Not one of those present expressed a desire to attend Toda's inauguration.

Although Toda waited for some word from Kiryu, no reply came. "If they fail to advance with me now, they will surely come to regret it for the rest of their lives. Try contacting them again," he commented to the leaders at the Soka Gakkai Headquarters.

Two or three more messages were sent, but still there was no reply. And when May 3, the day of Toda's inauguration, arrived, not one person from the Shoho-kai attended. Nevertheless, others who had been Mr. Makiguchi's disciples before the war took Toda's inauguration as an opportunity to renew their determination as Soka Gakkai members and launched themselves even more energetically into activities.

There was no malice in Miyata's stance. Indeed, in his own way, he felt respect and gratitude for Toda. The problem was, he could not grasp the vast state of life that Toda had attained in prison by awakening to his mission for kosen-rufu. He also failed to comprehend the significance of the Soka Gakkai, an organization that had appeared in accordance with the Buddha's will and decree. In other words, he did not understand the true lifeblood of faith.

Additionally, the Shoho-kai members came to have an overinflated opinion of themselves owing to the growth their organization had achieved on its own.

"Since we can do the same thing as the Soka Gakkai," they reasoned, "there's no need for us to join it or rely on Toda's guidance."

Eventually, however, rifts began to appear within the Shoho-kai. Disharmony reigned. No doubt partly because its membership comprised lay practitioners from two different Nichiren Shoshu temples, rival factions gradually formed, this rivalry eventually escalating into emotional infighting. Everyone came together when meetings were held, but afterwards, they would bad-mouth and maneuver to undermine one another. The atmosphere within the Shoho-kai became dark and oppressive. No longer were any experiences of benefit to be heard.

Miyata began to grow anxious. "Something's wrong," he thought. "There's something definitely amiss." The stress of the situation took such a toll on his nerves that his health faltered.

*I*N April 1954, while on a business trip to the city of Sendai, Shoho-kai Youth Division Chief Michio Terada, a dry goods salesman by profession, attended the Soka Gakkai's Sendai Chapter General Meeting, which he had happened to hear about.

Terada was overwhelmed by the energy and enthusiasm he witnessed at the meeting. And he was particularly moved by Toda's guidance, which brimmed with his profound knowledge of the Buddhist teachings and an unshakable confidence.

"The Soka Gakkai is incredible!" Terada thought. "It's completely different from the Shoho-kai. This is the true world of the Daishonin's Buddhism. Whoever is going to practice this faith had better listen to President Toda's guidance."

When he returned to Kiryu, Terada called on Yajiro Miyata at home, where he proceeded to tell him about the Gakkai meeting he had attended and his honest impressions and feelings.

"So that's what you think?" Miyata responded. "Actually, I've recently been thinking the same thing. I feel as though I've at last come to understand what President Toda told us. I guess only he can accomplish kosen-rufu. It's certainly not as simple an undertaking as I had imagined."

As Miyata said this, a look of deep pain crossed his face. He had begun to realize the irreversible error he had committed.

The two talked and decided they would ask to join the Soka Gakkai.

With Toda's inauguration, fresh waves of propagation spread throughout the country as people strove to achieve the membership goal of 750 thousand households. The number of Gakkai members in Kiryu was also beginning to increase steadily. Because of Miyata's responsibilities as Shoho-kai president, however, his decision to join the Soka Gakkai would affect not only himself but many other people. This troubled him deeply, and he agonized for days on end about what to do.

Ultimately, Miyata concluded that if things continued as they were, he could not teach the members of the group correct faith and help them become happy. That summer, he called together a hundred-or-so Shoho-kai members at his house and shared his resolution:

"I have decided to go with the Soka Gakkai," he announced, "for only the Gakkai has correct faith. I hope those who wish to continue with me will do the same."

Some Shoho-kai members, including a vice president, who knew that Miyata and others were intending to join the Soka Gakkai, had consulted with the chief priests of the two local temples and set about forming a new group. It was a desperate bid to prevent members from going over to the Gakkai. They branded Miyata and those who sided with him as "traitors." Despite these moves, Miyata went ahead and joined the Soka Gakkai. More than 100 Shoho-kai members eventually did the same.

MIYATA began devoting himself earnestly to practicing Buddhism as a Gakkai member, determined to learn the ABCs of faith from the Gakkai.

Some time after he joined, Miyata ran into Josei Toda on a walkway at the head temple while on pilgrimage.

When he recalled how he had failed to attend Toda's inauguration even though he had received several notices, Miyata felt so ashamed, he could not face Toda. He hung his head in remorse.

Toda was not the least bit reproachful toward Miyata. He said: "Mr. Miyata, you've had a really hard time, haven't you? I know about all that you've gone through."

As he said this, Toda placed his hands firmly on Miyata's shoulders in a gesture of warmth and understanding.

"President Toda...," Miyata said, as tears welled up in his eyes. Toda's clasp on his shoulders felt incredibly warm.

Thereafter, he persevered steadily in faith. As his understanding of the Gakkai deepened, he was filled each day with a renewed sense of the Gakkai's wondrous mission. He also came to appreciate the profound importance of the fact that the founding president, Tsunesaburo Makiguchi, had laid down his life to protect the Daishonin's Buddhism during the war, while the priesthood had allowed itself to become mired in slander out of fear of suppression by the country's militarist authorities.

He was also deeply impressed by the greatness of Josei Toda, Makiguchi's disciple, who had awakened to his mission as a Bodhisattva of the Earth by gaining a profound understanding of the meaning of the Lotus Sutra while in prison. Then, after his release, he had stood alone to accomplish kosen-rufu.

Miyata sensed with his entire being that the Soka Gakkai was indeed the sole body that had appeared in accord with the Buddha's will and decree and had inherited the lifeblood of faith of Nichiren Daishonin. Further, he became aware that the Gakkai possessed an indestructible unity, precisely because the great conviction in faith and the spirit to practice without begrudging one's life, which originated from Toda's enlightenment in prison, formed the essence of the Gakkai spirit. He was also convinced that kosen-rufu could only be achieved because of Toda's presence.

Years later, in 1978 and 1979, when the Soka Gakkai came under a barrage of unjust attacks from the priesthood,

Miyata visited the homes of many members who, ignorant of the truth, wavered in their faith, and earnestly explained to them the truth about the Gakkai. No doubt he was motivated by the strong wish never to allow any of his fellow members to repeat the mistake that he had once made.

In any event, these were the reasons the development of kosen-rufu in Kiryu had followed a rather circuitous route in spite of Toda's energetic efforts to give guidance in the area from the pioneering days of the organization.

FROM around 1955, the Kiryu Gakkai organization began to show substantial growth. Now, on April 20, 1961, Kiryu Chapter was at last to be formed.

The chapter's inaugural meeting was scheduled for 5:30 P.M. at the Industry and Culture Center in the city of Kiryu. Shin'ichi went there after attending the opening and Gohonzon-enshrinement ceremony for Muryo-ji, Kiryu's new temple, at 1:00 P.M.

Shin'ichi, who was familiar with Kiryu's past, said to local leaders while en route: "This is a new age for Kiryu. To create a new history, you'll have to unite harmoniously."

The assembly hall was filled with people, and the air was charged with excitement. Now, fifteen years after Josei Toda made his first postwar guidance trip to Kiryu, a fertile field of kosen-rufu had been cultivated and capable people were emerging from the earth there like fresh young shoots.

For his address there, Shin'ichi chose the subject of the fourteen slanders.[3] Hoping for the solid unity of the Kiryu members, he said: "The Gosho explains the principle of the fourteen slanders. Four of these, read literally, are: contempt for good, hatred of good, jealousy of good and bearing grudges toward good. Simply put, these mean to harbor contempt, hatred, jealousy or grudges toward those who uphold the True Law.

"These four slanders are all too easily committed. The Daishonin teaches that if people allow themselves to be consumed and dominated by grudges, jealousies and so forth toward their fellow believers, then although they may have been practicing strongly, they cannot tap the true, immeasurable benefit of faith.

"To illustrate, even if you buy a high-quality TV or radio, if you do the wrong thing, making a mistake with the channel selector or dial, you won't get a good picture or good reception. Much the same applies in the world of faith.

"No matter what our organizational position or social standing, we who exert ourselves in faith are all equally children of the Buddha. We should therefore trust and respect one another as we would the Buddha.

"If someone acts improperly, that person naturally should be reproved. But we must never revile our fellow members behind their backs. Also, it is never acceptable for leaders to use the people around them like servants simply because they have a high position in the organization.

"In the Gakkai, people are linked by bonds of faith and compassion. Therefore, let's advance cheerfully and harmoniously, warmly encouraging one another as members of a bright and caring family."

Kiryu was revitalized; it was now making a fresh start toward the future.

*A*PRIL 20 also marked the tenth anniversary of the *Seikyo Shimbun*, the Gakkai's newspaper. To commemorate, Shin'ichi wrote "Looking Back on the First Ten Years," a front-page article for the April 22 issue.

As the first anniversary of my inauguration as Soka Gakkai president approaches, I greet the tenth anniversary of the *Seikyo Shimbun* with profound emotion.

The *Seikyo Shimbun* chronicles the great and unprecedented endeavor of kosen-rufu. In correctly reporting the moment-by-moment development of kosen-rufu activities, in carrying guidance for leaders and members alike, and in all other areas, the *Seikyo Shimbun* has become a driving force for the Soka Gakkai.

It is said that the pen is mightier than the sword. And indeed, dialogue and debate should replace the role of brute force and military might. During Japan's Meiji Restoration (in 1868), a young generation awoke from the long slumber of isolationism and stood up burning with hope for the flowering of a new civilization. The energy and strength of this new generation came from the power of words. Soon, the power of speech and the written word came to oppose and challenge the power of authority and military might. And, to great popular acclaim, the newspaper emerged in Japan.

Today, the Soka Gakkai has made its existence known to the entire world. We have no authority. Nor do we have great financial wealth. We are simply a gathering of people who, with sincere and pure-hearted faith, follow the Buddha's golden words, lament the people's suffering, and wage an all-out struggle against the fundamental causes of unhappiness to construct a world of lasting peace and happiness. Can any other group of people match our purity and strength?

Our practice of sharing the Daishonin's Buddhism with others, our actions to lead individuals to enlightenment by correcting their mistaken religious beliefs — a fundamental source of so much unhappiness — arises from the power of words that resound with truth.

Shin'ichi went on to explain that the great work of kosen-rufu progresses through the power of the written and spoken word, on which the Gakkai has always placed the greatest importance. He pointed out that society had repaid the Gakkai's well-meaning efforts with misrepresentation, criticism and abuse. On this tenth anniversary of the *Seikyo Shimbun*, Shin'ichi wanted to reconfirm why the paper had been established in the first place:

We have advanced amid this storm clad in the armor of tolerance and forbearance. In doing so, the *Seikyo Shimbun* has at times directly admonished erroneous religions and magnificently asserted the correctness of Nichiren Daishonin's Buddhism. It has assuredly demonstrated its power as a most important weapon in the "war of words" to protect members within and to smash the despotism of unjust power without.

Shin'ichi also described how, in the summer of 1950, when Toda's business was in extremely dire straits, Toda and he had discussed plans for starting the newspaper.

*S*HIN'ICHI'S article concluded:

I express my sincere respect to all those who in these past ten years have struggled wholeheartedly day and night to produce the newspaper, manage advertisements, promote readership and deliver the newspapers to readers' homes.

Now is the time for us to recall the confidence of our mentor, who once remarked, "My wish is to make this paper available to people throughout Japan as soon as possible." And it is my hope that all members, not only those who are directly involved with the newspaper, will make this spirit their own and work to protect and develop the *Seikyo Shimbun*.

The *Seikyo Shimbun* began as a two-page paper, appearing every ten days with a circulation of 5,000. It was now published twice weekly, with four pages on Wednesdays and eight pages on Saturdays, becoming the organ for the Soka Gakkai's 1.85 million member households. Its development had been truly remarkable.

Further, the number of local editions — when they were first introduced in 1956, there were three: Tokyo, northern Japan and western Japan — had increased to seven. At the same time, local offices had expanded and developed. In July 1959, a system of six branch offices nationwide — located in the Kansai, Hokkaido, Tohoku, Chubu, Chugoku and Kyushu regions — was set in place. A system of volunteer correspondents had been established in 1954, and by 1961, the newspaper had a nationwide network of 49 correspondents and 215 associate correspondents.

In addition, construction of a new building to house the newspaper was almost completed at No. 18, Shinanomachi, a short walk from the Soka Gakkai Headquarters. The opening ceremony was scheduled for May 4. The new reinforced-concrete structure, with three floors above ground and one below, was to be equipped with modern, state-of-the-art facilities, far superior to other Gakkai buildings at that time.

When the newspaper first began publication, the editorial office was housed in a single cramped room in a building in Ichigaya, Tokyo, and the editorial department had only one antiquated camera.

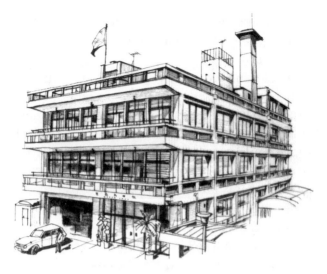

An editorial staff member once put in a request to Josei Toda to purchase a new, more sophisticated camera. Smiling, Toda replied: "Anyone can shoot good pictures with a good camera. But taking outstanding photos with a cheap, old camera is the test of a true photographer."

Had it been possible, Toda would have gladly bought any number of fine cameras for the newspaper staff. But at the time, the Gakkai simply couldn't afford it.

Those early days of the *Seikyo Shimbun* now seemed a lifetime away.

A FTER attending the Kiryu Chapter inaugural meeting, Shin'ichi began a guidance tour of the Chugoku region.

On April 22, he attended a district chiefs meeting at the Soka Gakkai Chugoku Headquarters in Okayama, before traveling to Matsue in Shimane Prefecture the following day for Matsue Chapter's inaugural meeting.

It was Shin'ichi's first visit to Matsue. When he caught sight of the new chapter chief, Gensuke Hamada

— who'd come to meet him at the station — Shin'ichi said with a smile: "I've come to Matsue at last! It's finally time for your fresh start!"

"Yes. Thank you very much," the solidly built Hamada responded with a rather tense expression.

Hamada lived right in front of the train station. Out of the first floor of his house, he ran an auto repair shop.

On completing elementary school, Hamada found a job. Through hard work and industry, he finally established his own company after the war and now had some thirty employees. He was one of the town's success stories.

But as his business got on track, he began to carouse. When evening approached, Hamada would leave the house, telling his wife that he had to meet with clients or business contacts. Often he would spend the night elsewhere and not return until the following day.

His wife, Yukiko, felt deepening mistrust for her husband, and each day as nightfall approached, the two would invariably quarrel.

While Hamada's behavior did not adversely affect his business, the discord at home intensified as time went by.

Each day toward evening, Yukiko's mental anguish over her husband's actions began to cause heart palpitations, shortness of breath and a tightness in her throat, as if she were choking on something. When these attacks occurred, her body would stiffen and her face turn ashen.

At first, Gensuke was alarmed and worried about his wife. But when he became accustomed to these episodes, he would accuse Yukiko of feigning illness. When she went to see a doctor, her condition was diagnosed as neurosis.

Around this time, Yukiko heard about the Daishonin's Buddhism from an acquaintance and, desperate to try anything to solve her problem, she joined the Soka Gakkai. That was in March 1957.

Receiving instruction in faith from the friend who introduced her, she exerted herself in sharing the teachings of the Daishonin's Buddhism with others. She was driven by a single-minded fervor. Those around her viewed her with curiosity, whispering behind her back, "Does she really think she can cure herself by doing that?" But with each passing day, she grew brighter and her health improved.

Gensuke, having witnessed this transformation, also joined the Gakkai on his wife's urging, as eventually did their three daughters and many of the employees of Gensuke's repair business.

When this happened, Yukiko thought: "Since my husband has taken faith, he will surely come back to me. Everything's going to be all right from now on!"

ALTHOUGH Gensuke had joined the Soka Gakkai, he neither did gongyo nor participated in Gakkai activities. He continued to stay out all night, just as before. The faint hopes Yukiko had cherished of her husband turning over a new leaf had been dashed, and she plunged once again into despair.

In July, four months after joining the Gakkai, Yukiko began to make wild statements, such as: "I'm so worried about my husband. My shoulders have been so stiff with all the tension that now the muscles in my neck have torn. I'm going to die, I just know it."

But when she was feeling well enough, she earnestly chanted daimoku with the thought that faith was the only way to change her destiny.

Gripped by intense anxiety, Yukiko continued to berate herself and think constantly about death. One day in August, she concealed herself in a closet where she attempted to commit suicide by cutting her tongue with a razor. Fortunately, her family soon discovered her and she escaped serious injury.

Her daughters were increasingly bewildered and distraught by her behavior. They had to hide all knives in the house and pay careful attention that she didn't leave the gas turned on.

In September, Yukiko made a second attempt to kill herself, by drinking pesticide, but again was unsuccessful.

Then, in October, she concealed herself beneath the flooring of the house and tried to starve herself. When she was discovered several hours later, she was babbling incoherently and had a deranged look in her eyes.

The following morning, the family had Yukiko admitted to a university hospital, where the doctors pronounced her schizophrenic.

While in the hospital, she suffered from hallucinations and would cry out incomprehensibly. But even in the midst of these bouts, she continued chanting daimoku with the determination that she would overcome her suffering.

Mysteriously, in the course of ten or twenty days, she gradually regained her composure and began to improve little by little.

Her treatment proved so effective that even her doctors were surprised; she was discharged from the hospital after a little more than three months.

Witnessing his wife's recovery, Gensuke sincerely awakened to faith. He completely stopped staying out all night and began doing gongyo with his whole family. Their home brightened and Yukiko was filled with life, having totally regained her health.

The transformation astonished their neighbors, who observed: "Old Hamada has completely given up his wild ways, and his wife has overcome her illness. They used to fight all the time, but now they're getting along fine. I wonder if it could be their religion?"

Hamada accompanied his wife as she went out and talked to others about the Daishonin's Buddhism. Seeing them beaming with so much proof of benefit in their lives, a steady stream of people who heard about Buddhism from them joined the Soka Gakkai.

GENSUKE Hamada opened his home as a meeting place and attended meetings with his wife, Yukiko.

Shin'ichi had met Hamada for the first time a year earlier, in February 1960. Hamada was then Matsue District chief. After attending a Chugoku General Chapter leaders meeting in Okayama, Shin'ichi spoke with a number of district chiefs at the home of Ittetsu Okada, the general chapter chief. Hamada was there. Shin'ichi had heard about him and his family from Okada.

Although Hamada was a district chief, he had been doing Gakkai activities largely at the urging of his wife, who was the women's division district chief. So, he wasn't exactly participating on his own initiative. Hamada felt himself somehow unworthy to lead all the members of the district, given his former dissolute lifestyle and lack of education.

When Okada introduced Hamada, Shin'ichi said: "So you're Mr. Hamada of Matsue? I'm always grateful for your efforts. I'm really sorry I haven't visited Matsue. I hope you'll look after the members in my stead. With you there, I know that Matsue is in good hands."

Shin'ichi then handed Hamada a mandarin orange he was holding.

"Mr. Hamada, let's dedicate our lives to kosen-rufu together. Someday I will visit Matsue."

Hamada took the orange from Shin'ichi and held it cupped between both hands, his eyes growing teary despite himself. He was deeply touched that Shin'ichi should have directed such heartfelt concern and encouragement toward even someone with a past like his.

The following day, Shin'ichi took the train to attend a meeting in Tottori and Hamada rode along. Aboard the train, he sought guidance in faith.

"Although I am district chief," Hamada said, "I have only an elementary school education and lack ability. What's more, I have trouble reading and writing."

Shin'ichi told him: "Neither educational background nor social status determine a person's value. In the Soka Gakkai, faith is the foundation. If you refine your character through faith, everyone will support you."

Shin'ichi gestured at the cherry trees outside the train window, their branches now black and barren. "Mr. Hamada, those cherry trees are now bare, but shortly, buds will emerge from their branches and they will produce flowers that charm people with their beauty. Likewise, though we cannot see what is in people's hearts, each of us possesses the life of the Buddha. This Buddha life will eventually emerge, causing us to display our true brilliance and our lives to blossom with happiness. Please have confidence in this."

Hamada was profoundly moved by Shin'ichi's guidance.

TREATING it like the most precious of treasures, Gensuke Hamada carefully brought the mandarin orange Shin'ichi had given him back to Matsue. When he arrived home, he placed it on his Buddhist altar and chanted daimoku sincerely to the Gohonzon. With all his heart, Hamada wanted to respond to Shin'ichi's expectations. He conveyed Shin'ichi's warm encouragement and high hopes for Matsue's development to the district's group leaders. He then divided the orange among them, and they ate it together.

Hamada had taken a resolute stand. At heart he was very sincere and honest. Now, inspired by Shin'ichi's words, he began taking action, constantly thinking of how to assist the members. The membership of Matsue District began to grow steadily, increasing by fifty, sixty and even seventy households each month. This growth continued, becoming the driving force for the formation of a chapter in the area.

Hamada had first heard about a Matsue chapter being formed some two or three months before the inaugural meeting. Several leaders had come from Tokyo, and a conference had been held at his home.

A leader from Tokyo (who later abandoned his faith) had announced, "It's been decided that you, Mr. Hamada, will be the chapter chief."

Hamada was stunned when he heard this pronouncement. Though he was firmly committed to working hard for kosen-rufu, he felt that he was just barely managing to fulfill his duties as district chief.

He therefore demurred, saying, "I haven't had much of an education, and even now as district chief, I have to rely on my wife to take care of administrative matters."

"What's that?" the senior leader yelled, outraged. "Who are you to complain? You've gotten benefit, haven't you? Well, then, you should just say 'I accept' with a spirit of appreciation. If you're not willing to become chapter chief, you should just quit practicing!"

It was a brutal and incredibly arrogant diatribe, demonstrating not the least bit of concern for Hamada's feelings. When she heard the heartless words "You should just quit practicing!" the color drained from Yukiko Hamada's face.

"If Gensuke were to abandon faith," she thought, "we could never become happy. We might even return to our former hellish existence. I have to convince him to take the position."

With a note of desperation in her voice, she fervently assured the leader on Gensuke's behalf: "I will do everything in my power to assist and support my husband so that he will fulfill his responsibilities as chapter chief. So, please, don't make him quit practicing."

"All right. That's what I want to hear. Well, your wife has spoken up. Now, what about you?"

*A*LTHOUGH these words came from an unreasonable and arrogant leader, Gensuke Hamada accepted them with faith and a pure-hearted seeking spirit. This was his strength.

"He must be speaking to me so strictly," Hamada reasoned, "because President Yamamoto wants me to become chapter chief regardless of the difficulties he knows I have with reading and writing. If that's so, then to accept the position is the correct thing to do from the standpoint of faith."

He resolved to accept the position.

It was thus agreed during the meeting that Hamada would become chapter chief and his wife, Yukiko, chapter women's division chief. Yukiko later had a chance to seek counsel from President Yamamoto while he was on a guidance tour of Kansai. She told him that while her husband had made a strong determination to take on the responsibility of chapter chief, he was worried about whether he could actually be effective.

"I was the one who recommended your husband for the position of chapter chief," Shin'ichi said. "Please convey my very best regards and gratitude for the great contribution he will be making. If you're worried about your husband, then please do gongyo with him and study the Gosho together. Please become his right hand and give him your full support."

This encouragement put the Hamadas' minds at ease once and for all, allowing them to pursue their activities with confidence.

The Matsue Chapter formation had been officially announced at the headquarters leaders meeting on March 27.

Now in Matsue at last, Shin'ichi was delighted to see Gensuke Hamada brimming with enthusiasm and energy. He first stopped by the Hamadas' home and then went by car to the meeting site. Approximately ten thousand people had gathered for the event — so many that the hall could not hold them all and a great many crowded outside. It was President Yamamoto's first visit to Matsue, and the air was filled with joy.

Chapter Chief Hamada stepped up to the podium amid explosive applause. Producing a manuscript from his breast pocket, he bowed and began speaking exuberantly.

"As of today, I am your chapter chief!"

There was a roar of applause. The hall gradually quieted. But Hamada did not continue speaking. He stood transfixed on the stage.

On the podium before him was the text of the speech that his eldest daughter, Kazue, had written out for him in a clear hand the previous day. But the almost illiterate Hamada was now so nervous that he could not read the words.

There was an interminable silence. The audience watched and waited with bated breath. Beads of sweat streamed down Hamada's brow.

From one part of the hall came the sound of someone chanting daimoku. It was Hamada's mother. As though on cue, other voices here and there throughout the hall began to join her in chanting daimoku.

THE participants were familiar with Gensuke Hamada's personality and his awkwardness as a speaker, yet they all loved him.

This was now revealed in their daimoku to support him as he stood frozen on the stage. The hall resounded with their voices, which grew louder still as more people joined in.

Hamada's silence lasted only a couple of moments, but to the audience it seemed an eternity.

After standing there helplessly for a while, Hamada raised a hand to wipe his brow and, summoning all his energy, said simply: "The chapter now has a membership of 7,200 households. I'm determined to make this 11,000 households before the year's end. Thank you for your support!" He then bowed deeply and returned to his seat.

Ear-splitting applause enveloped the room. It was a moving scene of harmony and joy born of the warm heart-to-heart bond of comrades.

Shin'ichi looked on, smiling warmly. At that moment, he knew that he didn't have to worry about the future of Matsue Chapter.

Eventually, when his turn came to address the audience, Shin'ichi stressed that Buddhism means being victorious and that achieving a state of true happiness in life necessitates courageous action based on faith.

After the meeting, Shin'ichi accompanied Hamada outside to encourage those members who could not fit inside the hall. As both of them stood on a raised platform, Shin'ichi patted Hamada on the shoulder and said: "Mr. Hamada has become chapter leader at my request. Please give him your utmost support."

Afterwards, Shin'ichi Yamamoto again visited the Hamadas' home.

Gensuke was somewhat downcast, perhaps because he couldn't say what he had wanted to at the meeting.

"What's troubling you now?" Shin'ichi asked him.

"Well, I can't speak very convincingly. So when I think of how I'm going to direct activities, I just feel...." His voice trailed off helplessly.

Hearing this, Shin'ichi asked a leader accompanying him from Tokyo to bring some paper and a writing brush and ink. He then wrote in Chinese characters: "The voice does the Buddha's work." When he had finished, he presented the calligraphy to Hamada, saying:

"The Gosho states, 'The voice does the Buddha's work' (*Gosho Zenshu*, p. 708). Speaking out and talking to others is an integral part of Buddhism. Just keep on chanting daimoku and encouraging others. By doing so, you will definitely gain the ability to speak with eloquence and confidence.

"But you don't have to make long speeches. Just a few simple words are fine. The important thing is that your voice reverberates with faith and sincere conviction."

GENSUKE Hamada never forgot these words. When he began his activities as chapter chief, the other leaders in the chapter rallied around him, lending their assistance in such areas as announcing and explaining activity guidelines to the members. Much of this support was due to Hamada's likable, warmhearted character.

And when he called out to the members, "Come on, let's give it our best!" this short impassioned cry from the depths of his being never failed to resound in people's hearts. Over the years, his words would inspire countless fellow members to stand up in faith, contributing to the great development of the kosen-rufu movement not only in Matsue but throughout Shimane Prefecture.

At the Hamadas' home, Shin'ichi told Yukiko: "You've really had your share of difficulties. But you don't need to worry anymore. Your husband will become a fine chapter chief. All of this is due to your unwavering determination. It is your victory."

He also courteously greeted the Hamadas' three daughters: Kazue, 18; Namiko, 14; and Kaori, 10.

"From now on, your parents will be helping us out as chapter chief and chapter women's division chief. This may cause you some added burden, but I hope you'll support them as well as you can," he said, bowing.

He then smiled and told them gently: "You don't have to worry about anything from now on. You're all my family. If something happens, I will look after you. The important thing is for you to accumulate good fortune and be happy throughout your lives."

The Hamadas' three daughters had suffered the most on account of their parents' discord and their mother's illness. Knowing this, Shin'ichi wanted to encourage them in some way. Gazing at their bright faces and shining eyes as they showed their readiness to follow his words, he prayed with all his heart for their great happiness.

As dusk approached, Shin'ichi headed for the inn where he would be spending the night.

Nearby Lake Shinji was ablaze with the golden light of the setting sun. It seemed to Shin'ichi that the Buddhist gods were celebrating the start of Matsue Chapter.

The inaugural chapter meeting of Fukuyama Chapter in Hiroshima Prefecture would be held the next day, April 24. Shin'ichi left Matsue in the morning and went by train to Fukuyama via Kurashiki in Okayama Prefecture. When he arrived at Kurashiki Station, a number of Gakkai members were waiting to greet him.

When Shin'ichi transferred to a train on the Sanyo Main Line, members did the same. They gathered around him and an informal discussion meeting was soon under way. Fortunately, the train was practically empty and there were virtually no other passengers on board.

Looking at the members, Shin'ichi said: "I hope you haven't taken time off work to come and see me. Those who neglect their work, no matter how they may seem to be exerting themselves in faith, are not practicing correctly. After all, faith has to be manifested in daily life."

*A*FTER stressing the importance of work and daily affairs, Shin'ichi said with a smile, "Well, since we're all here like this, if there's anything you'd like to ask me, please go ahead."

A member jumped in, saying, "I have a hard time introducing others to this Buddhism."

"It's the same for everyone," Shin'ichi assured him. "Propagation is the most difficult Buddhist practice. It's no simple matter. Teaching people the power of Buddhism today is just as challenging as it would have been trying to teach people a thousand years ago about atomic energy or explaining to them the wonders of radio and television. You can explain this Buddhism with all your might, but people still may not understand.

"But when someone actually tries practicing it, they can appreciate how wonderful it is. And, more often than not, they'll ask themselves why they didn't take faith sooner. This is probably true of many of you. So the important thing is to treasure your friendships and be steadfastly committed to continuing a dialogue."

Next, an elderly woman spoke up: "My son refuses to practice, no matter how I urge him. I'm at my wit's end. What can I do to get him to start practicing?"

"You probably didn't take faith until quite late in life, did you? There's no need to be impatient. Pestering your son to start practicing won't do any good. What's important first is that you, his mother, earnestly strive in faith and live an exemplary life. If you are cheerful and optimistic, no matter what happens, and always show warm consideration for your family, then your son will come to understand faith through your example.

"When all is said and done, it is through your behavior as a mother and as a human being that you can best introduce your family to faith. If you become a mother your son can be truly proud of, then he will eventually take faith of his own accord."

While their time together was brief, Shin'ichi put his heart and soul into guiding them. As they parted, he said: "I deeply respect your seeking spirit. I'd very much like to spend more time talking with you casually like this, and it pains me that this is not possible.

"There is one request I'd like to make of you, though. And that is that the men's division members exert themselves with a full sense of responsibility in all areas and thus lighten the burden of the women's division members. Women's division members are truly dedicated and hardworking. I'd like for them to relax occasionally, with the men showing their chivalrous spirit by saying, 'Don't worry, we'll do it.' Please become models of such conduct for others. Many thanks."

So concluded another informal discussion — one of a continuing stream that had punctuated this trip. Shin'ichi wished he could spend more time with the members. He wished he were more than one person.

SHORTLY after Shin'ichi arrived in Fukuyama, a light rain began to fall. When he thought about the members coming to the Fukuyama Chapter inaugural meeting, Shin'ichi couldn't help worrying about the weather. But by the time he reached the meeting place, the sky had cleared to reveal a beautiful sunset.

During his address that evening, Shin'ichi said:

"On the Gohonzon is inscribed, 'Those who make offerings [to the practitioners of the Lotus Sutra] will enjoy good fortune surpassing the ten honorable titles [of the Buddha]' and 'Those who bring trouble [upon the practitioners of the Lotus Sutra] will have their heads split into seven pieces.' These words indicate the great benefit of the Gohonzon and also the punishment that those who slander the correct teaching will incur.

"Buddhism expounds the law of cause and effect that governs all life; it teaches us the formula for becoming happy. If we reject this causal law of life and try to go against it, then before long we will find ourselves deadlocked. It is natural, therefore, that a valid and effective religious teaching is certain to generate two types of clear-cut actual proof: benefit and punishment.

"Also, regarding the Gohonzon's benefit (Jpn. *ku-doku*), the Daishonin says, 'The Chinese character *ku* means to extinguish evil and *toku* [read as *doku* in the combination *kudoku*] means to bring forth good' (*Gosho Zenshu*, p. 762). This means that the 'benefit' of our practice is eradicating the evil in our lives and cultivating good. In other words, while we speak of receiving benefit, it is not bestowed on us from without. It wells forth from within our own lives like water from a spring. Through the Buddhist principle of the oneness of life and its environment, we can also change our environment and 'gather fortune from ten thousand miles afar' (MW-1, 272).

"Propagating the Mystic Law is an act that extinguishes evil and cultivates good in others' lives. Our activities to teach people about Buddhism simultaneously open the path of benefit for them and for ourselves. This is the Buddhism of Nichiren Daishonin.

"Buddhism is a teaching of compassion that seeks to help people become happy. But the courage to fight against wrong is an indispensable component of compassion. If we allow injustice to go unchallenged, it will come to hold sway, and everyone will suffer. So I wish to state that fighting against evil constitutes compassion and is the mark of a genuine Buddhist."

One important mission of kosen-rufu is to create an era of human triumph by defeating the injustice that brings about human misery, establishing a world where justice and good prevail.

Shin'ichi wanted the members of Fukuyama to understand a truly living Buddhism, rather than the Buddhism of ritual and formality.

After the meeting, Shin'ichi said to Hiroe Ishizuka, the chapter women's division chief: "I'm going now to encourage the members standing outside."

"Thank you!" Ishizuka said, overjoyed. "It will mean so much to them."

HIROE Ishizuka had specially requested that Shin'ichi say a few words to the members forced to stand outside because of the venue's limited seating capacity.

Shin'ichi had first met Mrs. Ishizuka in early March at the Kansai Headquarters in Osaka. By then she had already tentatively been selected to become the women's division chapter chief. At that time, she had said to him:

"President Yamamoto, would it be all right if I asked you a favor? In Fukuyama, we don't have any facilities large enough to accommodate all our members for our in-augural chapter meeting. The hall we're now considering can only hold about 2,000 at most. This will leave several thousand more outside who will have to listen to your speech via loudspeaker. So would it be possible for you to go out afterwards and offer them some encouragement?"

Whenever possible, Shin'ichi tried to encourage those forced to remain outside on account of inadequate facilities. And he was delighted that the new chapter women's division chief was also concerned about these members.

"Thank you for your valuable input," he said. "Let me give you something as a memento." On the flyleaf of a book, Shin'ichi wrote "Peace and happiness" in Chinese characters and presented the book to her.

Concern for others is the heart of the Soka Gakkai. The world of Buddhism is a world of human harmony woven from the thread of mutual consideration. Accordingly, con-cern for others is the foremost requirement of leaders.

After the inaugural meeting, Shin'ichi went out to en-courage those who could not enter the hall. With a fervent prayer that Fukuyama (literally, "mountain of happiness")

would become a great fortress of good fortune, he com-
mended all the members for their hard work and called on
them to continue in their valiant endeavors.

One day shortly before May 3, Shin'ichi was at the Soka
Gakkai Headquarters in Tokyo deeply absorbed in thought.

His mind was filled with plans for the continued
development of kosen-rufu, including construction of the
Grand Reception Hall at the head temple and additional
new temples and community centers around the country.
Each of these projects was crucial for the Gakkai's movement to spread the Daishonin's teachings. But the biggest
hurdle was how to finance them all.

As with the Grand Lecture Hall, which the Gakkai
built during President Toda's day, the funding for the
Grand Reception Hall would probably be realized by
calling on members' support in the form of a special
donation drive. But Shin'ichi was of two minds as to
whether this was really the right thing to do. At the
Gakkai's current rate of development, to proceed with
the building of new temples and community centers the
Gakkai would have to expand the number of its financially contributing members. But Shin'ichi was reluctant.

Members were definitely receiving benefit as a result
of their practice, but few of them could be called "well
off." The majority, after all, had been motivated to
embrace faith due to financial hardship or illness.
Shin'ichi didn't want to add to their burden.

SHIN'ICHI turned his thoughts to how the Gakkai's organizational activities had been funded in
the past. From the outset, when the first president,
Tsunesaburo Makiguchi, had headed the organization,
responsibility for its finances had been borne entirely by

Josei Toda, then general director. At the beginning of the Gakkai's postwar reconstruction, Toda again used his own money to cover organizational expenses, so as not to put a financial burden on the members.

But shortly after Toda's inauguration as second president, several members insisted that they be allowed to bear a portion of the Gakkai's expenses. Indeed, given the pace of the kosen-rufu movement's development, it would not have been possible for him to indefinitely cover all of the organization's expenses on his own.

Donations to support the Gakkai's organizational activities represent offerings for the advancement of kosen-rufu. Faced with members' growing insistence that they be allowed to help finance the organization, Toda sensed that the time had finally come to open the door to such a development.

Still, Toda remained extremely cautious. He felt it imperative that finances for kosen-rufu derive from donations made with the utmost sincerity and purity of intention, and he was very strict as to which members could participate in making financial contributions to the organization. He initially chose seventy-eight persons whom he deemed to be both strong in faith and financially secure, and appointed them members of the Soka Gakkai's finance group, responsible for all the Gakkai's funds.

The finance group, officially inaugurated on July 3, 1951, grew steadily over the intervening years, becoming a great force in sustaining the Gakkai's economic foundation. The members selected to belong to the group were filled with pride, joy and appreciation at being able to make offerings for kosen-rufu. Nothing gave Toda greater pleasure than to see this spirit pulsing in the lives of the group's members. Financial contributions to the Soka Gakkai were not the same as donations to other organizations, because it was essential that offerings for kosen-rufu be based on faith. As long as the contributors possessed such sincere and ardent faith, they would not fail to receive immeasurable benefit and be praised by Nichiren Daishonin.

Toda wished he could give more members this opportunity, but the thought of calling for donations from members still struggling with financial difficulties pained him. Yet, in the eyes of Buddhism, to deprive them completely of a chance to support the organization in this way would be lacking in compassion.

Reluctantly, therefore, Toda decided to give members an opportunity to participate in fund-raising for such major projects as restoring the Five-Story Pagoda and constructing the Hoanden and Grand Lecture Hall at the head temple. Especially for the latter project, one of his most cherished undertakings, Toda allowed all members to participate provided that it did not cause them economic hardship.

SHIN'ICHI recalled something that Josei Toda had once told him: "Tokugawa Mitsukuni,[4] lord of the Mito domain, compiled the monumental *Dai Nihon shi* (The Great History of Japan), an undertaking said to have severely strained the finances of his domain. Mitsukuni was a man of utmost virtue; it surely must have pained him to have to fund the project, important as it was, with taxes earned by the people's sweat and toil. He must have shed inward tears.

"Similarly, I encourage our members, many of whom are very poor, to make financial contributions because it is necessary for their benefit and for accomplishing kosen-rufu. Nevertheless, each time, my heart, too, fills with tears."

Shin'ichi understood Toda's spirit. He felt exactly the same. Still, the benefit of making offerings for Buddhism is immeasurable.

One good example of this is the story of the wealthy merchant named Sudatta, who built the Jetavana Monastery as an offering to Shakyamuni Buddha. Several Buddhist scriptures relate that Sudatta converted to Buddhism after he had made his fortune. Another, however, offers the following account:

Long ago in India, there was a man named Sudatta, who lived with his wife. Although they were extremely poor, they cherished deep faith in the Buddha's teachings.

One day, Sudatta's wife boiled a small amount of rice that her husband had managed to obtain. She would share it with him when he came home. But just as she finished cooking the rice, one of Shakyamuni's disciples, Aniruddha, came to the door with a begging bowl in hand. When Sudatta's wife saw him, she bowed respectfully and placed a helping of freshly cooked rice in his bowl.

Soon, other senior disciples of the Buddha, including Subhuti, Mahakashyapa, Maudgalyayana and Shariputra, each with begging bowl in hand, came by one after another. Sudatta's wife made an offering of rice to each of these visitors. Finally, Shakyamuni himself appeared at her door. At his request for some food, Sudatta's wife gladly offered him all of the remaining rice. It was a selfless gesture of almsgiving, an expression of her faith to revere and seek the Buddha.

Had Sudatta been home, his wife would have naturally asked his consent, and he surely would have eagerly agreed to give the rice to the visitors. Yet because her husband had been away, she felt a tinge of unease.

A little later, Sudatta returned home, extremely hungry. "I'm starved," he said. "Can I have something to eat?"

His wife looked him straight in the eye and asked him, "If Shakyamuni's disciple Aniruddha were to come begging to our door, would you make him an offering?"

"Of course," he answered. "If we had any food, I would offer it. Even if it meant going hungry myself."

S UDATTA'S wife then asked, "And if Subhuti or Mahakashyapa or Shakyamuni himself were to come begging for food, what would you do?"

"You know the answer to that. If we had any food, I would naturally offer it to them."

A smile appeared on his wife's face. "As a matter of fact, Shakyamuni's disciples and Shakyamuni himself did visit today," she said. "I was so happy that I offered them all the food you worked so hard for. I worried about what you might say, but I am relieved to hear that you would have offered the food even if it meant going hungry yourself."

Sudatta, too, smiled and said: "What you did was wonderful. It is bound to eradicate our negative karma and bring us good fortune."

It is said that the benefit of his wife's offering of rice resulted in Sudatta becoming a person of great wealth and influence.

The wife's unhesitating decision, and her husband's joy at that decision exemplify the timeless spirit of joyful offering arising from pure faith. Such joy is the true spirit of offering and it is the wellspring of abundant good fortune.

The story of a supremely wealthy Sudatta donating the Jetavana Monastery to Shakyamuni is well known. One Buddhist scripture records the episode as follows:

Having resolved to build a fine monastery for Shakyamuni, Sudatta decided to find a site that was quiet yet conveniently located, neither too far from nor too close to Shravasti, the capital of the kingdom of Kosala.

After much consideration, he chose a grove that belonged to Prince Jetri. Sudatta met with the prince and

humbly requested that the latter sell him the land for his noble purpose. But the prince refused.

"That grove is my favorite place," he declared. "Even if you were to offer enough gold to cover its entire area, I would not sell it."

But Sudatta would not give up. After a heated dispute, they decided to bring the matter before a judicial minister for arbitration. After hearing what both parties had to say, the minister handed down his ruling. He decided that the prince should agree to sell the land — but only as much as Sudatta could cover with gold.

SUDATTA rushed home, loaded up a cart with pieces of gold and headed for the grove. There he solemnly began laying the gold out on the ground. Yet one cartload of gold covered only a tiny bit of land, so Sudatta set out to bring all the gold he had in his house.

Astounded by Sudatta's sincerity, Prince Jetri wondered: "Why is he so eager to throw away all his gold? Is

Shakyamuni that great? Could the talk of Shakyamuni being a Buddha, an Enlightened One, be true after all?"

The prince told Sudatta, who was intently bent over his task: "That's enough. You don't need to cover the ground with gold. I will give the grove to you."

Sudatta's earnestness and his unshakable conviction had moved Prince Jetri. Not only did the prince give Sudatta the grove, but he volunteered to erect and contribute an ornate gate. Sudatta's spirit of joyful offering had struck a resonant chord within him.

The monastery built was called the Jetavananathapindadarama (the Jetri Grove Supplier of the Needy Monastery). The full name combined the name of the grove and one of the names by which Sudatta was known among the populace: Anathapindada (Supplier of the Needy), owing to his great charity in providing food for the poor. The monastery later came to be known as the Jetavana (Jetri Grove) Monastery, for short.

When Sudatta informed Shakyamuni that he wished to donate the monastery to him, Shakyamuni replied solemnly, "I would ask that you donate this monastery not just to me but to the entire community of believers, so that it may be used by all practitioners."

Thus the Jetavana Monastery became a facility for all practitioners, a spirit perpetuated in the later construction of Buddhist temples and found today in the Soka Gakkai's community centers.

Sudatta's offering of the Jetavana Monastery is certain to have brought him even greater benefit and good fortune. The spirit of joyful offering elevates our state of life and produces immeasurable benefit. This, in turn, deepens our conviction in faith. It is an unchanging equation for consolidating the foundation of happiness in our lives.

Shin'ichi opened the Gosho. He wanted to thoroughly study again the true meaning of Buddhist offerings in light of the Daishonin's teachings. He first read "The Gift of Rice," a letter Nichiren Daishonin had written in response to an offering of rice and other items sent to him at Mount Minobu.

Praising the person's sincerity, the Daishonin says, "Even common mortals can attain Buddhahood if they cherish one thing: earnest faith" (MW-1, 268). He thus indicates that earnest faith, a sincere seeking spirit toward Buddhism, is the key to attaining Buddhahood.

*I*N "The Gift of Rice," Nichiren Daishonin praises the sincerity of someone who offered him food, which is needed to sustain life. He writes that the benefit of this offering is comparable to benefit received by such saints and sages of the past as Sessen Doji, Bodhisattva Yakuo or Prince Shotoku, who offered their lives for Buddhism.[5]

Shin'ichi Yamamoto then opened to another page in the Gosho — this time to "The Wealthy Man Sudatta" (MW-5, 307), a letter sent to Nanjo Tokimitsu on the twenty-seventh day of the twelfth month of the lunar calendar in the year 1280 (December 27).

At the time, Tokimitsu was in dire financial straits. Because he supported the Daishonin's followers during the Atsuhara Persecution, the authorities forced him to pay heavy taxes and supply workers for unpaid labor to the government. Though he could no longer maintain a horse for himself and lacked adequate food and clothing for his wife and children, he offered the Daishonin one *kan*[6] of coins out of his sincere concern for the Daishonin's well-being in the winter cold of Mount Minobu. This was the letter the Daishonin had written in response.

Looking at the many letters addressed to Tokimitsu, we find that his offerings to the Daishonin normally consisted of food and other provisions. That on this occasion Tokimitsu had instead sent money suggests that he no longer had anything in the way of practical items to offer the Daishonin. It may well be that the string of coins he sent was money he had set aside for an emergency.

The Daishonin expressed his deep respect and praised Tokimitsu's sincerity. Although Tokimitsu was almost destitute, his spirit was lofty and heroic. Offerings must always derive from a sincere spirit of faith.

In a letter addressed to Lord Matsuno (*Gosho Zenshu*, p. 1380), Nichiren Daishonin describes how a child named Tokusho Doji was reborn as King Ashoka and eventually attained Buddhahood because he offered a mudpie to Shakyamuni. For little Tokusho Doji, the mudpie had been the greatest offering he could make. Despite its humble nature, he had presented it to the Buddha with the utmost reverence. This was the cause that led to his being reborn as a great monarch in a future lifetime.

Shin'ichi Yamamoto next turned to the Gosho "The Bodies and Minds of Ordinary Beings." He stopped at a passage near the end of the letter. He read it over and over, sensing its profound meaning:

> Though one may perform meritorious deeds, if they are directed toward that which is not true, then they may bring great evil but they will never result in good. On the other hand, though one may be ignorant in mind and his offerings meager, if he presents them to a person who upholds the truth, his merit will be great. How much more so in the case of persons who in all sincerity make offerings to the True Law! (MW-6, 281)

*I*N short, the Daishonin's statement in "The Bodies and Minds of Ordinary Beings" indicates that offerings can bring about either good or evil, depending on to whom or for what cause they are made.

In light of this Gosho passage, Shin'ichi thought about the offerings made within the Soka Gakkai. The offerings and financial contributions the organization solicited were exclusively to accomplish the Daishonin's mandate to widely propagate the Mystic Law. Offerings made toward this end were equivalent to offerings made to the original Buddha. There was, then, no greater offering, no greater good. Certainly, nothing could bring greater benefit. This thought filled Shin'ichi with a sense of immeasurable good fortune and joy at having had the chance to make such offerings as a Soka Gakkai member.

The Daishonin concludes this writing by praising the spirit of this follower who had sent offerings to him at Mount Minobu: "Surely you are sowing good seeds in a field of fortune. My tears flow when I think of it" (MW-6, 282).

Dedicating oneself to kosen-rufu means "sowing good seeds in a field of fortune" — Shin'ichi had been strongly convinced of this since his youth. He recalled his days of earnestly striving to protect and support Josei Toda, who took leadership to widely propagate the Daishonin's teachings. Back then, Toda's business was experiencing severe difficulties, and for a long time payment of Shin'ichi's salary was in arrears.

Shin'ichi realized that to support this great lion of a man, who had arisen alone to spread the Law, was the way to protect the Soka Gakkai and to accomplish the goal of kosen-rufu.

He drastically cut his living expenses and made it his creed to use even a little of the money remaining from his pay to support Gakkai activities, to contribute to spreading the Daishonin's Buddhism. To do so was his joy and secret pride. Because of this, he even spent an entire winter without an overcoat. Whenever he received some of his back salary, he would use a sizable portion of it to support Toda's activities to promote kosen-rufu. Shin'ichi was absolutely convinced that the benefit and good fortune he had acquired as a result had enabled him to overcome his illness and today take on the Gakkai's leadership with confidence and composure.

He had not acted to support his mentor or the organization at someone else's behest. He had done so spontaneously, with a spirit of cheerfulness. It was an expression of his sincere faith, a reflection of his profound resolve to dedicate his life to spreading the Daishonin's Buddhism throughout the world.

After long consideration, and taking into account the Daishonin's admonitions along with his own experience, Shin'ichi decided to make it possible for all members to participate in making contributions for the Grand Reception Hall, their sincere offerings "sowing good seeds in a field of fortune" in their lives.

WITH construction of the Grand Reception Hall slated to begin, members were eager to contribute financially. Wherever he traveled around Japan, people had conveyed this to him personally. They were willing to scrimp and save to contribute for kosen-rufu. This clearly meant that many members now shared the same determination and awareness with which Josei Toda had personally assumed full responsibility for funding the Gakkai. To Shin'ichi, they exemplified noble bodhisattvas.

"These members," he thought, "are the Sudattas, the Tokusho Dojis and Nanjo Tokimitsus of our present age. Though they may be poor now, they are certain to become people of great wealth in the future. I'll do everything in my power to make sure this happens. I must praise their sincerity and warmly support them, revering them as I would Buddhas."

To Shin'ichi, nothing would add more to the splendor of the Grand Reception Hall — symbol of a new dawn of kosen-rufu — than the beautiful radiance of members' hearts brimming with the joy and sincerity of faith. It was vital, therefore, to correctly transmit the true meaning and spirit of making offerings, and that each member gain a deep awareness of his or her mission for kosen-rufu.

Shin'ichi decided to present his views about financial contributions for the Grand Reception Hall at the Soka Gakkai board of directors meeting and, if all agreed, to make an announcement at the May 3 general meeting.

On May 3, 1961, the Headquarters general meeting marking the first anniversary of Shin'ichi's inauguration as president was held at the Nippon University Auditorium in Ryogoku, Tokyo. The meeting was not scheduled to start until noon, but by 9:00 A.M., the hall was already packed with joyous, high-spirited members.

Shin'ichi arrived shortly after 11:00. Stepping from the car, he waved to the leaders and event staff who were there to greet him, calling to them: "Congratulations! Thank you!" Brimming with energy and resolve, he was eager to work for even greater development during the second year of his presidency.

Shin'ichi's start as president had been at the Soka Gakkai general meeting held at this very hall a year earlier. In his inauguration speech, he declared: "I am young and inexperienced, but from this day on, as a representative of Josei Toda's disciples, I will endeavor to lead us one step further to the actualization of kosen-rufu."

That "one step" had involved 365 days of intense struggle. It had been a great, bounding leap, an unprecedented period of advancement in the history of kosen-rufu.

And now Shin'ichi had returned to this starting place. It was truly a triumphal homecoming, celebrating a great victory in spreading the Law.

WHEN Shin'ichi learned that everyone had already entered the hall, he proposed that the meeting begin a little ahead of schedule.

At 11:40 A.M., the meeting began with a chorus of "Song of Indomitable Dignity," so powerful it seemed to rock the entire hall. As the audience sang as one, President Yamamoto and other leaders filed onto the stage led by someone carrying the Soka Gakkai Headquarters flag.

After the opening words, one leader reported on the Gakkai's progress over the past year.

Joy at President Yamamoto's inauguration the previous May had spread throughout the country in the form of boundless waves of propagation. By August 1960, three months later, a record 67,384 new households had joined in a single month. At present, the Soka Gakkai's membership stood at more than 1.91 million households, and its growth to 2 million households seemed imminent.

Over the past year, the number of chapters had increased from 61 to 139. Outside of Japan, chapters had been formed in Los Angeles and Brazil, and a district established in Hong Kong. These developments marked the dawn of a new age of kosen-rufu.

There had also been a great upsurge in Buddhist study, with more than 120 thousand members taking exams. As a result, the Study Department's membership — from assistant lecturers to professors — now exceeded forty thousand.

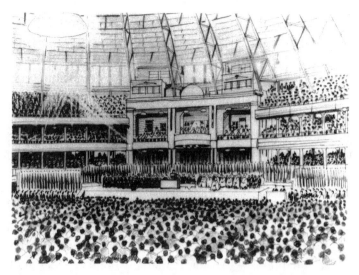

At the same time, construction of new temples progressed steadily. Six new temples had already been built, and another six would be completed in July 1961, including a new building for a temple relocating to a new site. There were also plans under way to build another thirty temples, for which the selection of sites had been nearly completed.

All the Gakkai's achievements over the past year represented a phenomenal accomplishment, which would have taken any other organization several years to realize.

Hearing what had been accomplished, the audience was filled with a fresh sense of admiration and excitement. It also gave them renewed courage and confidence: If they shared President Yamamoto's spirit and united solidly, then creating a new age of the people would not be a mere dream.

Announced next was an expansion and strengthening of the Soka Gakkai's organizational structure. The Gakkai's Culture Department would be upgraded to a Culture Bureau, incorporating departments of politics, economics, education and journalism, and charged with the mission of working for the creation of a new cultural tradition.

If Buddhism cultivates the soil of human life, then it follows that it will also support the flowering of humanistic culture. The value of religion is revealed in its ability to generate a renaissance of culture. The establishment of the Culture Bureau heralded the start of the Gakkai's broad cultural movement.

As for the structure of the Soka Gakkai Headquarters, a General Executive Office was instituted, incorporating the administrative as well as the overseas, editorial and publication departments, which were upgraded from divisions.

*A*LSO announced was the formation of a general chapter in Okinawa. It was made up of three new chapters — Nansei, Naha and Nankai — in addition to the existing Okinawa Chapter.

The current Okinawa chapter chief and women's division chief, Fukuyasu Takami and Tamako Uema, were also appointed as leaders of the new general chapter.

Shin'ichi had attended the inaugural meeting of Okinawa Chapter just ten months earlier, when the membership in Okinawa had been only 7,000 households. This number had now grown to 17,000.

After these announcements, chapter chiefs taking new positions returned their chapter flags. Newly appointed chapter chiefs, including those of new chapters, were then presented with their respective chapter flags.

Also attending the general meeting were members representing the United States and Brazil, countries Shin'ichi had visited for the first time the previous October. Chapter flags were now presented to the Los Angeles Chapter and the Brazil Chapter, both of which had been formed during Shin'ichi's visits.

When the emcee called out "Los Angeles Chapter!" all eyes turned to the stage. Although the Japanese members knew of the activities of their overseas comrades through reports in the *Seikyo Shimbun*, this was the first time any had seen them.

Next, divisional representatives shared their hopes and determinations for the second year of President Yamamoto's tenure. In particular, Youth Division Chief Eisuke Akizuki's remarks were infused with spirit and initiative. He declared that, as the Soka Gakkai's driving force, the youth division would generate a groundswell of Buddhist philosophy in society, as a current of the times. He also reported that, over the past year, the young women's division had grown from 120 thousand to 180 thousand members, and the young men's division from 180 thousand to 250 thousand. This represented an unprecedented jump to 430 thousand members in the youth division.

Then, touching on Toda's essay "Youth, Be Patriotic," which later came to be known as the "patriot" guidance, Akizuki remarked:

"In his 'patriot' guidance, our late mentor President Toda said: 'Youth, just one of you stand! A second and then a third will definitely follow. Once 100 thousand patriots gather in this way, then clearer than light, it will be possible to bring happiness to the suffering masses….'

"President Yamamoto is the one youth who has stood up just as these words instruct. And we members of the youth division are following in his footsteps. The time Mr. Toda refers to has now arrived. I am determined that we will at last carry out our mentor's words by bringing together 100 thousand patriots dedicated to saving people who are suffering. I vow to realize this epic meeting of outstanding young men's division members with President Yamamoto attending, and to open the curtain on a new phase of kosen-rufu."

SHIN'ICHI was the first to applaud Eisuke Akizuki's determination to hold a meeting with 100 thousand young men's division members. Nothing made him happier than the youth's spirit to cherish and sincerely strive to actualize the words of their late mentor, Josei Toda.

After speeches by representatives, the leaders of the America General Chapter were introduced. One of them reported on recent activities there.

When President Yamamoto visited America, the membership had been only about 300 families. But since then, members had stood up with a passionate determination for kosen-rufu and had succeeded in converting 350 more families to the Daishonin's Buddhism. Also, Soka Gakkai members were moving to the United States, and there were now 1,500 families actively participating in activities.

Next, Director Kazumasa Morikawa spoke of the development of the kosen-rufu movement in Southeast Asia. To follow up on President Yamamoto's trip to several of Japan's Asian neighbors earlier that year, it had been decided that Morikawa would lead the next overseas guidance trip to that region. His party would depart on May 16 for a ten-day trip that would include stops in Taiwan, the Philippines and Hong Kong.

Morikawa explained the plans for the trip and concluded with an energetic determination: "The day is now close at hand when a general chapter will be formed in Southeast Asia. The time for kosen-rufu throughout Asia has arrived. And I am determined to exert my utmost to lay its foundation."

Construction embodies hope and youthful vigor. Each day since Shin'ichi's inauguration, the Soka Gakkai had advanced dynamically, like a young eagle soaring through perfectly clear skies. It was leading people to a lofty realm of hope, and this hope continued to expand.

Following an address by High Priest Nittatsu, Director Katsu Kiyohara stepped up to the podium to announce that the Gakkai would be accepting financial contributions for the Grand Reception Hall. Kiyohara said animatedly:

"At the general meeting last year on the occasion of his inauguration, President Yamamoto proclaimed that he would build a Grand Reception Hall at the head temple by the sixth anniversary of the death of our late mentor, Josei Toda. Not only will the Grand Reception Hall be a place for offering prayers for kosen-rufu, it will also be the grand temple where a solemn ceremony shall be conducted at the time kosen-rufu is achieved. The construction of this edifice arose from President Yamamoto's determination to actualize President Toda's vision. Preparations are now proceeding steadily.

"We aim to make the Grand Reception Hall a magnificent modern building. It will be suitable in both its size and facilities for receiving visitors from other countries and for conveying a sense of the majesty of the Daishonin's Buddhism. This will prove most important in showing the greatness of this Buddhism to the world and establishing a new foundation for kosen-rufu."

KATSU Kiyohara spoke with even greater vigor: "Moreover, this great undertaking will be carried out by the Soka Gakkai. Ever since plans for this project were announced last year, I've been eagerly awaiting the day when I could make a donation to support it. Plans toward this end have now been completed, and I am announcing on this auspicious day that all members can make donations for this project!"

The hall roared with applause. The members had been looking forward to such an announcement. If there were any way to contribute to kosen-rufu, they wanted and were resolved to do so. This was the Soka Gakkai spirit, the source of the Gakkai's strength.

After announcing that donations would be collected in late July, Kiyohara went on to talk about the spirit of making offerings:

"Offerings should always express our sincerity based on faith. For that reason, we mustn't pressure people to make contributions. Also, even if we take the trouble to give an offering, if we do so merely because everyone else is, lacking a genuine sense of joy, then our benefit will be far less than those who make offerings joyously, of their own initiative.

"I hope that all the leaders here today will thoroughly explain the significance and correct spirit of making offerings to their members. Then everyone can participate proudly and joyfully. Helping people truly understand the importance of offerings through individual, heart-to-heart dialogue will spur them to joyful action. Let's join forces and resolve to write a fresh page in the history of kosen-rufu."

This was followed by greetings from the general director and other leaders. Thunderous applause erupted when President Yamamoto was announced to speak.

Shin'ichi rose slowly from his seat. Images came rushing back to him. In this hall a year earlier, he had first stood up as the third Soka Gakkai president, his gaze fixed on the photograph of Josei Toda high above him. The year seemed to have passed in an instant. Each day had been an intense struggle, packed with an overwhelming array of tasks. In that time, the kosen-rufu movement had experienced unprecedented growth. He savored a deep sense of fulfillment at knowing that he had scored a resounding victory.

In a manner befitting Josei Toda's disciple, Shin'ichi had forged a history of victory and returned to his place of inauguration in triumph.

WHEN Shin'ichi Yamamoto stepped up to the microphone and bowed to the audience, the thunderous applause ceased. In a moment, silence filled the hall. All present waited expectantly for this triumphant general of kosen-rufu to give a great lion's roar announcing their fresh beginning.

After expressing his deep appreciation to High Priest Nittatsu for attending, Shin'ichi said powerfully:

"I join all of you leaders here representing members throughout Japan in rejoicing at our holding this spirited Twenty-Third General Meeting. I am firmly convinced that our mentor, Josei Toda, is observing us today from his vantage point on Eagle Peak, and that he is smiling with pleasure and exclaiming, 'Well done, my disciples!'

"Where else in the world is there an organization comparable to the Soka Gakkai, whose members uphold a great philosophy, are true allies of the suffering, and advance with compassion, confidence and iron-like unity for the peace of all humankind? I declare that the Soka Gakkai is the 'pillar' of Japan and the 'sun' of the world!"

Shin'ichi was filled with great pride and confidence that the Soka Gakkai was the only organization thoroughly exerting itself as an ally of ordinary people and working for the lasting happiness and prosperity of Japan and the world. He then touched on the story of the monk Realization of Virtue and the great patron of Buddhism King Possessor of Virtue, which appears in the Nirvana Sutra.

Realization of Virtue lived in an age many years after the passing of the Thus Come One Joy Increasing. As the correct teachings of this Buddha were in danger of dying out within another forty years, the monk staunchly strove to protect and uphold them. He stood up resolutely, expounding the true teaching and admonishing those who broke the precepts. As a result, evil monks tried to kill him, attacking him with swords and staves.

Learning of these events, King Possessor of Virtue fought courageously to protect the Law and to assist the faithful monk. As a result of the king's efforts, Realization of Virtue escaped serious injury. But the king himself was killed in the struggle. He was so badly wounded, it was said that not even part of his body the size of a mustard seed remained unscathed. That was how fierce the struggle had been.

Due to the benefit they received for their devotion to Buddhism, King Possessor of Virtue was later reborn in the land of Buddha Immovable and became his chief disciple, while Realization of Virtue became that same Buddha's second disciple.

King Possessor of Virtue, who represents Shakyamuni Buddha carrying out his Buddhist practice in a previous lifetime, could be compared to lay Buddhist leaders in the present age who live and struggle in the midst of society and selflessly devote themselves to propagating the Law.

This story teaches not only the spirit Buddhists should demonstrate at a time when the teachings are imperiled but the immense benefit derived from protecting the Law.

AFTER sharing the story of Realization of Virtue and King Possessor of Virtue, Shin'ichi observed: "Day in and day out, morning and night, we of the Soka Gakkai struggle earnestly to propagate the Daishonin's Buddhism, to study Buddhist teachings, and to hold lively discussion meetings — all so that we can help those who are suffering. We also strive to protect the head temple and support High Priest Nittatsu. I am firmly convinced that, in terms of the unchanging principles of Buddhism, the actions and spirit of Soka Gakkai members correspond exactly to the actions and spirit of King Possessor of Virtue."

As he spoke, Shin'ichi thought of Tsunesaburo Makiguchi, who had steadfastly upheld the True Law and ultimately laid down his life in doing so during the war, when the priesthood had become tainted with slander and lapsed into corruption and decadence. Though he did not mention it, the thought occurred to him that Makiguchi's conduct embodied not only the actions of King Possessor of Virtue but the spirit of Realization of Virtue as well. Shin'ichi was determined that whatever lay ahead, the Soka Gakkai would always steadfastly continue to protect the correct teachings of Nichiren Daishonin with a selfless commitment to propagating the Law.

"On May 3 a year ago, on this same stage," Shin'ichi continued, "High Priest Nittatsu dedicated the following words of Nichiren Daishonin to me: 'Let the gods forsake me. Let all persecutions assail me. Still I will give my life for the sake of the Law' (MW-2 [2ND ED.], 174). As I once again engrave these words in my heart and brace myself for the struggles ahead, I ask all of you, my beloved comrades, for your cooperation. And I firmly determine to lead the way to further victory by May 3 next year. I pray that all of you, while maintaining solid faith in the Gohonzon, will join me and advance triumphantly toward kosen-rufu. That is all I would like to say. Thank you."

The hall echoed with cheers and vigorous applause. Having reached a momentous milestone of treasured victory, the Gakkai was now poised to embark on a second year of triumph.

As Shin'ichi exited the hall, the entire audience joined in a grand chorus, singing a favorite Gakkai song. The blazing fighting spirit burned even higher in his heart. There could be no defeat nor turning back on the course to achieving kosen-rufu, to which he had committed himself. No matter what hardships lay in store, he would have to keep pressing forward, forging his way through all obstacles and winning in every struggle he encountered. Shin'ichi keenly sensed that this was his destined mission.

He gazed up at the sunlight streaming in through one of the windows high above that encircled the hall at the base of its great domed ceiling.

"Above even the darkest clouds," Shin'ichi thought, "the sun always shines. My sun is President Toda. With this sun forever blazing in my heart, I will strive again tirelessly, in a manner worthy of a disciple of Josei Toda."

Illuminated by the sun's rays, Shin'ichi's face glowed with a serene smile.

"Triumph" Notes:

1. Joetsu region: Area in central Honshu, Japan's main island, encompassing Gumma and Niigata prefectures, but excluding Sado Island.

2. Takasaki: City in southern Gumma Prefecture.

3. The fourteen slanders: Fourteen types of slander enumerated by the Great Teacher Miao-lo of China based on "Simile and Parable," the third chapter of the Lotus Sutra. They consist of fourteen attitudes that believers should avoid in their practice of the True Law. They are: 1) arrogance, 2) negligence, 3) arbitrary, egotistical judgment, 4) shallow, self-satisfied understanding, 5) attachment to earthly desires, 6) lack of seeking spirit, 7) not believing, 8) aversion, 9) deluded doubt, 10) vilification, 11) contempt, 12) hatred, 13) jealousy and 14) grudges. While the first ten describe attitudes toward the Law itself, the last four describe attitudes that disparage those correctly upholding it.

4. Tokugawa Mitsukuni (1628–1700): The second lord of the Mito domain (now part of Ibaraki Prefecture), who gained fame for his effective and benevolent rule. He assembled a large number of scholars to compile a comprehensive history of Japan. Popularly known as Mito Komon, he is portrayed in fictional accounts as traveling incognito throughout Japan in his later years to detect and punish wrongdoers in high office.

5. In "The Gift of Rice," the Daishonin lists Sessen Doji, Bodhisattva Yakuo (Medicine King) and Prince Shotoku as examples of saints and sages who have ungrudgingly offered their lives for the Law. Sessen Doji offered his body to a demon to receive half a verse from a Buddhist teaching. Bodhisattva Yakuo burnt his elbows as an offering to the Buddha. And Prince Shotoku (574–622), a highly revered political and cultural leader in Japanese history, who was a devout

believer of Buddhism and did much to contribute to the religion's establishment in Japan, according to legend, peeled off the skin of his arms to copy down a portion of the Lotus Sutra.

6. *Kan*: An old monetary unit consisting of 1,000 coins, or *mon*, strung together with a cord through square holes in their centers. The *kan* was the basic monetary unit of rice exchange.

Fresh Leaves

FRESH leaves exhibit the brilliance of youth. Bathed in radiant sunlight beneath a cloudless sky, they perform a carefree melody of hope. Their delicate veins pulse with the beat of new life, hardily drawing up nutrients for the future. Enduring wind and rain, they mature from their tender state into lush green foliage.

Shin'ichi Yamamoto's great vision for kosen-rufu lay in creating a burgeoning forest, a forest teeming with the fresh verdure of youth.

The Chinese classic *Guan Zi*[1] says, "The best life-long plan is to raise people," thus extolling the endeavor of fostering capable people as the most important project of one's life.

It would surely be another thirty or forty years before the Gakkai's efforts to develop the kosen-rufu movement worldwide took off in earnest. And it would be today's young generation, spearheaded by those now in the youth division, who would be the leaders of society at that time.

Shin'ichi keenly sensed, therefore, that without fostering young people right now, substantial future development would be impossible.

After attending the May 3 Headquarters General Meeting, Shin'ichi had an informal discussion with Youth Division Chief Eisuke Akizuki and other youth division leaders who had overseen the meeting's planning and coordination. In the course of this exchange, Shin'ichi said: "Well, we're off to a new start. As a tribute to the great strides the youth division has been making, I propose that as of today we designate this year the 'Year of Youth.' What do you say?"

"Yes! I think that's great," Young Men's Division Chief Shoichi Tanida replied enthusiastically.

"Any organization," Shin'ichi continued, "whose youth are dynamic, whose youth are freely and fully giving rein to their potential, will never reach an impasse. The Soka Gakkai's future and the task of forging a permanent path to kosen-rufu rest on the shoulders of the youth division. That is why I wish to devote even more serious attention to raising youth. My main focus during this second year of my presidency will be to create a fresh tide of kosen-rufu centering around the youth division. As a first step, I plan to attend every regional general meeting of the young men's and young women's divisions held throughout Japan this year. I am totally committed to fostering the youth of the Soka Gakkai."

These general meetings of the young men's and young women's divisions were scheduled around the country that year from May until early July to mark the tenth anniversary, in July, of the youth division's formation.

For the young men's division, these meetings also marked the effective commencement of preparations for the planned gathering of 100 thousand young men's division members that fall. Since the young men's division now had more than 250 thousand members, only a portion could participate in the fall gathering. It was decided that representatives from chiefly the Tokyo area would attend the main gathering, and that the regional general meetings would hold the same significance for the young men in other parts of Japan.

"**I**N President Toda's time," Shin'ichi continued, his voice resounding even more powerfully, "the youth division members shouldered full responsibility for the Soka Gakkai and were always the driving force in its development. They possessed the ardent spirit to realize President Toda's goal of 750 thousand member households, even if it meant having to accomplish it on their own. Youth spearheaded propagation efforts in every chapter and district. And when some problem arose, the youth division members were the first to come forward and address it. They took responsibility in all areas. That's why President Toda declared, 'The youth division members are my direct heirs,' and held the greatest expectations for their growth.

"But I can't help feeling that, as the Soka Gakkai has grown larger and its organizational structure has solidified, our youth division members have gradually come to stand in the shadows of our men's and women's division members. As a result, they no longer can fully manifest their abilities. Frankly, I am concerned about the youth's growing tendency to be concerned only with their own divisions and not the Gakkai as a whole. Youth who do not recognize that the Gakkai's future rests on their shoulders will never develop into leaders who can carry on our movement in the future.

"Many graduates of the youth division now hold top leadership positions in our organization and bring all their capabilities to play in meeting the challenges that face them. But each of them, since their youth, has worked earnestly alongside me with the determination to take full responsibility for the Gakkai. Because of this awareness and the efforts they have made, they can now splendidly take the lead as central figures of our organization."

This was Shin'ichi's sincere feeling.

Even before being appointed to a leadership position, Shin'ichi had striven to realize his mentor's vision for kosen-rufu with the spirit to take full responsibility for the Soka Gakkai. His sense of commitment had never changed, through the time he was a group leader and, later, youth division general chief of staff.

Of course, his functions and duties had varied according to the organizational positions to which he had been appointed. But, as a disciple who strove to make his mentor's heart his own, he felt a deep sense of personal responsibility for every aspect of the Gakkai. As a result, he could fully utilize all the training Toda had given him and realize tremendous personal growth. Such determination, though intangible and invisible, is the very seed of growth.

A seed that is nurtured, watered and exposed to sunlight will one day sprout to grow into a tall tree. But where there is no seed, all the effort in the world will not yield a sprout.

Shin'ichi wanted to plant the seed of growth in the hearts of his beloved youth division members — that seed being a deep awareness of their mission to assume responsibility for every aspect of the Soka Gakkai.

KYUSHU was the first region in the country to hold its youth division general meetings for that year. First, the Kyushu young women's division held a general meeting shortly before 10:00 A.M. on May 7 at the Fukuoka Sports Center, with eleven thousand members attending.

Shin'ichi Yamamoto drew on a familiar metaphor to explain the nature of Buddhism to the young women:

"Let's take traffic laws, for example. These are rules designed to ensure the smooth flow of vehicular traffic and to protect lives. If we familiarize ourselves with these rules and learn, for example, that we must stop at a red light and may proceed at a green light, then by following them we can get around safely.

"But what would happen if a pedestrian — either unaware of the rules, or aware but simply determined to ignore them — were to cross the street against a red light? There is a very strong likelihood that one day he or she will get hit by a car or meet with some other kind of accident.

"Many other kinds of man-made laws govern human affairs. Those caught stealing or committing fraud will be put on trial and brought to justice. By breaking the law, they cause suffering not only to their victims but also ultimately to themselves.

"Also, many natural laws and principles operate in the realm of nature. One of these is the cycle of the four seasons. People use their knowledge of this principle to determine the optimum time for planting and harvesting rice and other crops. But if we are ignorant of this law of the seasons and plants crops in autumn, for example, we cannot expect to harvest anything.

"Similarly, there is a fundamental law of life that pervades the universe. This is the Buddhist Law, and its essential force is Nam-myoho-renge-kyo."

The eyes of the participants shone as they listened to President Yamamoto.

"People know the laws of the land. They also study the laws of the natural world, their knowledge fueling the advance of science. But most are ignorant of the fundamental law of the universe, the causal law of life, which they need to understand to become happy. To create true happiness, we have to understand and live in accordance with this fundamental law.

"The purpose of our kosen-rufu movement is to teach others about this law."

There were smiles and nods of agreement in the audience.

Shin'ichi concluded by urging the participants to continue building a solid core of happiness in their lives by, based on faith, carrying out their own human revolution, while at the same time striving unceasingly to lead the people of Japan and the world to happiness.

THE young men's division was scheduled to hold its general meeting at the same location that afternoon. When the young women's meeting ended, young men's division members began entering the hall and, within a short time, filled it to capacity, the arriving participants overflowing into the area outside.

At 2:00 P.M., the meeting began.

Hironori Kawanaka, chief of the Kyushu YMD 1st Corps, rose to offer greetings and declared: "Some 17,000 Kyushu young men's division members out of a total of 23,800 have gathered here today!"

There was a storm of cheers and applause.

This meant that more than seventy percent of the young men's division members in Kyushu had come together in one place. It was truly a magnificent turnout.

The high attendance had resulted from all the Kyushu YMD leaders uniting and taking great pains to personally encourage each member, determined to not let even one person fall by the wayside. Kawanaka had been the key person behind these efforts.

Born and raised in Amakusa, in Kyushu's Kumamoto Prefecture, Kawanaka had moved to the city of Tobata in neighboring Fukuoka Prefecture in 1948, when he was 19. There he had worked in a glass factory during the day while attending night classes to earn his high school diploma. Later, he changed jobs and became a salesman at a paint store, this time studying in the evening for a university degree.

He joined the Soka Gakkai in 1955. Once he took faith, he dedicated his life to the ideal of kosen-rufu, regarding it as his personal mission. He worked hard at his job, in his studies and in Gakkai activities.

Living by the motto "Life is a battle," he faced every challenge head on with an impassioned seeking spirit. Once he made up his mind to do something, he would plow ahead tirelessly and wholeheartedly to accomplish it.

An honest, good-natured and unpretentious young man, Kawanaka came to play a leading role in his company, achieving brilliant results as a salesman and bringing in many new clients. He was equally enthusiastic and hard-working in his Gakkai activities, using what little free time he had to travel to different places to tell others about the Daishonin's Buddhism and encourage fellow members.

Kawanaka was highly regarded in the organization for his trustworthiness and reliability and at one time was a group chief for both the young men's and the men's divisions — with overall responsibility for an entire group in one district. In those days, a group would average a membership increase of around five or six new households per month at most. But Kawanaka's group scored record numbers of up to fifty or sixty new households a month.

In August 1960, a few months after Shin'ichi Yamamoto's inauguration as third Soka Gakkai president, Kawanaka, then a young men's division chapter chief, spearheaded a campaign in which his chapter's young men's division members succeeded in converting 514 new households. This accounted for one-third of the entire chapter's new membership for that month and was celebrated as a landmark achievement in the history of the young men's division.

WHEN Shin'ichi came to Kyushu, Hironori Kawanaka was always the first to welcome him. Shin'ichi often discussed the future of kosen-rufu with this youthful leader.

On one occasion after Shin'ichi had become president, Kawanaka said to him:

"A person who seeks growth and self-improvement needs a mentor in life. I will fight throughout my life as your disciple, President Yamamoto. This is what I have decided.

"Inspired by the relationship you shared with President Toda, I have given some thought to the action and behavior required of a disciple. But the truth is that the mentor–disciple relationship involves something so profound, I find I cannot penetrate its innermost essence. At the same time, my situation makes it impossible for me to always be near you.

"From your deeds and actions, however, I know that a disciple is one who strives to actualize the mentor's vision

— in this case, for the happiness of all people and the realization of world peace. Therefore, I am determined to successfully accomplish all the goals and objectives you set forth for kosen-rufu. I will reply to your expectations by winning in these endeavors."

In fact, Kawanaka always came with news of some laudable success or achievement when he met Shin'ichi.

Often during meetings or informal gatherings, Shin'ichi would say to the members, "Everyone, please go home early tonight and get a good night's rest."

While Kawanaka would urge his fellow members to do so, he himself never thought of relaxing or slackening his efforts. He modeled his behavior after that of Shin'ichi, whom he looked up to as his mentor; in any situation, he would ask himself what Shin'ichi would do if Shin'ichi were in his place. In other words, he did not stand looking toward his mentor, thinking of himself as one of the crowd; he instead strove to live side by side with his mentor, facing the same direction in which his mentor's gaze was focused. This was his philosophy as a disciple.

Kawanaka had also been the driving force behind the great turnout for this Kyushu YMD general meeting. In the weeks leading up to the meeting, he had rallied his fellow young men's division members, telling them:

"The first of this year's scheduled regional youth division general meetings will be held here in Kyushu. What this means is that we hold the key to victory or defeat for the entire country. That's because if Kyushu gets things off to a successful start, then members in other regions will throw themselves headlong into their activities, determined not to be shown up by Kyushu. I say: 'Let us now demonstrate to our fellow youth division members throughout the country the passion and power of the sons of Kyushu!'

"The only way we can do this is to put our utmost effort into visiting our members and offering them encouragement in faith. I regard all of the young men's division members as younger brothers of President Yamamoto. I take the view that when we accept a position of responsibility in the YMD organization — no matter how minor that position may be — we are being entrusted by our mentor with the task of looking after his beloved younger brothers."

HIRONORI Kawanaka candidly related his feelings: "I think that if President Yamamoto were to ask any of us to look after his younger brother, we would be concerned not only about that young man's faith but also about his work situation and even his eating habits. We would go every day to encourage him. If we learned that our president's younger brother was not doing gongyo, then we would certainly sit down with him and have a frank talk.

"But if we in fact look at our division's members in each area, I think we will find that there are any number of members who are not doing gongyo. To turn a blind eye to their situations is irresponsible and lacking in compassion.

"Of course, giving individual guidance is no simple matter. There may be some who, failing to appreciate the greatness of the Daishonin's Buddhism, have a negative attitude toward faith. And some may even get angry and start yelling when we try to talk with them. But my hope is that through conducting tenacious dialogue, with the thought that each of these members is a precious younger brother of our mentor, we can raise every young men's division member in Kyushu to become a person of matchless strength and ability, and have each of them attend the general meeting."

Kawanaka's appeal moved the hearts of his fellow members. With a fresh awareness all earnestly applied themselves to giving individual guidance.

Kawanaka, too, went around by motorbike from one member's house to another. When he returned home, he would chant daimoku, offering prayers for each member's attendance at the general meeting. He literally "cut short his sleep by night and curtailed his leisure by day" (MW-5, 173) to carry out his activities. He strove to challenge his own limits.

His determination and effort in faith inspired YMD members throughout the length and breadth of Kyushu, known in ancient legends as the "Land of Fire." With Kyushu's great victory, flames would further spread to engulf the entire country.

Courage spreads like waves. Vitality and enthusiasm are infectious.

In his speech at the Kyushu Young Men's Division General Meeting, Shin'ichi Yamamoto said:

"Recently, the Soviet Union succeeded in sending a person into space — a feat that is a first for humankind. The pilot of the spacecraft, Yuri Gagarin, is still a young man like all of you. Unlike Gagarin, however, you are not in the spotlight of attention — you are not being written about in newspapers or interviewed on television. But I declare that your activities for kosen-rufu, your unceasing efforts day and night to spread the Daishonin's teachings for people's happiness, are a great undertaking that is in no way inferior to Gagarin's heroic feat."

A little less than a month earlier, on April 12, the Soviet spacecraft *Vostok I* had blasted off with Gagarin on board, successfully completing a single orbit of the Earth in one hour and forty-eight minutes. This was the first manned space flight in human history.

Gagarin, who spoke the famous words "The Earth was blue," was then a youth of just 27.

THE vast majority of youth now gathered before Shin'ichi had little money or standing in society. Hardly any were members of the professional elite. Yet they understood the hearts of ordinary people and were passionately committed to helping their friends who were suffering. This is the most important requirement for genuine leaders.

Shin'ichi's wish was to raise these youth to be the next generation of leaders.

After going explaining that the road to a life of great achievement lies not far away but where we are right now, Shin'ichi closed his address urging each participant to strive to distinguish himself in his job or sphere of endeavor, playing a leading role and scoring great success.

After attending the two general meetings in Kyushu, Shin'ichi flew from Fukuoka to Osaka.

Then, on May 9, he traveled to Maizuru, a city in northern Kyoto Prefecture. His schedule that day included the opening and Gohonzon-enshrinement ceremony for the newly completed Jitsudo-ji, a temple donated by the Soka Gakkai, and the Maizuru Chapter inaugural meeting.

This was Shin'ichi's third trip to Maizuru. On his first visit, in January 1958, he had come on behalf of Josei Toda, who was then bedridden with illness. While there, Shin'ichi had put all his energy into holding guidance meetings and encouraging the members.

His second visit had been in June of the same year — two months after Toda's death. While on a trip to Kyoto, he suddenly decided to squeeze in a quick visit to nearby Maizuru. He wanted to impart hope and courage to the members there, who were deeply saddened by the loss of

their mentor. During the short four hours he spent in Maizuru on that occasion, he held a question-and-answer session at the district chief's home — the focal point for local activities — and threw himself into giving guidance and encouraging the members.

During the war, Maizuru had been a bustling center of activity as the site of a naval base and dispatch point to the Asian continent for troops. After the war, it was designated as a clearance port through which some 660 thousand repatriating soldiers made their way back to Japan.

Now on this first visit to Maizuru in three years, Shin'ichi was welcomed by a cloudless, deep blue sky and the members' smiles.

The opening and Gohonzon-enshrinement ceremony for Jitsudo-ji commenced at 1:00 P.M. Because Maizuru had once been a naval base, Shin'ichi described in his address how the Gakkai had stood up to the militarist authorities during the war. He also declared that the Soka Gakkai was a religious organization representing a powerful creative force for an age of genuine peace.

Shin'ichi said that although in the past soldiers had embarked for war from Maizuru's shores, he hoped that in the future, practitioners of the Daishonin's Buddhism would venture from Maizuru into the world as emissaries of the Buddha and messengers of peace.

A FTER the ceremony, Shin'ichi removed his jacket and went out in the garden. There he saw some youth who had been working as event staff for the ceremony and beckoned them to join him.

Twenty or thirty young men and women gathered around Shin'ichi.

"I'm determined to spend even more time meeting and talking with young people from now on," he began, and then inquired, "Are all of you studying hard?"

Looking at the young people around him, he saw that some nodded while others blushed and dropped their eyes.

"Studying is what counts. No matter how busy you are, you still should read one or two books a month. Those who realize great success in society, even if they've had no formal schooling, all study very hard. This is the time when you need to work hard, study earnestly and develop your abilities.

"Buddhist study is particularly important. Through your efforts in Buddhist study, you establish your path in life. If you cease to apply yourselves to Buddhist study, you will forget why you are practicing, be swayed by your emotions or self-interests, and ultimately come to live and act in a disingenuous and calculating manner.

"By the way, do any of you have any questions?"

One young man, who looked rather fatigued, said:

"President Yamamoto, I'm having a hard time participating in Gakkai activities as much as I would like to because of a busy work schedule. How can I find a way to do both?"

This was a problem that had once given Shin'ichi himself quite a bit of anguish. He immediately replied:

"To get right to the point, it boils down to making a decision to do your best in everything and then having the determination not to retreat a single step. When placed in severe circumstances, people all too easily tend to give up, convinced that the situation is hopeless, before even considering what concrete actions they could take. In their hearts, they have already conceded defeat without even putting up a fight. That, in fact, is the cause of all failure.

"The crucial thing is to determine to do your absolute best both at work and in Gakkai activities, and to find time to earnestly chant daimoku about your situation. You have to bring forth your wisdom and life force, and then exercise your ingenuity.

"How you go about resolving the dilemma will differ according to the kind of work you do, conditions on the job and your position. For instance, leaders who cannot get around to see their members because they have to travel frequently on business can encourage them by writing them letters regularly while on the road. Or, if they have to work overtime until late at night six days a week but have Sundays off, they can do a week's worth of activities on that day. A hundred people will come up with a hundred different creative ways, but in every case the basic principle is the same."

THE eyes of the young man who had asked the question gradually brightened. Shin'ichi's guidance was specific and to the point. He continued:

"If you are the central figure in your organization, it is particularly important to train someone who can lead activities in your absence. It's vital that you be determined, no matter what, to achieve the targets everyone has agreed on as an organization. You must not allow the organization to come to a standstill simply because you can't be as active as you would like.

"Often, curiously enough, the leaders of those areas making the most remarkable progress — regardless of their division — are people who have very demanding work schedules. Their all-out dedication moves others, with the result that those around them become serious and start working hard, too."

Because this was a very important issue, Shin'ichi wanted to discuss it from a variety of angles.

"Again, in trying to strike a balance between work and activities, you have to consider the problem of time. It is only natural that a student, for example, should study hard before an examination. And there are similar critical times on a job. At such times, it is natural to devote most of your time to work.

"So how to balance things has to be considered on a case-by-case basis. Also, rather than viewing things only in the short term, it's important to have a long-range perspective.

"While we are young, however, we should exert ourselves so that we can honestly say that we've done our best in both our work and Gakkai activities. That's because our efforts during this time will become the foundation for our entire lives. President Toda often said, 'In faith, do the work of one; in your job, do the work of three.'

"Since there are only twenty-four hours in a day and each of us is only one person, some of us probably feel it is a contradiction to say we should make an all-out effort in both our work and Gakkai activities."

Some of the youths nodded at this.

Smiling, Shin'ichi continued: "But if this is a contradiction, then everything is a contradiction. We live in a world where all kinds of demands are constantly pulling us in different directions. If our job entails manufacturing something, then we will be told to make a good product. But even though doing so will require more time, we'll still be pressured to complete the work quickly.

"There are even proverbs that contradict one another. For instance, one says, 'The warrior betrays no weakness when starving,' while another says, 'An army travels on its stomach.' And then there is the saying, 'If you see a stranger, assume he is a thief,' while another proverb says, 'There are no demons in this world.'"

THE youths listened intently, nodding each time Shin'ichi made a point that struck home. Some were taking notes.

"Even in the Gosho, the Daishonin makes statements that might at first glance seem contradictory. For example, in one letter, he says that we can attain Buddhahood by just chanting a single daimoku. But elsewhere he warns that if we commit slander, then no matter how much daimoku we chant, we'll see no benefit at all.

"Again, in one letter he says that it is better to live a single day with honor than to live to 120 and die in disgrace. Yet, elsewhere he says to die young is a terrible waste.

"There are two sides to everything. Not seeing things just one way is very human. Life involves striking a balance amid the tensions of conflicting issues while striving always to improve ourselves and move ahead. While we may think that concentrating on one thing — work, for example — would make life a lot less complicated, it's a mistake to cast aside other commitments or pursuits on that account.

"I'm well aware what a challenge it is to hold down a job, to study and do Gakkai activities all at the same time. But true Buddhist practice and training lie in working hard and succeeding in each of these areas. Moreover, all of these struggles will become precious lifelong treasures.

"If we feel that our lives are painful or agonizing, then let's find a spare moment and pray about our situation. If we pray, then the energy to challenge our circumstances will emerge, and we will definitely find a way to break through. Eventually we will attain a life state where we can do activities and devote ourselves to kosen-rufu to our heart's content, free of all hindrances.

"We may think there's no advantage to working hard. But hard work pays off in the long run. All our efforts will become valuable assets in life. So let's work really hard! And let's relish doing so!"

Bright smiles appeared on the youths' faces.

There are schools for teaching young people knowledge and technical skills. Yet there are no educational institutions that teach life or how to live, no schools that help people truly cultivate themselves. However, such training lies at the core of human education.

Shin'ichi worried about the narrow-mindedness caused by Japanese society's overemphasis on higher learning at the expense of building human character. The Soka Gakkai was a "university of ordinary people" — a school with no classrooms. Here, Shin'ichi strove to promote education that would develop the character and inner fiber of each individual, for when young people who were fostered and trained in this way became mainstays in each field of society and in every locality, they would create a tide of true prosperity for their country and the world.

A FTER talking with the youth, Shin'ichi left to attend the Maizuru Chapter inaugural meeting and then a district leaders guidance meeting.

The following day, he went for a drive around the city with Hyozo Tagawa, the chapter chief. Tagawa ran his own express freight business. His wife, Keiko, was the chapter women's division chief.

As Tagawa explained the sights, Shin'ichi gazed out the window at the scenery. Before them stretched the blue waters of an inlet, tranquil amid the fresh greenery of the surrounding mountains.

They stopped at a spot that commanded a clear view of Maizuru Bay and got out to have a look.

"Maizuru has a fine natural harbor," Shin'ichi remarked to Tagawa. "It's wonderful. Let's make Maizuru the best 'harbor of kosen-rufu' in all Japan."

Shin'ichi then asked, "Do you know why we formed a chapter here in Maizuru in addition to the one in Kyoto?"

Tagawa was silent.

"It's because growth and development arise where there is friendly competition, where people inspire one another through their efforts. If the members in Maizuru stand up and take action, this will encourage those in Kyoto to work hard, too. Hyogo and Osaka will then want to show their strength. And if the entire Kansai organization encompassing both these regions exerts itself fully, then Tokyo, too, will rise to the occasion. From there a wave of growth and progress will spread through the entire country. That's why Maizuru is important. From here you can set the entire Soka Gakkai in motion."

As he listened to Shin'ichi, Tagawa felt a whole new perspective open up for him. He was inspired by the thought that his sphere of activity — this port city surrounded by mountains and sea — was in fact a primary port of departure for the growth of the entire country. A fighting spirit blazed anew within him.

Later that day, Shin'ichi traveled to Nara where he was scheduled to encourage local members. After spending the night in Nara, he went on to Kobe the next day, May 11, to attend the joint inaugural meeting of Kobe and Hyogo chapters at the Oji Gymnasium.

Here in Kobe, he was planning to make an important announcement. It concerned the production of films to document the Gakkai's activities.

Each step forward for the Soka Gakkai constituted a brilliant, enduring page in the history of kosen-rufu. But those who could attend even the largest meetings were only a small handful compared to the Gakkai's total membership, now fast approaching 2 million households. The kosen-rufu movement was also spreading to other parts of the world, where the large majority of members could not witness or appreciate this with their own eyes.

While he was still youth division chief of staff, Shin'ichi pondered how to enable all members to more directly share and personally savor the Soka Gakkai's spirit of dynamic progress. From that time on, he had begun to pursue plans to record major Gakkai events and activities on film and make them available for all members to enjoy.

WITH Shin'ichi's proposal, the Gakkai began recording all of its important events — starting with the Youth Division Sports Meet in September 1956 — on 8- or 16-millimeter film. There was historic footage capturing Josei Toda delivering his declaration for the abolition of atomic and hydrogen bombs, the opening ceremony for the Grand Lecture Hall, and the burial of a memorial plaque dedicated to the kosen-rufu of Asia and other items at Bodhgaya in India.

The power of film is truly immense. As the saying goes, "Seeing is believing." Film brings distant images to life before millions of people, wherever they are. Well-made movies record not only the bare facts but the underlying truth; the thought and philosophy behind the events portrayed.

One person who demonstrated most brilliantly the power of the motion picture was the great comedian Charlie Chaplin. In his film *The Great Dictator*, which opened in 1940 during World War II, Chaplin, through scathing criticism and hilarious parody, deftly exposed the true nature of the dictator Adolf Hitler, whose forces were then sweeping across Europe.

The United States — where Chaplin then resided — had not yet entered the war and there was a general reluctance to publicly criticize Hitler's actions. Chaplin was widely denounced for making such a film. Nevertheless, he forged ahead alone with his project and in this single film magnificently exposed Hitler's lies and facade to the entire world.

In a sense, the twentieth century can be described as an "age of film." From early on, Shin'ichi had appreciated the immense potential of this medium.

A few weeks earlier, at the organization's board of directors meeting, he had brought up the matter of in-house film production for the express purpose of documenting the Gakkai's great popular movement of kosen-rufu. The matter was discussed and deliberated at length, and was now being implemented.

Shin'ichi had been inspired to announce this development in Kobe because of his conviction that this port city, long a principal center for trade with other countries, would become the site of a brilliant new cultural renaissance. Moreover, of Japan's six largest cities — Tokyo,

Osaka, Kyoto, Nagoya, Kobe and Yokohama — only Kobe, in Hyogo Prefecture, had been without a chapter. Now, Shin'ichi wanted to celebrate Kobe's new beginning as a chapter with an announcement that would inspire and give hope to the members.

Despite the pouring rain outside, there was an electric atmosphere inside the hall where the joint Kobe and Hyogo chapter inaugural meeting was being held.

Shin'ichi's words on that occasion were like a bright ray of hope breaking through the rain clouds. He began by announcing plans for the construction of a community center in Kobe.

AFTER waiting for the applause to subside, Shin'ichi said: "I imagine you might wonder at times what kind of headquarters building the members in Hokkaido have, or under what conditions they are carrying out activities. And I think many of you might want to know what the members in Okinawa are like, or what activities are being conducted in the

Tohoku or Chubu regions. Or you may wish to know what it's like to practice in the United States, Brazil or in Southeast Asia.

"For precisely this reason, I would like to form what might best be described as a film crew — to record images of these places on 16-millimeter film and present them to you as chronicles of the activities of members throughout Japan and the world. What do you think?"

Cheers and applause again filled the hall.

"Since my friends of Hyogo approve, I will move ahead confidently with this project. I hope you'll enjoy watching these films when they're finished."

Shin'ichi then stressed that in the realm of faith it is always crucial to engage in activities for kosen-rufu with a thoroughly pure spirit that is untainted by self-interest. He closed by voicing his hope that all present would strive to build truly happy lives.

From Kobe, Shin'ichi returned briefly to Tokyo on May 12, only to leave again the next day for Okinawa, where the inaugural meeting of Okinawa Chapter would be held on the 14th.

Only ten months had passed since his last visit to Okinawa the previous July. Shin'ichi's wish was to visit Okinawa every year in order to lay a solid foundation for the southern archipelago's future.

When he arrived at Naha Airport, Shin'ichi declared to the members who had come to welcome him: "Spring has come at last to Okinawa."

The dynamic development the Okinawan members had realized over the past ten months had completely transformed their expressions. Each face was lit with a dazzling smile and radiated self-confidence and joy.

When people change, society changes, too. When people sparkle with life and vitality, the realm of the environment does as well. Buddhism teaches that life and its environment are inseparable.

Shin'ichi was now confident that a glorious future lay in store for Okinawa.

He used every moment of his short, two-day visit to encourage the Okinawa members, taking time out to talk with the leaders of each district in particular.

At the new chapter's inaugural meeting, he announced plans to build a Gakkai community center in Okinawa and promised to pay a third visit for the center's opening and Gohonzon-enshrinement ceremony.

For the kosen-rufu movement in Okinawa, these plans marked the arrival of a new spring, the unfurling of fresh buds of hope.

*A*FTER the Okinawa General Chapter inaugural meeting, the general chapter chief, Fukuyasu Takami, remarked to Shin'ichi, "President Yamamoto, tomorrow I'll finally be setting off for the guidance tour of Southeast Asia."

Shin'ichi had envisioned such a visit by leaders from Japan when he was on a tour of Asian countries in January and February that year. After his return to Japan, the plan was discussed and approved at a board of directors meeting. Apart from his own trips abroad, this was the first time a delegation of leaders from the Soka Gakkai Headquarters was to be dispatched overseas. Shin'ichi had proposed that Takami and another leader from Okinawa be included.

"Yes, that's right!" Shin'ichi exclaimed. "Thank you for all your efforts. Okinawa is the gateway to Asia. I want to create a growing stream of people traveling from Okinawa to Southeast Asia to encourage members there. Among all the Japanese people, the citizens of Okinawa suffered the most during the war. The people of Southeast Asia suffered much as well.

"Because of this, your going forth to encourage our friends in Southeast Asia, while working to build a paradise of peace in Okinawa, will be the most persuasive of testimonies to the greatness of faith. By the way, will you be going to Taiwan first?"

"Yes, that's right. We arrive in Taipei on the 15th, and the following evening we are scheduled to meet up with Director Morikawa and other senior leaders from the headquarters," Takami replied.

"I'd like to go to Taiwan, too, and encourage the members there," Shin'ichi said. "But since that's not possible now, please meet with each of them on my behalf and do everything in your power to encourage them. I'd like you to help them forge a deep and solid spiritual foundation so that they can maintain faith throughout their lives and never be defeated.

"Eventually, we will see an 'age of great voyages for kosen-rufu,' a time when many members from Japan will go out into the world and fellow members from all parts of the globe will come to visit Japan. This trip to Southeast Asia is a harbinger of that time. Therefore, please unite with Director Morikawa to bring about a new phase of kosen-rufu, while remaining alert against accidents or mishaps. I will be sending you daimoku."

Shin'ichi's words deeply inspired Takami with the profound significance of his upcoming trip.

The following day, May 15, Takami and the other leader from Okinawa participating in the delegation set out from Okinawa and met up with Morikawa's group in Taipei.

During their stay in Taiwan, the leaders visited a number of cities, including Kao-hsiung; met with and encouraged more than 130 families and individuals who were practicing the Daishonin's Buddhism; and established three districts in Taipei and two in Kao-hsiung. They also set aside time to look into purchasing cypress timber in Taiwan for the Grand Reception Hall. It had been Josei Toda's express wish that Taiwanese cypress be included among the construction materials for this building.

A FTER leaving Taiwan, Kazumasa Morikawa, Fukuyasu Takami and the other delegates visited Manila, Bangkok and Hong Kong, returning to Japan on May 25.

During the trip, they established a district in Manila and one in Bangkok and met and held discussions with members from Indonesia, Vietnam and Burma (now Myanmar) who had been invited to rendezvous with the delegation, forming a district in each of those countries as well.

The unfolding of kosen-rufu in Asia that Shin'ichi had pioneered was expanding rapidly; the foundation was steadily being laid for the lasting peace and happiness of people throughout the region.

In the meantime, Shin'ichi had returned directly to Tokyo from Okinawa and was meeting with the directors about the immediate future course the organization's activities would take. He was pouring his energy into setting the stage for the next advance. The first issue on the agenda was the collection of donations for the Grand Reception Hall.

Katsu Kiyohara reported the details of the plan that had been worked out: She explained that the campaign would be implemented nationwide, and that donations would be accepted by each district during a four-day period beginning July 21.

After listening to her report, Shin'ichi asked, "Who will be responsible for the collection at each district?"

"The district chiefs."

Shin'ichi looked concerned.

"Aren't you, the directors, going to take responsibility yourselves?" he asked. "It's outrageous that you should think of saddling the district chiefs and women's division chiefs with all the responsibility! They'll be busy enough as it is just going around to encourage members and convey to them the significance of making donations for this project. The responsibility for the collection itself should naturally fall on the leaders of the chapter level and higher, including our directors. It should also be their job to greet the members with utmost courtesy and deference when they come to make their donations, sincerely thanking them on my behalf and offering warm words of encouragement.

"Our members are leading busy lives with many demands and pressures, spending what spare time they have on doing Gakkai activities and striving with all their might for kosen-rufu. They'll be going out of their way to make their donations — with money they've earned by the sweat of their brows. How praiseworthy they are! Their very actions are those of bodhisattvas. Their behavior is that of the Buddha. It is the duty of leaders to support and serve these members. By doing so, they can accumulate benefit and good fortune.

"'What can I do to raise people's spirits?' 'What can I do to give people joy?' — these should be a leader's constant thoughts. You couldn't possibly have come up with a plan like this — a plan that leaves everything up to others — if you had this kind of attitude."

SHIN'ICHI was always strict in his guidance to top leaders. This was because the entire responsibility for the Soka Gakkai rested on their shoulders.

Next on the agenda for discussion were the activities of the culture bureau, which had been inaugurated at the

May 3 general meeting. In addition to his other responsibilities, youth division chief and director Eisuke Akizuki had been appointed to head the writers department within the culture bureau.

Shin'ichi turned to him and asked, "How is the activity plan for the writers department coming along?"

"Yes, we're still looking into that," Akizuki replied, looking apologetic.

Shin'ichi shot back in a stern tone: "That's too slow. Our purpose in forming the writers department is clear, so you should already be coming up with concrete plans and discussing things with me if there is a problem. Just standing by until I give you instructions is irresponsible. If youth are passive, they will lose in their struggles in society. Being reprimanded for something when you've actively done your best is no disgrace, but being reprimanded when you haven't done anything out of fear of failing is shameful."

"I'm sorry," Akizuki replied. "What happened was that our executive staff was split on the direction the writers department should take. As a result, we couldn't reach a consensus on an activity plan. One view is that the department should comprise authors and screenwriters who are presently active in their fields, to provide them an opportunity to develop their faith. Another view is that the department should aim broadly to educate many young people as writers and journalists for the future. I was hoping to get your opinion as to which focus the writers department should take."

"Both are necessary," Shin'ichi said. "We have to raise great authors who possess a solid grounding in the Daishonin's Buddhism. At the same time, it is important to develop each member of the youth division to be an accomplished writer and speaker. From now on, it will be increasingly important for leaders to have good writing and speaking skills. If those who become top youth division leaders can neither write a speech nor an article, nor speak persuasively, they cannot hope to lead society.

"In that respect, too, youth division leaders should not simply entrust such activities to a select group of specially trained individuals; rather, they should ensure that all members hone their general abilities as speakers and writers. In light of that, why don't you adopt a dual structure: one section comprising youth division leaders and another consisting of professional writers?"

Shin'ichi's thinking was very flexible in this regard. In an instant, Akizuki's worries about the direction of the new department were resolved.

SHIN'ICHI next asked about the education department, which was headed by the women's division chief and director, Katsu Kiyohara.

Kiyohara outlined the progress of preparations to set up the department, and said:

"We've asked each local organization to provide us with the names and addresses of any members in the teaching profession. Once we have finished compiling our list — which shouldn't be long now — we will contact those individuals. At this stage, we're hoping to hold the department's first meeting in June, the month of President Makiguchi's birth."

"That's a good idea," Shin'ichi responded. "Let's hold it at the Gakkai Headquarters. President Makiguchi began his struggles to save people from misery by advocating educational reform. And he found the philosophy that would provide the underpinnings for his educational theories in Nichiren Daishonin's Buddhism. At the most fundamental level, Buddhism is the highest form of humanistic education. I think that education also will be my final undertaking.

"Japan is certainly becoming affluent. But delinquency and other problems involving young people are becoming increasingly severe. This is because the nation, the schools and teachers lack a clear philosophy of how to go about educating human beings. I fear for Japan's future and for the twenty-first century if things continue as they are.

"Providing good facilities and a proper environment is certainly important to education. But teachers themselves are the most crucial aspect of a child's educational environment. The education department of the Soka Gakkai must develop those teachers."

Kiyohara sensed President Yamamoto's vast expectations for the education department, as well as its important mission.

Shin'ichi then turned to General Director Koichi Harayama and said: "I'll make one proposal today. To raise the next generation of core leaders, I would like to appoint some new directors from among the top leaders of the youth division. Youth don't grow just by our urging. It's important to give them responsibility and areas where they can actively contribute.

"You are all seasoned directors, so I imagine that young people with little experience often give you cause for worry. But unless they're given responsibility, they'll never grow. We'll never know if they can really do something unless we let them try. So I'd like you to bear that in mind from now on when you nominate new directors."

Resting his gaze on Eisuke Akizuki, Shin'ichi said:

"By the way, Mr. Akizuki, I want you to be responsible for the production of the documentary films we've been discussing. Since it's a completely new field, I'd like a young person to take it on. I know it will be difficult for you, having so many different responsibilities already

— but I want the youth to shoulder everything and pave the way for greater progress."

"I'll do my best!" Akizuki replied, his voice conveying his resolve.

*T*HE young men's division leaders meeting for May was held on the 16th. Shin'ichi had not been scheduled to attend the meeting, but to encourage these young members he made arrangements to join the meeting halfway through. It was the first time he would attend a young men's division leaders meeting in almost a year.

When his car reached Asakusa Station, he saw a number of young men running toward the Taito Gymnasium, the meeting site. The meeting itself had already begun, and these members had surely rushed to finish their work and come as soon as they could. They were running at full speed, panting heavily as sweat streamed down their faces. But no matter how fast they ran, the meeting had already started, and their rushing would save them no more than five or ten minutes at the most. Nevertheless, Shin'ichi sensed a passionate seeking spirit in their earnest haste.

Running to a meeting place was not exactly a good idea if you wanted to avoid having accidents and creating a negative impression. But the spirit behind doing so was important. Though a meeting might already be under way, the determination to arrive even a minute or second earlier to absorb just that much more is a cause for growth. This attitude should not be forgotten. Shin'ichi pondered how best to teach each person this spirit in the pragmatic times in which they lived.

Shin'ichi's attendance caused the energy level at the meeting to soar. The president's attendance drove home the significance of his statement after the May 3 general meeting that "This year will be the Year of Youth."

In his speech, Shin'ichi shared his personal feelings:

"I am an imperfect human being lacking any special ability. I imagine that many of my faults may be obvious to you. But I'm confident that I am second to none in the trust I place in you, the great hopes I have for your future, and my ardent spirit to save Japan from misery and accomplish kosen-rufu. This year, as one of the more than 400 thousand youth of the Soka Gakkai, I am determined to struggle and advance directly among the members of the youth division. Thank you very much."

It was not Shin'ichi's intention to instruct the youth from the lofty office of president. He wanted to inspire them with his own spirit and actions as an ordinary person no different from themselves. Such inspiration is the most potent force for human development.

ON May 17, the next day, Shin'ichi Yamamoto traveled to Koriyama in Fukushima Prefecture, where meetings were being held to inaugurate three new general chapters in the Tohoku region.

On the way back to Tokyo, he remarked to a youth division leader who was accompanying him:

"About the writers department, I think it's important that it begin its activities by focusing on the youth division. Membership could initially consist of young men's division and young women's division chapter leaders. Their next gathering is on the evening of the 19th, isn't it?"

"Yes, chapter-level leaders of both the young men's and young women's divisions of the Tokyo area will be meeting at the Gakkai Headquarters."

"Good. I'll attend. Let's make it a kickoff for the writers department," Shin'ichi proposed. Wherever he went, the matter of raising youth never left his mind.

On the 19th, Shin'ichi told the young men and women who gathered at the Gakkai Headquarters:

"Unarmed and without any political power or wealth, Nichiren Daishonin bravely employed the power of words to fight against the nation's wholesale attempts to suppress him. Words have the potential to create, influence and determine the direction of the times. But journalism in Japan today has become corrupt and irresponsible. This, I think, lies at the root of Japan's moral decay.

"Against this backdrop, the role of the Soka Gakkai writers department will be to develop a tide of discourse to illuminate the correct course for humanity, to protect the people, and to create a groundswell toward peace. As the writers department prepares to launch its activities, I especially ask you, the youth division leaders, to take on this important mission as the department's first members.

"As for specific activities, I'd like you to discuss them thoroughly with Youth Division Chief Akizuki, who is heading the department. At any rate, I hope each of you will work to the full extent of your ability to write articles that champion the cause of the people and attest to the virtue of the Soka Gakkai in a variety of forums, including the Gakkai's newspaper and magazines. I will write, too. I will stand and fight in the vanguard."

Besides writing the editorial for the Gakkai's monthly study journal, *The Daibyakurenge*, Shin'ichi wrote articles for the monthly Soka Gakkai-affiliated current affairs journal, *Ushio*, and other publications.

Now, in the second year of his presidency, Shin'ichi continued tirelessly to travel the country, speaking and taking action with the development of youth always his primary focus. So hectic was his schedule that he had barely finished attending a leaders meeting of Hokkaido General Chapter on May 21, when he was off again to

Nagoya for the kickoff of three new general chapters in the Chubu region on the 24th. Three days later, he was back in Tokyo for another Headquarters Leaders Meeting.

A T the May Headquarters Leaders Meeting at the Taito Gymnasium on the 27th, the appointment of six new directors was announced. They included Young Men's Division Chief Shoichi Tanida and two other youth division leaders. Such youthful additions to the Soka Gakkai's Board of Directors reminded the participants that the age of youth was truly at hand.

Also announced was the establishment of the Southeast Asia General Chapter. Kazumasa Morikawa was appointed the general chapter chief and Ryoko Nakahara of the women's division Headquarters staff became the general chapter women's division chief. Kenji Mikawa was assigned to the general chapter staff.

A news bureau was established within the Gakkai Headquarters and Eisuke Akizuki was appointed bureau chief. It was to be responsible for the production of films documenting the organization's activities. Shin'ichi's dream of chronicling the Soka Gakkai on film had now become a reality.

The dual structure of the writers department — with one section consisting of youth division leaders and another of professional writers — was also officially announced.

Shin'ichi was laying the groundwork for developing youth in one arena after another.

When the board of directors met on May 29 to discuss activities for June, Shin'ichi made another proposal:

"I don't think we should leave the task of fostering youth to only the leaders of the young men's and young women's divisions," he said. "Young people may encounter problems in life that leaders of the same generation cannot adequately address. Also, if the young men and young women concern themselves exclusively with their own divisions, they may lose sight of the bigger picture — of the Soka Gakkai as a whole.

"To better support the youth division, therefore, I would like all members of the board of directors, myself included, to attend monthly leaders meetings of the young men's and young women's divisions beginning in June, according these meetings the same importance as the monthly Headquarters Leaders Meetings."

Shin'ichi's proposal came from his fierce resolve to work for the welfare and happiness of the youth. The directors expressed their unanimous agreement. Fostering the youth was now becoming a common concern of the entire board of directors.

The film production project was also absorbing a great deal of Shin'ichi's attention around this time. Two young men had been assigned to the news bureau as permanent staff along with Eisuke Akizuki. The team was working as fast as it could to produce its first film for public screening in early June.

The series would be titled *Seikyo News* and the first film would document the May 3 general meeting marking the first anniversary of President Yamamoto's inauguration. It would also cover the formation of Okinawa General Chapter and other activities that took place in May. The plan for the time being was to produce one thirty-minute newsreel each month.

*T*HE film production staff had begun working even before the official announcement of the news bureau's establishment. At Shin'ichi's suggestion, they had filmed all of the May events and had enough film to edit and compile a newsreel of some

twenty to thirty minutes. But when they viewed the raw footage at the pre-production stage, they found that most of the indoor scenes, such as the coverage of inaugural general chapter meetings in various parts of the country, were too dark.

One of the young bureau members, Yoshio Iizaka, had worked as a film director, but he was not a professional cameraman. Nor did the Soka Gakkai own sufficient lighting equipment for shooting films. But there was no turning back now. While editing the first film, they began shooting the second.

With so many tasks to complete — filming, audio recording, editing and script writing for the narration — each member of the group had to wear several hats. Late one evening, Shin'ichi dropped by their workroom. The two young staff members were hard at work and didn't even notice the president's arrival.

When he greeted them, the two looked up with a start. They must have been working late like this for several days in a row and fatigue showed on their faces. They began to rise from their chairs, but Shin'ichi motioned for them to remain seated. "Don't get up," he said. "Just tell me what your biggest problem is right now."

"To tell the truth, we're out of film," Iizaka replied. "We've already used up our entire budget."

Having just been established, the news bureau did not have a sufficient budget, and its members had been doing their best to economize. For example, a thirty-minute newsreel equaled about one thousand feet of film. Normally, about ten thousand feet had to be shot to obtain one thousand feet of usable film. But to economize, they had done everything possible to minimize the amount of film that would be discarded when editing. In spite of such painstaking care, they had still run out of film.

"I see," Shin'ichi said. "I'm sorry you have to work under such austere conditions." He then asked Iizaka how much money was needed for film for the time being and, opening his wallet, made a personal donation to the group.

Flashing a broad smile, Shin'ichi encouraged them, "Mr. Iizaka, I know things are tough now, but that's always the way it is when you're breaking new ground."

SHIN'ICHI'S sincere concern in coming by in the middle of the night to see how they were doing warmed Yoshio Iizaka's heart.

"I'm sorry," Shin'ichi continued, "that your limited budget has caused you so much trouble. But I'm sure you understand that we have to supply projectors for each general chapter, and there are numerous other outlays as well. In addition, since all the operating expenses of the Soka Gakkai are funded by the members' sincere donations, it's natural that we always make every effort to economize.

"Soon we can increase your staff, but until then, please be patient, use your wisdom and ingenuity, and do the best you can. The true spirit of youth is that of challenge, to determine to produce the best work you can under the worst conditions. If you can produce something truly excellent in spite of all the shortages you face — shortages of staff, of funds, of equipment, of time — it will be something you can be proud of for the rest of your life. That's what it means to be a pioneer. If you keep in mind that you are creating a memory that you can treasure for the rest of your life, it will be fun, too."

He then asked them, "How is your health?"

"Fine!" both replied.

"Remember to take good care of your health. This, too, is using your wisdom. Anyway, whenever you start to feel that it's just too much, think of your fellow members and how delighted and inspired they'll be when they see your films.

"The audience may not see those working behind the camera, but the influence you have will be profound. We can't see the foundation of a house, either, or the engine of a car. Nor can we see the human heart. All the important things, the things that support existence and keep it running, are hidden.

"When you've finished this film, you will have written a new page in the history of the Soka Gakkai. Hundreds of thousands will be inspired to take action. All this rests on your shoulders. In that sense, you are functioning as great leaders."

Shin'ichi went on to discuss future plans for the news bureau. "Let's make a color film soon. From now on, all films are going to be in color," he told them. At the time, almost all newsreels were in black and white. "And in the future," he continued, "let's make dramatizations of the experiences of our members — and documentaries, too. If films can help people understand the true nature of the Soka Gakkai, they will be a major force for kosen-rufu."

The exhaustion Iizaka and his workmate had felt was banished by Shin'ichi's warm encouragement, and they felt new courage to pursue their work. With tears of gratitude in their eyes, the two young men watched Shin'ichi as he left the room.

I N preparation for the screenings of *Seikyo News,* a projection group of mostly young men's division members was organized in each general chapter.

A trial print of the first *Seikyo News* film was finally completed in early June after much hard work, though some of the images were too dark or unclear.

After the preliminary screening, Shin'ichi told the news bureau staff: "You've done a fine job, especially in such a short time. The content is excellent. This is a historic achievement."

Bright smiles lit the young men's faces, which had been a bit wan from all their hard work.

There was certainly a lot of room for improvement and much work still to be done, but Shin'ichi was happy knowing that these young people had earnestly tried to respond to the hopes he had placed in them.

The first showing of *Seikyo News* was on June 9, at the end of a meeting of district leaders from the Kanto First General Chapter at the Ota Industrial Hall in Ota Ward, Tokyo.

The auditorium lights went out and, against a background of lively music, the words *Seikyo News* appeared on the screen, triggering a wave of applause. Images of the May 3 Headquarters General Meeting filled the screen as the narration declared, "On a beautiful, sunny day, the

Twenty-third Headquarters General Meeting, marking the first anniversary of President Yamamoto's inauguration, was held with great success at the Nihon University Auditorium in Tokyo."

The participants gazed intently at the screen. In a corner of the auditorium, two young men were watching the audience as intently as the audience was watching the screen: Yoshio Iizaka and his news bureau companion. They found it impossible to go on with their work until they had seen the audience's reaction with their own eyes.

On the screen, President Yamamoto was passionately describing his goals for his second year. Those watching applauded enthusiastically — an energetic response to the scene in which Shin'ichi invited the members to share this challenge.

The scene switched to the inaugural meeting of Okinawa General Chapter. Everyone earnestly took in the Okinawa members' firm resolve to transform their "island of tragedy" into an "island of peace." During a scene in which Shin'ichi praised the valiant efforts of the Okinawa members and affixed the Soka Gakkai gold pin to the lapel of a representative, the melody "Okinawa Kenji no Uta" (Heroes of Okinawa) played in the background. Many eyes brimmed with tears among the film's audience, and sniffles could be heard here and there.

TEARS filled the eyes of Yoshio Iizaka, too, as he observed the audience watching his film *Seikyo News*. More moved than anyone, he began to weep. He managed to choke out the words "It's…it's incredible" to his companion seated next to him, before being overcome by emotion.

When the film ended, a storm of applause shook the auditorium. Their eyes red from crying, the two film

staff members joyfully shook hands. Iizaka had directly experienced the tremendous significance of filming Soka Gakkai activities, and he felt enormous joy and pride at his involvement. From that moment on, he could not help but feel that the heavy weight of the camera cutting into his shoulder was equivalent to the weight of his mission.

In later years, the filmmaking section was set up as an independent unit, and eventually established as a Gakkai-affiliated company under the name Shinano Productions. It would go on to produce many films about the Soka Gakkai and contribute to a broader understanding of Buddhism in society. With the energy of youth, both the writers department and the news bureau thus began their endeavors for the future realization of kosen-rufu.

On June 5, Shin'ichi attended the young women's division leaders meeting at the Taito Gymnasium in Tokyo, and on June 6, he appeared before a similar young men's division meeting at the same location.

The youth of the Soka Gakkai were achieving remarkable growth. In their activities for May alone, the young men had brought 12,400 new households into the Soka Gakkai and had increased the membership of their division by 12,900, reaching a new total membership of more than 270 thousand. The young women had brought in 6,300 new households and increased division membership by ten thousand, for a total membership of nearly 200 thousand.

Moreover, from June onward, the leaders meetings of the young men's and young women's divisions would be given the same significance as the Headquarters Leaders Meetings, and President Yamamoto was to attend. This also strengthened the youth's awareness and sense of responsibility as the prime movers of kosen-rufu.

The secret to nurturing young people, first and foremost, is to make them aware of their mission. The next step is to clarify the goals they are to challenge.

The goals of the youth division were very clear: to continue sharing the Daishonin's Buddhism with others and increase their membership, as they devoted their energies to holding regional general meetings and, in the case of the young men's division, a grand gathering of 100 thousand representatives in one location.

It is vital that leaders pay attention to details so that all activities can proceed smoothly. For example, Shin'ichi gave careful thought even to the starting times of the leaders meetings. In those days, meetings of both the young men's and young women's divisions frequently started shortly after 6:00 P.M., but it was difficult for many members to make it to the meeting places so quickly after work. Shin'ichi therefore suggested beginning the meetings half an hour later, at 6:30.

*O*N June 11, Shin'ichi attended the Chubu region youth division general meetings in Nagoya. The Chubu general meetings were as successful as the earlier Kyushu meetings: some sixteen thousand members attended the young women's division meeting, which began at 11:30 A.M., and eighteen thousand participated in the young men's division meeting at 3:00 P.M.

But Shin'ichi received some bad news on June 13, while visiting the head temple on his way back to Tokyo from Chubu. Miyoko Shibayama, the Kyushu First General Chapter women's division chief, had died that day of heart failure during a women's division meeting at a Nichiren Shoshu temple in Kumamoto City. According to the report he had received by phone from Kyushu, Mrs. Shibayama had finished giving a Gosho lecture and, after answering several questions, suddenly collapsed on the desk at which she was seated. There, in front of the Gohonzon and surrounded by friends and comrades, she quietly breathed her last. She was 49.

She and her husband, Kunio, had been playing pivotal roles in Gakkai activities in Kyushu. A vivid picture came to Shin'ichi's mind of Mrs. Shibayama participating in meetings with her baby at her side, back when he had gone to Yamaguchi Prefecture to take the lead in developing Gakkai activities there. She was always simply but neatly dressed. She set her own hair in an attractive style and had a bright smile for everyone she met. Though she spoke softly, her strong conviction toward faith was evident in her words, and her fellow members placed great trust in her.

What impressed Shin'ichi most of all was the consideration Mrs. Shibayama showed her family. When she took the train with her husband up to Tokyo to participate in the Headquarters General Meetings, she never forgot to press her husband's trousers under the mattress in the sleeping car they shared. Whenever she returned home from Gakkai activities, she courteously greeted her husband and thanked him sincerely for his cooperation and understanding.

Mrs. Shibayama had four children. Whenever Gakkai activities required her to leave the children at home on their own, she thoughtfully prepared some sweets for each child and set them out in small neatly wrapped paper bundles. Her children undoubtedly appreciated this loving touch.

She was never heard to carp or complain, and she never appeared tired. In her home, she fulfilled her duties as a wife and mother while for her fellow members, for kosen-rufu, she traveled widely across Kyushu.

Shin'ichi was taken aback by this unexpected, sad news. Nothing was more tragic or painful for him than the death of a comrade in the struggle for kosen-rufu.

SHIN'ICHI recalled a visit he had made to Fukuoka in Kyushu a year earlier. On that occasion, he relayed his plans to go on a guidance tour of North and South America that October and asked those gathered where they would like to go if they had the chance.

Mrs. Shibayama had replied: "My dream has always been to go to Europe to spread the Daishonin's Buddhism. But that may well have to wait till my next lifetime.

"While you are visiting America, President Yamamoto, we will work hard to see that Fukuoka takes the lead in activities for kosen-rufu in Japan; we'll watch the home front while you are away."

And in fact, Fukuoka Chapter, of which Mrs. Shibayama had been women's division chief, added a total of

2,030 new member households in October that year — a brilliant achievement that led all other chapters in Japan.

Mrs. Shibayama had truly been the "mother of kosen-rufu" in Kyushu.

Though it may have been her destiny to die young, Shin'ichi thought she doubtless had died after completing her mission in this lifetime. Yet he continued to ask himself whether there wasn't something he could have done to ensure that Mrs. Shibayama was still alive and active.

When Shin'ichi received news of the death of this beloved women's division leader, her husband, Kunio, happened to be at the head temple for the monthly pilgrimage. With great sensitivity to Kunio's emotional state, Shin'ichi comforted him:

"The saddest and most painful thing that can happen to a man is to lose his wife. But if you succumb to grief, it is your late wife who will surely be the most saddened. She is watching faithfully over you and your children. Please take heart and overcome your sorrow. I will go to Kyushu, too."

Shin'ichi was certain that Mrs. Shibayama had attained Buddhahood. What worried him was the children. There were three girls, ages 19, 17, and 15, and a boy of 6.

On June 16, Shin'ichi attended the funeral service for Mrs. Shibayama in Fukuoka. There, he heard the details of her last moments from those who had been with her. The oldest daughter had rushed to Kumamoto when she heard the news, and was said to have spoken the following words to her mother:

"Mom, you worked real hard. I know that it was your wish to die in just this way, in the midst of activity, surrounded by all these friends and comrades."

When Shin'ichi learned how Mrs. Shibayama's daughter had taken her mother's death, he felt some relief.

THE funeral ceremony was solemn and dignified. Many members from throughout Kyushu came to pay their last respects to Mrs. Shibayama. The crowd that gathered seemed endless; there must have been some ten thousand present.

At the service, Soka Gakkai Women's Division Chief Katsu Kiyohara read the eulogy: "Please rest peacefully, Miyoko. I want to die just the way you did — in the midst of the struggle for kosen-rufu, surrounded by all my friends."

These were Kiyohara's heartfelt sentiments. Miyoko Shibayama's life came to end all too soon, but she was a shining example of the spirit to not begrudge one's life for the sake of the Law. Upon seeing her photograph on display before the altar, many vowed to carry on her mission and devote their lives to kosen-rufu as she had done.

After the funeral, Shin'ichi Yamamoto called the Shibayamas' three daughters over to his side and told them:

"Your mother was a great woman. She was a fine mother, of whom you can be proud for the rest of your lives. I know that your hearts are filled with pain and sadness now, but I am sure your mother's dearest wish would be that you don't allow this to dampen your spirits, that you grow up to be happy and fulfilled. She would also have wanted you to devote yourselves to the happiness of others, just like she did. There may still be suffering and hard times ahead of you, but if you persist in your faith and stay close to the Gohonzon, you will certainly attain happiness in the end. So please, don't ever be defeated, and keep your faith alive.

"Your fellow members are looking out for you. If you should have any troubles, please feel free to come and discuss them with me at any time. Also, I'll see to it that a fine tomb is built for your mother."

Holding back their tears, the daughters nodded in appreciation.

Shin'ichi took some loquats that had been set out on the table for him and gave one to each of the daughters, urging them to cheer up.

When Shin'ichi left for Kansai the following day, the Shibayama family saw him off at the airport. Shin'ichi offered heartfelt encouragement to the Shibayama daughters until boarding time.

"Life is eternal," he told them. "Your mother will be reborn quickly, and close to you, I'm certain, so she can watch over you. There's nothing to worry about."

The departure time arrived, but even as he walked to the gate, Shin'ichi kept looking back and waving to the daughters, assuring them that everything would be all right.

His entire bearing emanated a determination to do all in his power to help these young women become happy.

*O*N the evening of June 17, Shin'ichi was in Kyoto to attend the inaugural meeting of the Kansai Fourth General Chapter, which comprised four chapters: Kyoto, Heian, Kyoraku and Maizuru. The following day, the 18th, the general meetings of the Kansai youth division were held. Both the young men's and young women's divisions meetings were held in the Minato Gymnasium in Osaka. Thirty thousand members gathered for the young women's meeting and forty thousand for the young men's. These youth meetings perfectly demonstrated the deeply rooted strength of the Soka Gakkai in Kansai.

At the young men's division meeting, Shin'ichi clarified the Soka Gakkai's basic stance toward Japan's labor movement. There was a tendency in society to think that the aims of the Soka Gakkai and the labor movement were not compatible, and members of the young men's division frequently inquired whether it was acceptable for a Gakkai member to also become involved in labor activities.

"I am often asked by members of the young men's division wishing to take part in labor activities, whether, as members of the Soka Gakkai, it is actually right for them to do so." Shin'ichi said. "It is a mistake to think that Soka Gakkai members may not participate in the labor movement. You are, of course, free to do as you please. Nichiren Daishonin taught that 'All phenomena in the universe are manifestations of the Buddhist Law' (*Gosho Zenshu*, p. 563). Faith alone is the basis of true happiness, but since most of the young men's division members are workers, it is perfectly natural for you to be active in the labor movement or union activities. Nor is that in any way incompatible with Buddhism.

"President Toda once said, 'If my own children were to take up the cause of labor to work for the good of society, and for their own proper rights, I would take up the banner of the working class myself and join the movement.'

"Meanwhile, we see emerging in the labor movement today a sort of 'labor elite,' the professional organizers who set themselves up above the actual workers.

"So, if you are going to participate in labor activities in your workplace or hold a union post, however high — and, in contrast to the labor elite, protect workers rights — then as long as you maintain a solid basis in faith, there is absolutely nothing in the least wrong with your doing so. The movement for kosen-rufu makes use of every element of society to create happiness for all."

Shin'ichi wanted to teach the members that Buddhism was not some narrow doctrine seeking to confine or limit them. Buddhist practice lies in actively working for the benefit of others and making contributions to society.

*S*HIN'ICHI Yamamoto's efforts to foster capable young people were not limited to the young men's and young women's divisions but also extended to the student division.

On June 20, Shin'ichi attended the Fourth Student Division General Meeting at the Hibiya Civic Hall in Tokyo. The meeting celebrated the division's achievement of a membership of 6,000, the division's one-year goal set at the previous year's general meeting. At that time, the student division had only 2,800 members. The membership, therefore, had more than doubled in the space of a year. In terms of percentage growth, the student division had outpaced even the young men's and young women's divisions. Over the past year, it had been steadily developing its activities, including publication of a new magazine, *Daisan Bunmei* (The Third Civilization).

Student division members had also earned high marks in the March sudy department examinations. Of the 571 people who advanced to the level of assistant professor alone, 45 were from the student division. At the end of March, after the exams, the division still had a membership of only 4,600, in contrast to the Soka Gakkai's 1.85 million member-households. For the student division members to have comprised around one-thirteenth (almost eight percent) of those who passed the assistant professor exam was therefore a remarkable feat.

At the meeting, Student Division Chief Goro Watari announced the goals they would work toward for the Fifth General Meeting: a membership of twelve thousand and enrollment of the entire student division in the study department.

Shin'ichi was pleased by the student division's vibrant energy and dynamic growth. When it was time for him to speak, he did so in a friendly and relaxed manner:

"Recently, many non-Japanese have been visiting the Headquarters, and since I don't speak any foreign languages, it puts me on the spot. So I've come up with a plan. When an American visits, I'll say that I studied German, and unfortunately don't speak any English. But then I worry what to do if a German happens along!"

His audience roared with laughter.

"Last night, I was engaged in discussions with the youth and student division chiefs until quite late. As time wore on, everyone got hungry and tired — spirits seemed to sink. So, throwing in an English word for good measure, I suggested: 'Let's lighten this discussion up a bit. We need more humor and more wet.' A student division leader jumped in and said: 'President Yamamoto, wet means "damp" in English. I'm sure that what you meant to say is wit.'"

Shin'ichi spoke without vanity or pretension, not pretending to be anyone other than who he was.

DRAWING wave after wave of laughter with his disarming humor, Shin'ichi continued: "I ask you all to study foreign languages and then make many friends around the world. Nichiren Daishonin's Buddhism is destined to spread throughout the world as a natural consequence of history. There is no need to be overly hasty in propagating it overseas. It is more important for you to make friends from many countries and build bonds of mutual trust, person to person.

"We are working hard to increase our membership, but not simply to increase our worldly influence. We are doing it to bring happiness to as many people as we can and to bring peace to the planet. Peace can never be achieved without the forging of strong bonds of friendship between human beings. As you become close friends with people from other countries, and your new friends come to know you and your way of life, they will be impressed and moved. That will naturally lead to a deepening understanding of Buddhism around the world.

"Only those who have truly mastered foreign languages can perform this role, which is why I am turning to you, members of the student division. It is to you that I entrust the propagation of Buddhism outside Japan.

"In the fall, I'll be visiting Europe, but I will leave the European languages to you; I'm afraid I'll just have to make do with Japanese. And if someone says to me in a disappointed voice, 'Why, President Yamamoto, you only speak Japanese!' I have my answer ready: 'No, you should hear my Martian!'"

Another wave of laughter warmed the hall.

Shin'ichi's message — to join all the world's people with bonds of friendship — might have seemed very simple, but behind it rested the essence of the Buddhist way of life. Buddhism develops people's inherent goodness and nurtures in them concern and empathy for others' pain and suffering. Where a Buddhist walks, therefore, the fragrant flowers of friendship bloom. Sharing the teachings of Buddhism with others is just a natural expression of that friendship.

Most of the student division members at the general meeting thought of a Buddhist as someone who did nothing but passionately discuss religion. Of course, to distinguish the correct teaching from the erroneous, a certain amount of discussion is necessary. But that is only a part of what it means to be a Buddhist.

Shin'ichi was concerned that these bright young people, who would be leaders of the next generation, might become too narrow-minded and fall victim to the delusion that people exist for the sake of religion — instead of the other way around. A true Buddhist is always flexible, with a mind as vast and accepting as the ocean. Shin'ichi wanted to raise the young members of the student division to grow straight, tall and broad-minded.

T HE northern island of Hokkaido was clothed in the fresh greenery of spring. In the capital, Sapporo, the lilac blossoms had already faded, and the young lilac leaves rustled in the breeze, hinting at summer's not-too-distant arrival.

On June 25, Shin'ichi attended the general meetings of the Hokkaido youth division at the Nakajima Sports Center in Sapporo. The young women's division met in the morning, and the young men's division in the afternoon.

When he arrived at the site, Shin'ichi was greeted by the dazzling smiles of the young women. But Shin'ichi's gaze was quickly drawn to the gaunt form of Haruko Arashiyama, the Hokkaido young women's division chief. When they entered one of the waiting rooms, he asked her, "Are you all right?"

"Yes, I'm fine. Please don't worry about me," she replied, standing erect and smiling.

But it was clear to Shin'ichi that Arashiyama, who was suffering from tuberculosis, had considerably weakened.

"What are you scheduled to talk about at today's meeting?" Shin'ichi inquired.

"I'm giving a progress report," she replied.

"I see," he said. "I don't want you to strain yourself. Let the vice chief give the report today."

Arashiyama looked disappointed, but Shin'ichi said to Yoshiko Urushibara, the Hokkaido young women's division vice chief, seated beside her, "I'm sorry to call on you so suddenly, but please deliver the report today in Miss Arashiyama's place."

Shin'ichi looked again at Arashiyama, and tried to persuade her of the seriousness of her situation:

"Please, try to rest a little. You need to concentrate on getting well. I sincerely want you to recover your health and live a long time — for the sake of Hokkaido and all your fellow members who are counting on you. Please do so, as a favor to me."

Arashiyama nodded silently. Tears glistened in her eyes.

Shin'ichi had first met Arashiyama when in Hokkaido for the Otaru Debate[2] in March 1955. The day after the Soka Gakkai's great victory in that debate, the young woman had visited the inn where Shin'ichi and his companions were staying. The neatly dressed Arashiyama had radiated a quiet inner strength. Her clear eyes shone with seeking spirit, and a powerful will to fight emanated from her slight form.

She was the eldest daughter in a family of three girls and one boy. Her father had died in the war when she was still in elementary school, leaving her mother alone to raise the four children. Arashiyama held down part-time jobs all the way through her school years, from the time she was in elementary school straight through high school, which she successfully completed.

Though she had been a Soka Gakkai member less than a year when Shin'ichi first met her, Arashiyama was extremely active as a leader of the young women's division in Rumoi, while working full time at a bank.

*A*T their first meeting at Otaru, Shin'ichi said to Haruko Arashiyama: "I've heard all about your hard work from other members. I am 100 percent behind you. Let's dedicate our youth to Buddhism, to our friends, and to our own achievements, and together build a beautiful garden of happiness in society."

"I'll do my best!" she promised in a clear, energetic voice. Her eyes shone with passionate determination.

From that day on, she worked harder than ever, traveling all over the vast and often rugged region of Hokkaido. Riding on trains and making her way through drifts of snow, she visited fellow members in Haboro and Mashike. Nothing stopped her — neither blinding blizzards nor bitter north winds. She devoted her youthful energies to spreading the Daishonin's teachings — to this and this alone.

Arashiyama cared about others. In a hospital near the bank where she worked, there was an elderly woman afflicted with asthma. Her family rarely visited her. After becoming acquainted with the woman, Arashiyama visited her every day at the hospital, offering her words of comfort and encouragement. She brought her flowers, and would leave nourishing foods, such as cheese and butter, by her bedside.

One day, the elderly woman grasped her young visitor's hand firmly and said, with tears in her eyes, "No one has ever been so kind to me."

Arashiyama herself was suffering from tuberculosis. She was regularly stricken with coughing fits, congestion and low-grade fevers. But when meeting others, she never gave the slightest hint of illness. She always had a smile for her friends, spoke passionately about the Daishonin's Buddhism, and warmly encouraged others.

Eventually, the arena of her activities shifted to Sapporo. In August 1956, four chapters were established in Hokkaido: Sapporo, Hakodate, Asahikawa and Otaru. With this development, Arashiyama became the central figure for the young women's division in Sapporo Chapter. She was only 21.

At that time, she was working at the small restaurant her mother had started. She had some difficulty dividing her time between work and her Soka Gakkai activities, but she organized her schedule efficiently and could stir the spring breezes of kosen-rufu across Hokkaido.

When she finished her daily activities, she pushed her tired body beyond its limits to chant daimoku and write daily letters of encouragement to fellow members. Everyone looked up to her as a kindly elder sister, and Sapporo's young women's division made remarkable progress under her leadership.

SHIN'ICHI frequently sent letters of encouragement to Haruko Arashiyama. She valued his advice and responded to his sincere concern by making every activity a great success. At the Fourth Young Women's Division General Meeting in December 1956, she had reported on the activities of the Hokkaido young women's division. The activities of these young women in the snowbound region of Hokkaido moved and electrified the listeners, triggering a wave of response that spread all across Japan.

Whenever Shin'ichi visited Hokkaido, Arashiyama sought his guidance with a dedicated passion. But she did not just go herself to see Shin'ichi; she constantly brought capable new members along to meet him. She was always concerned with and took action for the progress and growth of others. Such is a true leader.

When the Coal Miners' Union trouble in Yubari broke out in 1957, Arashiyama sprang into action, determined not to permit the union's unjust treatment of Gakkai members to continue. She rushed from one member's house to another, perspiration streaming down her brow. Her unwavering determination to fight for her friends, as long as her strength held out, recalled the courage of Joan of Arc.

Shortly after this was the Osaka Incident, in which Shin'ichi, then youth division chief of staff, was arrested on trumped-up charges of election violations filed by the Osaka District Prosecutors Office. Arashiyama, shaking with anger and frustration, had declared to her fellow members: "How dare they arrest Chief of Staff Yamamoto, an ally of the wretched and suffering who prays for and gives his entire life to the realization of human happiness! How I hate the authorities for persecuting the Soka Gakkai and Mr. Yamamoto this way!"

She prayed: "Mr. Yamamoto, a true champion of justice, has been falsely arrested. If I could, I would happily take his place in jail, but all I can do now is pray for his health and safety. Please let him be released as soon as possible."

Her tear-filled prayers continued day after day.

While chanting daimoku, Arashiyama became convinced that the way to prove Mr. Yamamoto's innocence and the Soka Gakkai's integrity was to make further strides in kosen-rufu and raise the banner of the people's victory.

"I will fight," she decided. "I will be victorious in every struggle. Only through victory will the truth be proven!" Her fighting spirit flared up, and she set down her determination in a letter to Shin'ichi.

The first thing Shin'ichi read after his release from prison was Arashiyama's letter, her passionate pledge.

*A*RASHIYAMA went into action again when Shin'ichi announced his vision for the Soka Gakkai's future in terms of the Seven Bells, seven seven-year periods of development. He made the announcement at the Headquarters General Meeting on May 3, 1958, just a month after the death of the second Soka Gakkai president, Josei Toda. She said to her fellow members: "Mr. Yamamoto has now taken his stand as President Toda's disciple. This is not a time for sadness. We, too, must do our part."

The day after the meeting, Shin'ichi sent a poem to Arashiyama, who had communicated her pledge to support him on the Gakkai's fresh departure:

May you blossom
As the white lotus
Of Hokkaido,
Who will live long
And build the future.

Arashiyama took Shin'ichi's poem to heart and worked harder to ensure the success of the First Hokkaido Young Women's Division General Meeting, scheduled for June 22, 1958. She rallied her fellow members, telling them, "Now is the time for the Hokkaido young women's division to prove itself!" Her cry resounded all across Hokkaido.

She announced her determination to meet the Hokkaido young women's division's membership goal for that year by the time of the general meeting. She also proposed establishing a Fife and Drum Corps by then and personally took on the responsibility of training its members. When the day of the meeting arrived, she welcomed Shin'ichi with more than 3,500 members and a wonderful Fife and Drum Corps performance.

Some people make resolutions when swept up in the excitement of the moment that ultimately amount to little more than empty posturing. Arashiyama, on the other hand, spoke from a deep-seated commitment. She saw to it that everything she promised came true. This is the mark of integrity.

Unfortunately, from about this time her illness began to worsen, and she was visibly weakened. As would later become apparent, she was already in need of complete bed rest, but she didn't let anyone else know it. Her slight fever persisted, and when she awoke each morning her sheets were soaked with sweat. Her coughing fits grew more violent, and she was plagued with increased congestion.

Each time he saw Arashiyama, Shin'ichi said with concern: "Don't worry about attending meetings. Please rest. You must stop overexerting yourself and allow yourself to heal."

But a young women's division member had only to ask her and she would go anywhere. She had resolved to be a leader who would always be there for the members, and she simply could not remain still when she knew she was needed somewhere. She would go to freezing Asahikawa, to Kushiro, or to Hakodate, panting from exertion as she made her way to encourage friends.

*I*T pained Shin'ichi whenever he received news of Haruko Arashiyama's condition. "I must get her to rest," he thought.

On a visit to Hokkaido, Shin'ichi told her: "I want you to stop participating in Soka Gakkai activities for a while and get some rest. You mustn't underestimate the importance of fighting this illness. Buddhism means being reasonable."

But Arashiyama pleaded with Shin'ichi: "Please let me stay active. Please!" In the spirit of not begrudging one's life for the sake of the Law, she was determined to give her entire being to the struggle for kosen-rufu.

"No," insisted Shin'ichi firmly. "You are being selfish." Shin'ichi was well aware of Arashiyama's earnest wish to remain active. He, too, had suffered from tuberculosis earlier in his youth and had felt just as she did now. But he wanted to do everything in his power to ensure that she would not die.

Shin'ichi changed his tone to one of gentle persuasion: "I know how you feel. But you are irreplaceable both to your family and to the Gakkai, so you must regain your health. You have to survive this illness and live to a ripe old age. That is why you must rest; so that you can make a fresh start in the future. To rest does not mean to retreat, by any means." It pained Shin'ichi to have to give such guidance.

As she watched Shin'ichi intently, large tears rose in her eyes. "All right. I'll do as you say," she finally replied.

At the Seventh Young Women's Division General Meeting in November 1959, Haruko Arashiyama stepped down from her leadership position. Immediately before the meeting, Shin'ichi sent her a letter of encouragement, in which he wrote:

"The journey to achieve kosen-rufu is a long, long one. There is no need to rush. Young people such as you are the future of the Soka Gakkai, of society and of Japan. For that very reason, now is the time to heal yourself. Instead of overexerting yourself and making it worse, you should calmly devote yourself to fighting this illness without reservation. This, too, will be an opportunity to create a wonderful experience in faith. So that you may fully participate in the struggle to spread the Law, as an heir to Mr. Toda's legacy, I pray that you will win over the hindrances of sickness and death and regain your former health and energy."

Shin'ichi continued to send her daimoku, fervently praying for her to recover and rejoin the forefront of Soka Gakkai activities.

Rest brought a new vigor to Haruko Arashiyama, and gradually her health returned.

WHEN Shin'ichi was inaugurated as third president, Haruko Arashiyama prayed with renewed determination to defeat her illness as quickly as possible and resume her activities for kosen-rufu.

Her wishes came true that autumn, when she returned to the front lines of the organization. In November, at the Eighth Young Women's Division General Meeting, she was appointed the Hokkaido young women's division chief. She had great plans for the Hokkaido young women's division. At her home she would sit up all through the night with Vice Chief Yoshiko Urushibara, a map of Hokkaido spread out before them, discussing the future. They made little flags out of paper and matchsticks and affixed them to the map, saying, "Let's form a young women's division group here, too." Soon there were forty or fifty flags. Her eyes shining, Arashiyama told her friend: "Let's work together to make our plans come true. President Yamamoto has placed such great trust in the young women's division of Hokkaido — we must become a model for the rest of the country." Arashiyama burned with resolve.

She traveled tirelessly throughout the vast area of Hokkaido. Her immediate focus was the Second Hokkaido Young Women's Division General Meeting, to be held on June 25, 1961. The young women's division membership in Hokkaido had grown fantastically. By the time of the general meeting, it exceeded 8,500 members — an astonishing increase from just over 3,500 members only three years before. More than 7,000 young women — over eighty percent of the entire division — attended the meeting. Just as Arashiyama had resolved, the Hokkaido young women's division had become a model for all Japan.

The general meeting had been a great success — but illness had struck Arashiyama once again, with a renewed vengeance. Shin'ichi, who had been present, persuaded Arashiyama not to overtax herself by giving a speech. But knowing how she must have felt, it had been extremely painful for him. He wondered if he shouldn't have let her go ahead and speak, just this once, and fretted that he had made the wrong decision. But how could he have let her appear on stage? She was so emaciated that her clothes hung loose on her, and her breath came only in gasps.

The Hokkaido young men's division general meeting, held that afternoon, had also been a great success.

That evening, Shin'ichi attended a joint inaugural meeting for Higashi-Sapporo and Nishi-Sapporo chapters, devoting all of his energy to giving the members guidance and direction.

*A*FTER the chapter kickoff, Shin'ichi talked again with Arashiyama about her future. On the plane back to Tokyo, he kept thinking about her. "She must know," he thought, "that she doesn't have long to live. She must want to spend her remaining time carrying out her mission in a final burst of glory." Shin'ichi's heart ached for her. "I want her to live. I cannot let her die," he thought. But that meeting in Hokkaido was the last time Shin'ichi ever saw or spoke to Haruko Arashiyama.

The June Headquarters Leaders Meeting was held at the Taito Gymnasium in Tokyo on the evening of the 27th. When the meeting began, Director Hiroshi Yamagiwa took the stage to announce the results of the month's activities. The audience waited expectantly for his report.

"In June, 37,556 new households received the Gohonzon and started practicing with the Soka Gakkai," he said. "Since our total membership at the end of May was 1,965,000 households, we have now reached a membership of more than 2 million households! Congratulations! Thank you all very much for your efforts!"

A great roar filled the gymnasium, followed by long, thunderous applause. A membership of 2 million households had been the goal set for the end of the year, but it was reached in just half that time. It was another unprecedented, golden milestone along the road to kosen-rufu.

These new members had not joined the Soka Gakkai due to the influence of rank, wealth or power. Ordinary people, wishing only for others' happiness and a peaceful world, had talked sincerely and passionately with them about Buddhism, in their own way and capacity. Everything had been achieved through the continuation of such steady efforts. It was a great accomplishment, won through the passionate spirit of members who had forged ahead, one in spirit with Shin'ichi.

In every region of Japan, the youth division members had led this advance. They were responsible for thirty to forty percent of the new membership each month, proving again that young people were the driving force for the fresh development of kosen-rufu. Indeed, this is an unchanging principle for the spread of Nichiren Daishonin's Buddhism.

Shin'ichi felt as if a thick canopy of fresh young leaves had sprouted on the great tree of the Soka Gakkai and was rustling gently in the early summer breeze. Just as leaves protect people from the burning heat of the sun and from the driving rain, offering a place to rest and take shelter, the young people of the Soka Gakkai would act as a great canopy to protect the people.

*T*HE outline of activities for the rest of the year was announced at the June Headquarters Leaders Meeting. Focus would be placed on maximizing the effectiveness of discussion meetings at the unit level, the front line of the organization. Also, youth division sports meets planned around the country for the second half of the year were canceled, and in their place the youth division was to take the lead in developing and strengthening the discussion meetings.

As the membership approached 2 million households, Shin'ichi emphasized the importance of improving the Gakkai's discussion meetings. The purpose of sharing the Daishonin's teachings was not simply to increase the membership but to enable all people to become happy. It was vital, then, that as the membership increased more care and attention be focused on each individual. Guidance and encouragement had to be given to deepen the members' understanding of Buddhism and allow them to advance in faith with courage and joy.

The discussion meeting was the place where this human contact took place. Such meetings held at the most basic level of the Gakkai organization — at the unit

level — would be an oasis of unfettered dialogue and human interaction. At this time, the average unit consisted of about a dozen households, providing an intimate setting for discussion. Precisely because unit meetings were small, people felt free to ask questions. Such small gatherings were very flexible and informal, making it possible to focus on the needs of any new members who might be present. As the sphere of happiness within each unit expanded and the members' conviction in faith grew, the solid grass-roots base of the Soka Gakkai developed even further.

Essential to the success of each discussion meeting were not only the efforts of the leaders but the members who would become the core of these meetings in inspiring and encouraging all those present. That was the main reason why Shin'ichi had asked the young men's and young women's division members to involve themselves actively in discussion meetings. He held boundless hopes for what they could contribute, since they had demonstrated remarkable growth in such a short time.

He looked to the youth to bring the vital pulse of kosen-rufu to every corner of the very forefront of the Gakkai organization.

The radiant faces of youth inspire hope; their passionate words awaken courage in people's hearts.

If young people were confined to displaying their potential only within the youth division, they could not become a true driving force for the times. Their training in the youth division was significant precisely because it enabled them to lead and inspire members of all generations. Youth represent the light that leads us to a hope-filled future.

SHIN'ICHI was the last to speak at the Headquarters Leaders Meeting. He bowed deeply to all the members, and then began to speak in a vibrant tone:

"First, I want to rejoice with all of you at having successfully reached our goal for the year of 2 million households — in only six months. Thank you all for your hard work."

The auditorium erupted with applause.

"But though I can thank you," Shin'ichi continued, "I'm afraid I have nothing to give you for your efforts. Instead, I hope each of you will claim lavish benefits from the Gohonzon!" Warm laughter filled the hall. Everyone there felt the joy of having accomplished a challenging task.

"As the Gakkai continues to grow," Shin'ichi went on, "some people may join with impure motives, aiming to use the organization for their personal ends. But the Soka Gakkai is an organization whose members advance based on faith and who purely embrace the spirit of Nichiren Daishonin, making it their own. We must neither permit anyone to exploit the Gakkai nor allow his or her actions to disrupt our unity.

"As leaders, if you notice anyone attempting to exploit the organization, you must first give firm guidance while continuing to communicate pure and correct faith to all our members. If that should mean that a million of our 2 million households withdraw from the Gakkai, please remember: The unity of members truly bound by strong faith has the power to achieve ten, no, twenty times what one would normally expect. We must preserve this purity of faith within the Gakkai for all eternity.

"Let us meet again, just as cheerfully and energetically, at the July Headquarters Leaders Meeting."

Having reached the goal of 2 million member-households, the Gakkai began its spirited ascent of the next summit — 3 million households. Many of the top leaders were euphoric at having achieved their goal. Only Shin'ichi was gazing soberly at the various problems he knew the organization would confront as it expanded. The social responsibility that he carried as president of the Gakkai was also growing.

The path of kosen-rufu was an endless struggle.

Shin'ichi knew that devious plots to persecute the Soka Gakkai were certainly being spawned, and disturbances lay along the road ahead. Only the brave — those undaunted by raging waves or tempests — would make their way through. Shin'ichi felt the weight of his responsibility as he pondered how to ensure that every member of the 2 million households, without a single exception, reached the shore of happiness.

"Fresh Leaves" Notes:

1. *Guan Zi*: A treatise on ancient Chinese politics and economics attributed to Guan Zhong, prime minister of the kingdom of Qi during the Spring and Autumn Period (700–403 B.C.E.). This work contains the passage: "The best yearly plan is to raise crops. The bestten-year plan is to raise trees. The best lifelong plan is to raise people."

2. Otaru Debate: A public debate between Soka Gakkai representatives and priests of the Minobu sect of the Nichiren School of Buddhism, held at the Otaru Civic Hall on March 11, 1955. The incident is described in detail in *The Human Revolution*, vol. 9.

Rissho Ankoku

*T*HE rainy season showed no sign of ending. A thick mist hung over the pathways of the head temple. On July 3, 1961, Shin'ichi Yamamoto traveled to the head temple to pay his respects at the grave of his mentor, Josei Toda.

The next morning, he stood before the tomb and chanted three daimoku infused with deep prayer. He remained there for some time, seemingly engaged in a silent communion with his mentor.

Precisely sixteen years earlier, on July 3, 1945 — just weeks before the end of World War II — Toda was released from prison, having inherited the commitment of his mentor, Tsunesaburo Makiguchi, to spread the Daishonin's

Buddhism. After two years of incarceration by Japan's militarist government, his health was greatly weakened. He was painfully thin and his stride was unsteady. Beneath his protruding ribs, however, a ferocious commitment to kosen-rufu burned like a flame. It was also fueled by a fiery anger at the evil of authoritarian power, which had killed his beloved mentor and subjected the Japanese people to the extremes of suffering.

Under pressure from the authorities, most of his fellow members had renounced their faith, and there was no one for him to turn to. Toda knew that the future of kosen-rufu rested solely on his shoulders. He resolved to stand alone and single-handedly raise the banner of Nichiren Daishonin's Buddhism. From that day on, the water of the Law flowed forth abundantly — what had been an underground stream began to spring forth from the earth to nourish the parched soil of postwar Japan. July 3 was the day on which the Soka Gakkai was reborn, the day the lion king of kosen-rufu broke free of the chains in which the military dictatorship had bound him and began to roam proudly again.

Shin'ichi was keenly aware that spreading the Daishonin's teachings meant struggling against the insidious nature of authority. The mission of a true Buddhist is to rise up against the external threats of dictatorship and military might, which violate the dignity of human life, and triumph over them with internal spiritual power, with true humanity.

Makiguchi and Toda were arrested for their refusal to accept a Shinto talisman dedicated to the Sun Goddess. But that was little more than a pretext. The real reason for their persecution was that the military, trying to enslave the people with State Shinto as the nation's spiritual pillar and carry out its bloody war, could not tolerate an organization that spread a Buddhism teaching the ideals of human dignity, freedom and equality.

Though the war was long over and a democratic system had been established in Japan, Shin'ichi knew that the treacherous tendency of authority seeking to enslave people remained unchanged.

Shin'ichi had personally experienced this during the Osaka Incident, when the authorities falsely accused him of election law violations and had him arrested. By a remarkable coincidence, the day of his arrest was July 3, 1957, the same day that twelve years earlier his mentor had been released from prison.

WHEN Shin'ichi recalled the interrogation he had been subjected to at the Osaka District Prosecutors Office, he quaked with indignation. Despite his innocence, the investigators had threatened to arrest Toda unless Shin'ichi confessed. Such unscrupulous tactics made the authorities' dark intent all too clear: They were determined to undermine the Soka Gakkai by whatever means necessary.

The government feared the emergence of a new populist movement. It felt gravely threatened by the Gakkai's efforts to awaken people to their social mission — to the fact that they were central — and encourage them to influence the way the country was run.

Traditionally, Japanese religions, including Buddhism, had been co-opted by the ruling powers. They received protection and sponsorship by actively supporting the government's policies and wishes.

The great nineteenth-century Japanese thinker and educator Fukuzawa Yukichi observed in his *An Outline of a Theory of Civilization*:

Religion works within the hearts of men. It is something absolutely free and independent, not controlled in any way or dependent upon their powers. But while this is the way religion ought to be, such has not been the case here in Japan.[1]

And of Buddhism's acquiescence to secular authority, he noted:

If you inquire into the basis of this power, you will find it is not religion. They have simply borrowed the government's power. Ultimately, they are nothing else but a branch of secular authority.

Buddhism has flourished, true. But its teaching has been entirely absorbed by political authority. What shines throughout the world is not the radiance of Buddha's teachings but the glory of Buddhism's political authority.[2]

This has been the means by which every school of Japanese Buddhism has escaped persecution from the authorities and guaranteed its survival and prosperity. If the Soka Gakkai had followed the wishes of those in power, shut its eyes to social injustice and suffering, and become a "dead" religion, concerned only with a peaceful afterlife and solace here on Earth, it would never have come into conflict with the government.

But such a religion cannot realize religion's most basic purpose: to bring happiness to the people and peace to society. As long as religion advocates building a society dedicated to people's happiness and well-being, it must be prepared for persecution by corrupt and unscrupulous authorities bent on subjugating the people to their will.

For Shin'ichi, arrest and imprisonment were a point of departure for his lifelong activities to realize the triumph of humanism.

He would never forget his mentor's fervent and unceasing love for him, his young disciple. At Haneda Airport in Tokyo, just before Shin'ichi had boarded a plane to present himself voluntarily for questioning at Osaka Prefectural Police Headquarters, Mr. Toda had said to him:

"Shin'ichi, should death overtake you, I will rush to your side and throw myself upon you and accompany you in death."

WHEN Shin'ichi thought of what Toda must have been feeling as they parted at Haneda Airport, tears filled his eyes.

Moreover, Toda had personally gone to the Osaka District Prosecutors Office while Shin'ichi was in detention to protest his young disciple's unjust arrest. He had felt compelled to do so. Before that, on July 12, he convened a general meeting of members in the Tokyo area at the National Sports Arena in Kuramae to condemn the actions of the Osaka Prefectural Police Headquarters and the Osaka District Prosecutors Office.

On his arrival in Osaka, Toda requested a meeting with the chief prosecutor. By that time, the Soka Gakkai president had already become alarmingly emaciated. His steps were unsteady and he had to be supported on either side by the leaders accompanying him. The effort of climbing the stairs to the prosecutor's office made his breath come in painful gasps.

Toda was prepared to take Shin'ichi's place in jail. He was a mentor who would not hesitate to cast away his own life for his disciples.

Once admitted to see the chief prosecutor, he demanded strongly: "How long do you intend to keep my innocent disciple locked up?! If it is me you want, arrest me now!" He sought Shin'ichi's immediate release.

On the way back from the prosecutor's office, Toda murmured with deep frustration, "Can't they see just by looking at Shin'ichi that he isn't the sort of person who could commit a crime?"

Shin'ichi learned of his mentor's actions after his release. When he did, he wept. Toda's confrontation with the chief prosecutor also provided Shin'ichi with a shining example of how a leader defends and protects the people.

Now, as he stood before his beloved mentor's grave, Toda's words rang out in his heart: "Fight against the insidious nature of authority! Protect the people!"

Shin'ichi chanted three daimoku infused with a profound pledge.

The Osaka Incident trial, now in its fifth year, was approaching a crucial juncture. On behalf of his late mentor, he vowed to win and prove his innocence.

After Shin'ichi returned to Tokyo that day, he attended the July young men's division leaders meeting in the evening. It was a gathering of determined and committed young men who were the future of the Soka Gakkai and were actively involving themselves in the discussion meeting movement.

Youth Division Chief Eisuke Akizuki's call for the young men to do their best to promote and ensure the great success of small group discussion meetings — forums for heart-to-heart dialogue — was met with enthusiastic applause. These youthful leaders had begun to advance in earnest, raising the banner of the Law and carrying it into the midst of the people. The struggle to achieve kosen-rufu takes place on the forefront of the organization, among the people.

ON July 9, the youth division general meetings being held in each area around Japan came to a climax with the youth gatherings in Tohoku.

The Chugoku Youth Division General Meeting (which included Shikoku) had been held with great success on July 2; twelve thousand young women and fourteen thousand young men had attended. Record turnouts had thus been achieved in each region to date. For that reason, all eyes were turned to the Tohoku meeting, with expectations for a glorious finale.

When Shin'ichi arrived at the meeting place, the Sendai Municipal Leisure Center, a little past 9:00 in the morning, the building was already overflowing with participants. Those outside were all sitting on round straw mats — the lids of cylindrical-shaped bales of rice.

Shin'ichi guessed that these makeshift straw cushions had been distributed by the meeting organizers out of concern for the members' comfort. In any event, they were a perfect symbol of the rich agriculture of the Tohoku region, and Shin'ichi couldn't help but smile.

The YWD general meeting was scheduled to begin at 10:00. Out of concern for the members outside, however, Shin'ichi proposed that it begin earlier. It was a bright, sunny day, and he knew it would soon get hot. The meeting thus commenced half an hour early at 9:30, with more than twelve thousand young women attending.

As soon as the meeting ended, Shin'ichi hurried outdoors. He couldn't help but worry about the overflow of members who were waiting outside in the sun. The mercury had already hit ninety-two degrees.

The area outside the hall was packed, not only with young women but also young men, who would meet that afternoon. Shin'ichi climbed a platform that had been set up outside and spoke to those assembled:

"Thank you all for coming on this very hot day. The membership of the youth division, counting both the young men's and young women's divisions, is approaching 500 thousand. We are now the largest peace organization of youth in Japan. With this youthful energy, let's build a realm of peace and prosperity in Japan and all the world! That is the Soka Gakkai's lofty mission."

After speaking for about five minutes, Shin'ichi held up a Japanese fan in his right hand and said, "Let me lead you all in a Gakkai song." The Fife and Drum Corps began playing "Song of Kosen-rufu in Asia." Shin'ichi led the chorus, waving his fan with all his might. The voices of the young people reverberated into the blue skies of the north country. Large beads of sweat formed on Shin'ichi's brow.

Then came the afternoon and the young men's division general meeting, for which sixteen thousand members assembled in grand fashion, providing a wonderful climax to the nationwide regional general meetings.

A T the Tohoku Young Men's Division General Meeting, Shin'ichi Yamamoto declared to his listeners, "I want to leave completion of the task of kosen-rufu to you, the sturdy young men of Tohoku."

The great undertaking of kosen-rufu could not be accomplished in a day. Shin'ichi knew that it would require tremendous patience and perseverance. The process would be like the growth of a majestic tree sending powerful roots deep into the earth. Persistence, consistent effort to create opportunities, and the wisdom to know the right time were needed to achieve it. Each aspect had to be steadily and meticulously brought to completion. These qualities of patience and perseverance were special characteristics of the people of Tohoku, and that is why

Shin'ichi sought to entrust the finishing touches of kosen-rufu to the youth of Tohoku.

So it was that the regional youth division meetings came to an end. A total of 115 thousand young men and 88 thousand young women had assembled throughout Japan. Later, in autumn, representatives from throughout the country, mainly active around the Tokyo metropolitan area, would meet for one grand gathering. It was already decided that some 100 thousand representatives of the young men's division would assemble for a general meeting at the National Sports Stadium in Tokyo on November 5. The young women's division was scheduled to meet soon after in November, in a general meeting of Tokyo area and regional representatives.

With the wonderful success of the regional meetings, the members of the youth division showed remarkable growth. Shin'ichi was confident that if the organization could expand one step further before the general meetings in November, the youth division would establish an unshakable base.

Having come into contact with young people all over Japan at the youth meetings, Shin'ichi was strongly impressed by their search for a sound philosophy on which to base their lives, and by the passion and enthusiasm with which they sought it. He continued to ponder how he could best respond to these young people's needs. He felt keenly that, though he was Soka Gakkai president, he was himself young and couldn't begin to be as effective a leader as his beloved mentor, Josei Toda, had been.

But he recognized his responsibility to be the pillar that supported the Soka Gakkai after President Toda's death, not only to protect his fellow members across Japan but to educate and nurture young people so that they would become even more effective leaders of kosen-rufu — more effective than he himself. Precisely because he felt that responsibility so keenly, he was deeply concerned.

Nothing was more difficult than to keep young people continually inspired. Shin'ichi knew that the only way to accomplish this was to never lose sight of his own source of inspiration, his mentor, Josei Toda. No great river can survive and flourish when cut off from its source.

And he also knew that he must never forget his own spirit to seek Buddhism and challenge his limitations — that he must continuously educate and improve himself, and keep growing as a human being. Certain that the best way to inspire young people was through his own example, Shin'ichi vowed to act unselfishly and devote his life to bringing happiness to all humanity.

*A*IMING toward the November general meetings, the Soka Gakkai youth's efforts to introduce others to Nichiren Daishonin's Buddhism gathered further momentum. At the monthly young women's division leaders meeting held on July 10, it was announced that a divisional membership of more than 200 thousand had been reached. The young men's division, meanwhile, with a membership now close to 300 thousand, had launched an intensive drive to surpass that goal, determined to push themselves to new limits during the steamy summer months.

At last, the rainy season came to an end, and beginning July 21 donations for the construction of the much-awaited Grand Reception Hall at the head temple were accepted at each district over a four-day period. With pure-hearted joy, members everywhere brought their sincere donations — often saved by cutting their living expenses to the bone — to meeting places in their respective

areas. Some 1,419,532 — or seventy percent — of all member households contributed, their donations totaling approximately 3.27 billion yen. The goal set by the Soka Gakkai Headquarters had been 1 billion yen. More than three times the target amount had been collected — the indisputable outcome of the members' passionate commitment toward realizing kosen-rufu.

The July Headquarters Leaders Meeting was held on the 27th. Shin'ichi took the opportunity to express his deep appreciation to all members for their sincere contributions for the Grand Reception Hall.

"Let me begin," he said, "by expressing on this occasion my most humble appreciation for your unstinting support of our donation drive. Thank you very much. I am deeply grateful to you all.

"Now it is our responsibility, as the executive leaders of the Soka Gakkai, to live up to your expectations by building a truly magnificent Grand Reception Hall that will shine as an architectural masterpiece of our times. And we will not let you down. I hope all of you will look forward to its completion and, on that occasion, without a single exception, let us gather at the head temple as the happiest people in the world, our lives pervaded with boundless benefit and good fortune.

"As announced earlier, our donations have far exceeded our goal. In anticipation of an increase in members visiting the head temple, I dedicate the additional funds to the construction of several large, modern lodging temples on the head temple grounds, each capable of accommodating from one to two thousand guests.

"And, with your permission, I would also like to use these donations to purchase land adjacent to the head temple for future construction projects, and to build local temples throughout Japan."

The audience responded with applause.

*S*HIN'ICHI replied to the members' enthusiastic response with a deep bow, then continued, "In any event, please be assured that I will discuss exactly how your sincere donations may be put to the best use with High Priest Nittatsu and ensure that they all contribute to the prosperity of the head temple."

Shin'ichi's heart warmed when he thought of the sincere faith of his fellow members in making these donations. Many of them had scrimped and saved to contribute amid already tight financial circumstances. He had even heard a report of one earnest, elderly member, who needed a walking stick to get about, traveling several miles on foot across mountainous terrain to make a donation at the local meeting place. Shin'ichi was profoundly aware of the moving dramas of genuine faith that lay behind each member's endeavors.

He felt that the Daishonin watched over and praised this sincere faith. Shin'ichi fervently hoped that the

priests would appreciate the members' precious donations, and not merely regard them as something that was
their due; he hoped they would show warm compassion
for the members and their struggles.

At the Headquarters Leaders Meeting, forty-two new
chapters were born, among them Amami Oshima Chapter, bringing the number of Soka Gakkai chapters to 205.
In addition, a new headquarters system for each region
was introduced. With the expansion of membership, the
organization itself had grown, and most regions now had
more than one general chapter. The new headquarters
would function to consolidate and unite the general
chapters in each region, while allowing for the development of activities giving full play to each region's unique
character. This additional structure was designed to
strengthen the organization's overall effectiveness in its
efforts to promote kosen-rufu in each region.

On July 29, Shin'ichi attended the sixth outdoor
training session of the Suiko-kai at Kirigamine Heights in
Nagano Prefecture. Meeting with these energetic and
enthusiastic young people was one of Shin'ichi's greatest
pleasures. He arrived at the campsite a little before 6:00
in the evening.

"President Yamamoto! Thank you for coming!" Members who had already arrived greeted him cheerfully. It
seemed to Shin'ichi that the young men were more energetic and had matured enormously since the outdoor
training session at Inubosaki the previous year. They were
determined, after the strict training they had received
from Shin'ichi at that session, not to repeat their past mis-
takes. With a renewed commitment to their mission as
Suiko-kai members, they had worked hard over the past
year to improve themselves toward today's gathering.

Each face shone with a passionate spirit to achieve the goal of realizing a meeting of 100 thousand valiant young men.

S HIN'ICHI walked around offering words of appreciation and encouragement to the event staff who were busily preparing for the gathering. Near a small stream, the members of the kitchen crew were seeing to the dinner.

"Thanks for your hard work!" Shin'ichi called out. "You must be the kitchen crew, right? By the way, who chose this particular spot?"

"I did," replied the head of the kitchen crew, Kurazo Tateyama, stepping forward.

"You picked an excellent site," Shin'ichi said. "Securing a water source is the first thing you have to think about. This is especially true in the case of a natural disaster, when a lot of people have to be evacuated to a safe place. With a clean stream, you have a source of drinking water, too. And you can also use it to cook meals and wash clothes. That's why your choice is such a good one." Shin'ichi's endeavor to instruct and educate the young people was already under way, even before the official training session had begun.

"Now, aside from water, what else must you prepare for a shelter or site where a large number of people will gather?"

The members thought for a while.

"Food," suggested one young man.

"Of course, food is important," Shin'ichi admitted, "but anyone knows that. And in a tight spot, we can all go without a meal or two. But we can't go without toilets. So whenever you have a large gathering of people, you have to think about setting up toilets. Mr. Toda taught me this, and I hope you'll all remember it as well."

A white veil of mist flowed over the campsite, leaving only a faint outline of the mountain ranges in the distance.

Shin'ichi vividly recalled his first visit to Kirigamine in August three years earlier. Deeply moved by the beautiful, majestic mountain scenery, he wished he could have brought Josei Toda here. He had also thought of inviting young people here in the future to refresh and enliven their spirits. That is why he chose Kirigamine as a site for the outdoor training sessions of the Suiko-kai, a group of young people in whom Toda had placed much faith.

Though it was the middle of summer, the mountain air was chilly. Shin'ichi looked up at the sky, clouds blanketing its expanse in the gathering twilight. He hoped it would not rain. The members worked together with seamless teamwork to prepare the evening meal. Shin'ichi was pleased at their strong spirit of unity.

*M*OMENTS later, they sat in a circle and began to eat. A pile of firewood, which they would light when it grew dark, was stacked in the center.

Arriving at his seat, Shin'ichi said to everyone with a smile: "Thank you for all your hard work. Let's enjoy ourselves today!"

Smiles appeared in return on the faces of the youth. A warm and friendly atmosphere pervaded as they ate their dinner. Nothing could have tasted better than the simple meal of vegetable pork soup and canned fare with rice provided by the kitchen crew in the fresh air of this magnificent natural setting.

Not long after they began their meal, rain started to fall — faintly at first, then growing steadily heavier. They had no choice but to quickly finish eating and take shelter in their tents to wait out the downpour. But soon the rain lightened to a drizzle and stopped altogether.

Venturing outside again, the members lit the campfire and gathered around it for their training session. The youth division leaders and several Soka Gakkai directors rose one after another to say a few words. Rain started to fall again, though, gradually becoming heavier. The campfire continued to burn through the downpour.

Shin'ichi opened an umbrella the young men had given him and urged everyone to cover their heads with the straw matting on which they had been sitting. He began to speak over the sound of the falling rain:

"Please take care not to catch cold. What is my greatest desire? That you will become leaders who work actively on the global stage for the peace and happiness of all humanity. That was also Mr. Toda's wish. I want you to know that all of my actions are directed toward that end, that your developing into such outstanding leaders is my greatest source of joy, and that I am preparing the way for you with all of my strength.

"As Mr. Toda's disciple, I am fully prepared and determined to carry out his objective, which was to banish unhappiness from this earth. But I cannot do it alone. My life is limited, and that is why I have decided to entrust the completion of this task to you, the youth division. Even if something should happen to me, I want you to carry on this spirit and realize Mr. Toda's vision for me."

For a moment, Shin'ichi's voice was nearly drowned out by the fierce rain. But the young men listened intently so as not to miss a single word.

SHIN'ICHI continued: "Mr. Toda once said that if the members all support the third president, kosen-rufu will surely be achieved. This may rightly be called his last testament and guidance to us. Just as Mr. Toda instructed, President Makiguchi's direct disciples —

our esteemed seniors — are also supporting and assisting me. That is why I can lead with such confidence.

"When we look at other religious organizations, we see that they often split into factions as soon as the leader dies. But by observing Mr. Toda's instructions, we have moved forward with strength and ironclad unity. This is the way to ensure that kosen-rufu endures for eternity.

"The fourth and the fifth presidents of the Soka Gakkai will without a doubt emerge from our youth division. When that happens, I hope you will all protect and support them even more than you have me, and proceed to advance our movement even further.

"I also hope that you, the members of the Suiko-kai, will study, work hard and develop yourselves to become the very best you can be in your chosen fields. I would like you to become the core of the Soka Gakkai and take on the responsibility for the future of kosen-rufu. That is my fondest hope and my most cherished wish."

Excitement coursed through the young men's veins as they realized again the enormity of President Yamamoto's expectations for them.

Soon, the training session came to a close. The driving rain had thoroughly soaked them all, Shin'ichi included. The youth joined together in a rousing Gakkai song as the president made his way to his lodging, an inn a short walk from the camp.

Shin'ichi wanted to talk more with the members and encourage them further. So, after a brief rest, he invited some representatives to the inn's main room for a question-and-answer session. The young men assembled eagerly.

Shin'ichi's and the directors' shirts had been soaked by the rain, so they held the session in their undershirts.

"Please, ask anything you'd like," Shin'ichi urged.

Several hands shot up. Most of the questions concerned how to ensure a lasting peace given the troubled state of the world or how to proceed toward global kosen-rufu. Each was infused with an earnest sense of mission and passionate concern for the future of the world and the kosen-rufu movement. Pleased with the young men's spirit, Shin'ichi answered each question with great sincerity and care.

THE questions asked by the youth included the following: "When I read the Gosho, I see that the key to attaining Buddhahood lies in devoting one's life to Buddhism; in other words, in offering one's life for the Law. If there is ever a major persecution, I am prepared to fight and die, if need be, as Mr. Makiguchi did. But it seems unlikely, judging from the present, that we will encounter such a situation. How, then, should we interpret this concept of devoting one's life to Buddhism?"

It was clearly a question arrived at through long and serious thought about how a Buddhist should live.

Shin'ichi replied: "Let me begin to answer your question by making it clear that in taking leadership it is my intention that none of our precious members should ever have to lay down their lives because of faith-related persecution. That is why I am working so hard. I don't want to sacrifice even one member. This is my spirit.

"Nevertheless, no matter how wisely or skillfully one takes the helm, a major life-threatening persecution — as is described in the Gosho — might still occur. If that should happen, my wish is that I be the only sacrifice. This is the spirit of a true leader. In striving to spread the Daishonin's teachings widely for the happiness of all, I am always gazing squarely at reality, carefully paying attention to everything and deeply pondering the best way to proceed, with prudence, determination and speed.

"If one just rushes ahead without thinking, there is a great risk of making an irreversible error. A leader's responsibility is truly heavy."

Everyone listened seriously.

"As far as dedicating one's life to Buddhism is concerned," he continued, "in the present circumstances it means to make kosen-rufu our fundamental purpose in life and to live a long and useful existence in pursuit of this goal. This is what it means to offer your life for Buddhism. Once you resolve, as a Soka Gakkai member, to make kosen-rufu your life's foundation, it is essential that you become an outstanding person at your place of work. If you do poorly at work, you cannot demonstrate to others how wonderful Buddhism is, and no one will want to take faith. For the same reason, you should strive to create a happy and harmonious family life and take good care of your health. To live a life devoted to kosen-rufu means to be a success in society and to attain personal happiness. Dedication to Buddhism does not mean living a tragic life."

WITHOUT them noticing it, the sound of the rain had ceased. Shin'ichi Yamamoto continued explaining what it means to dedicate one's life to Buddhism, this time from a slightly different angle.

"Perhaps another way of looking at it," he said, "would be in terms of how much time you can spend engaged in activities for kosen-rufu. This may be an extremely empirical view, but if, for example, you were to spend two hours a day doing Gakkai activities, over sixty years you would have given five years of your life to Buddhism.

"When all is said and done, living with the commitment to make kosen-rufu your life and striving to carry out your mission equals dedicating your life to Buddhism."

Shin'ichi cherished the young people's frank questions and answered them with great sincerity. Questions are a sign of a seeking spirit. Asking a question in front of a group requires courage. And the presence of those who ask questions is important, for in raising questions they help to resolve not only their own doubts but those of countless others, leading everyone to a greater understanding of Buddhism.

By the time the question-and-answer session at the inn was over, the rain had stopped completely and the moon was shining in the night sky.

The weather was fine the following day. From early that morning, the Suiko-kai members played hard in a series of sports events that included dodgeball and sumo wrestling. After the sports finished at 9:00 A.M., Shin'ichi promised them that they would hold another outdoor training session the following year. Then, on horseback, he headed for the area where the young women's division Kayo-kai members, having arrived at Kirigamine early that morning, were holding their outdoor training session.

The sky was blue and clear and rolling green mountains stretched out in the distance. A mountain breeze blew gently as Shin'ichi urged his horse forward. When the Kayo-kai members came into view, Shin'ichi waved to them from horseback. A short time later, he joined them in informal discussion.

"I hope you will all exercise your bodies and minds today," he said. "At the same time, please enjoy yourselves and refresh your energy. Buddhism teaches us to enjoy our lives to the fullest. The Daishonin, even while in exile on Sado, wrote, 'I feel immeasurable delight even though I am now an exile' (MW-1, 94). These words come from the lofty state and immense conviction of the original Buddha. Even when undergoing the persecution of exile, the Daishonin was filled with boundless joy. Faith means enjoying our lives to the fullest under any circumstances."

THE young Kayo-kai members' eyes sparkled as they listened to Shin'ichi: "Mr. Toda often said that Buddhahood is a state where one is filled with a deep and irrepressible joy at just being alive. Of course, we have to work hard in life; this is unavoidable. As students, you have to study diligently. Then, when you join the work force, you have to apply yourselves seriously to your jobs. Nor is marriage a guarantee of an easy life; it inevitably entails taking on a host of new responsibilities, not the least of which are household chores and raising a family. These can at times make life seem like a war zone!

"But those who have really mastered the art of living find meaning in such struggles, cultivate a sense of purpose, set goals and rise eagerly to life's challenges. They make each minute as meaningful and enjoyable as possible. Happiness does not exist outside of us. It is inside. Buddhism teaches us this.

"Today, we are lucky enough to be in this beautiful natural setting. I hope you will all have a wonderful time, one that you will always remember."

After the discussion, the young women began their sports activities, splitting up into several teams to play volleyball. When the games were over, Shin'ichi suggested, "Let's form circles and see which one can make the most successful volleys."

The volleying began, but none of the groups could keep it going very long: Someone would inevitably drop the ball after only three or four hits.

Seeing this, Shin'ichi joined one of the groups, telling them, "No one seems able to keep the ball up for long, so let's aim for 100 volleys in this group!"

"One hundred?" a member cried out incredulously.

"Yes, 100," Shin'ichi replied. "If we set our minds to it and all work together, we can do it. It's important to set goals and achieve them. OK, let's go!" He served the ball.

In unison the group counted off the successful volleys. When the ball went to someone who wasn't strong in volleying, neighboring teammates helped her out, sending the ball back up into the air. The count reached 20, 30 and then 40. Then two members tried to hit the ball at the same time and nearly collided.

"Make sure to call out to each other so that you know who has the ball covered," Shin'ichi advised.

Gradually the players found their rhythm.

"We're doing fine now," he announced. "We'll definitely reach 100."

EIGHTY volleys came and went. The other groups gathered around the one Shin'ichi was in, and began to join in the counting. As their goal approached, the group's members began to tense a little.

Shin'ichi called out to them: "Let's relax. You'll be fine as long as you pay attention. You're just repeating the same thing again and again."

Ninety passes. The counting echoed louder around the circle. The air was charged with their determination not to drop the ball as they neared their goal. Even volleys that seemed almost impossible to return were skillfully intercepted and the ball sent flying back into the air.

"Ninety-six, 97, 98, 99, 100!" The volley continued even after they reached their goal of 100 volleys.

"One hundred three, 104, 105, 106…." They managed to keep it going through more than 110 volleys before the ball finally hit the ground. Applause rose from the crowd in response to the group's achievement.

Wiping his brow, Shin'ichi congratulated them: "None of you thought you could keep the ball up for more than 100 volleys, did you? But you did it. When everyone works together toward the same goal, you will find you can bring about unexpected results. This is how the Gakkai advances."

After a brief rest, they were to assemble again for lunch in the great outdoors. When Shin'ichi arrived at the place where they would be eating, not all of the members had appeared yet.

When one YWD leader saw Shin'ichi, she grabbed a hand mike and began shouting at the others: "Everyone, come immediately! Hurry up! Let's get going!"

Chuckling, Shin'ichi spoke to the leader: "It's better not to get all excited and make a fuss. Just say, quietly, 'Shall we assemble?' A real leader can get everyone to gather on time without shouting."

Within a short while, most of the young women had taken their seats. But Shin'ichi didn't see Yumie Kaga, one of the top young women's division leaders.

"Miss Kaga isn't here," he noted.

A member seated nearby informed him, "She's preparing the food."

"I see," he said. "She's a devoted behind-the-scenes worker. She's one of those who energetically exerts herself outside the limelight. That's very important. As leaders, you must always be aware who is making efforts behind the scenes, and who is working the hardest."

*E*DUCATION that is truly practical arises from natural interaction among people. Shin'ichi made use of any suitable situation or event to teach the young women of the Kayo-kai what it meant to be a good leader. He used the example of Yumie Kaga to remind them to be considerate of those who work behind the scenes.

"Leaders who notice only what's happening in the limelight, on center stage, who see only the surface of things, do a great disservice to their fellow members," he said. "Eventually everyone will care only about appearances, more concerned with presenting themselves in the best light than actually doing their best.

"For example, when you attend a meeting and there's a lovely theme poster or specially crafted decoration on display, a good leader immediately thinks about who created it and how. What distinguishes good leaders is their degree of concern for those who are not there — for instance, those posted outside ensuring the orderly flow of members into the venue. Are they cold? Did they have lunch?

"Human kindness and consideration are keys to building a good organization. When people feel appreciated, they do their best. Neither hierarchy nor rules make for a smooth-running organization."

After lunch, they entertained themselves with folk dances. The young friends, cheerful and brimming with life, looked like beautiful dancing blossoms.

As he watched, Shin'ichi told the YWD leaders: "The young women's division is the flower of the Soka Gakkai. I hope you will always approach your activities with joy and good common sense, as we see here today. Being bright and cheerful, in a way that delights everyone you encounter, is wonderful proof of faith."

At the time, the Kayo-kai members, the core of the young women's division, were busy day and night with propagation activities. This was only to be expected if the Gakkai were to achieve its goal of 3 million member-households. But Shin'ichi did not want these young leaders to charge ahead heedlessly without sensitivity to others or their surroundings, looking put-upon. He knew such members wouldn't last long, that others would find them unpleasant.

The purpose of faith is to bring our humanity to full bloom. A single blossom brightens its surroundings and gives pleasure to those who gaze upon it. In the same way, true faith means that the more an individual strives, the more considerate toward others and the more cheerful and lively he or she will become.

The outdoor training session ended at 3:30 that afternoon. The members spent an enjoyable and productive time in the breathtaking natural setting of Kirigamine, and left with a renewed sense of well-being. Shin'ichi felt very strongly that, if it were possible, he would like to nurture each member of the Soka Gakkai youth division as he had here during these outdoor training sessions.

WITH the young men's division leaders meeting on July 31 and the young women's division leaders meeting on August 1, the youth division members got their activities for August off to a dynamic start. The young men announced at their meeting that the division's membership surpassed 300 thousand.

Immediately after the youth division meetings, the annual summer training course was to be held at Taiseki-ji in four separate sessions, August 2–10.

Shin'ichi Yamamoto was scheduled to lecture on one of the most important of Nichiren Daishonin's writings, the "Rissho Ankoku Ron." He had decided on this topic in early July. Now that the Gakkai had attained a membership of more than 2 million households, it was time, he felt, to reaffirm their goal and mission as Buddhists to secure a peaceful society based on the Daishonin's teachings.

Rissho means "to establish the true," in other words, the propagation of the True Law. It means to ingrain such tenets as the sanctity of life and respect for human dignity in people's lives and establish them as guiding principles in society. The purpose of this is "to bring peace to the land" (*ankoku*), to bring about the security and prosperity of society.

The Soka Gakkai's mission is to achieve this goal of the Daishonin. When religion averts its gaze from its mission of relieving suffering in the real world, it dies. The earnest wish of Josei Toda, who raised the banner of kosen-rufu in the grim days after Japan's defeat in World War II, was to bring the light of eternal happiness and peace to the Japanese people, whose lives were filled with misery.

Since becoming Soka Gakkai president, Shin'ichi had prayed constantly for world peace, for freedom from natural disasters such as earthquakes, and for rich harvests. Both Toda and his young disciple Shin'ichi had constantly pondered and asked themselves what they should and could do for the prosperity and peace of society.

In 1957, Josei Toda called for the abolition of atomic and hydrogen bombs. He said that the use of nuclear weapons, for whatever purpose or outcome, was indefensible; those who did so were fiends, monsters. And he entrusted the youth with spreading this idea around the world.

Toda also encouraged qualified Gakkai members to run for local and national political offices to restore power to the people, to improve the people's lives and to establish Japan on a path of lasting peace. The Soka Gakkai's opportunities to serve society and work for peace were bound to increase in the future. As those opportunities arose, misunderstanding and confusion might occur unless all members had a thorough grasp of the principle of *rissho ankoku* — of achieving a peaceful society through the teachings of Nichiren Daishonin's Buddhism.

This is why Shin'ichi selected the "Rissho Ankoku Ron" as his topic for the summer training course.

*A*S the summer training course approached, Shin'ichi devoted every available moment to study of the "Rissho Ankoku Ron." He read and pondered the Gosho whenever and wherever he could: in his offices at the Gakkai Headquarters, in his home late at night and in his lodgings when traveling.

He had studied the "Rissho Ankoku Ron" many times before, but now he came to it as if for the first time, reviewing it carefully, starting with the Daishonin's motivation to write it. In the "Postscript to the 'Rissho Ankoku Ron,'" the Daishonin writes, "I began the work during the Shoka period (1257–59) and completed it in the first year of Bunno [1260]" (MW-2 [2ND ED.], 45). He goes on to say that a major earthquake that struck the Kamakura region on the evening of August 23, 1257, prompted him to begin compiling the lengthy treatise.

Nichiren Daishonin was 36 and living in a small dwelling at Matsubagayatsu, an area in Kamakura, when the earthquake struck. Four years earlier, in 1253, after proclaiming the establishment of his teaching, he was driven from his home in Awa province by the local steward, narrowly escaping assassination. Thereafter, he made Kamakura, the seat of Japan's government, the base for his propagation activities.

During that period, the country was ravaged year after year by famine and epidemics. The *Azuma Kagami* (Mirror of Eastern Japan) and other historical chronicles from that period describe countless natural disasters occurring even in just the short period from 1257 to 1260.

Aftershocks persisted for several months following the devastating earthquake of August 1257, and another major temblor occurred in November the same year. In June 1258, an unseasonable cold wave literally turned summer into winter, gale-force winds lashed Kamakura, and driving rains pounded the Kyoto area — all of which combined to severely damage the year's crops. Then, in October, torrential rains caused floods in Kamakura that washed away homes and killed many people. Epidemics attacked the populace, and famine struck many provinces.

In March 1259, the third year of the Shoka period, the authorities decided to change the name of the period in an effort to improve the land's fortunes. But epidemics continued unabated in succeeding months and on into the next year, leading to yet another change in the period name, in April 1260, to Bunno. Nevertheless, that same month, a great fire razed much of Kamakura and, in June, the city was subject once again to violent gales and flooding.

As a resident of Kamakura, the Daishonin was in direct and daily contact with the suffering people, and he was deeply pained by their plight. People wandered the streets aimlessly, injured and starving. Children wailed; homeless mothers clutched their infants to their breasts, not knowing where to turn. Some collapsed at the roadside, but there was no one to help. Death waited at every turn.

The government ordered Shingon priests to perform rituals and prayers to ease the situation, but these were of no help.

W HAT did we do to invite such suffering?" This was the question on everyone's minds. Yet no one could provide an answer. Nichiren Daishonin, too, must have been deeply troubled by the misery around him and given long and measured thought to how this living hell — this anguish, pain and despair — could be transformed.

As Shin'ichi Yamamoto read the Gosho, he tried to imagine Nichiren Daishonin's life. He vividly pictured him responding to the sight of the people's sufferings, sharing in their pain and agony and acting on their behalf.

Around 1258, the second year of the Shoka period, a solitary monk made his way from Kamakura to Suruga (in present-day Shizuoka Prefecture). There was a look of deep sadness in his eyes. That monk's name was Nichiren. He visited Jisso-ji, a Buddhist temple of the Tendai school located at Iwamoto in Suruga, which possessed a complete set of the Buddhist scriptures.

In the temple library, Nichiren carefully perused the texts of each scroll of those teachings. He was determined to find documentary and theoretical proof that would show unmistakably that the fundamental cause for the continuing onslaught of natural disasters, epidemics and famine lay in the confusion in the religious realm, the basic spiritual foundation of human society. Day after day, he stayed in the library poring over the sutras. When he came to the Daijuku Sutra (Sutra of the Great Assembly),[3] his eyes gleamed with an intense light: There before him was a detailed description of the natural disasters that would occur when

Buddhism was in decline. It matched exactly what he had witnessed since the Great Earthquake of 1257.

"It is just as it says!" he exclaimed inwardly.

Nichiren himself was keenly aware of the decline of Buddhism and deeply regretted it. Because Kamakura was filled with the temples of many Buddhist schools, it seemed that Buddhism was flourishing. But neither the genuine Buddhism that Shakyamuni taught nor any vestige of its spirit was to be found there.

The sutras were clear as to what Shakyamuni's true teachings were. For example, in the Muryogi Sutra (Sutra of Immeasurable Meanings), which serves as a prologue to the Lotus Sutra, Shakyamuni Buddha declares, "In these more than forty years, I have not yet revealed the truth." This clarifies that, of Shakyamuni's five decades of preaching, the first forty-or-so years were devoted to expounding preparatory teachings in which he did not yet reveal the truth. Whereas the Lotus Sutra teaches the true nature of life in its totality, these pre-Lotus Sutra teachings are merely provisional, employing examples and parables that elucidate a partial view of life's reality. In addition, the "Simile and Parable" chapter of the Lotus Sutra insists on "not accepting a single verse of the other sutras" (LS3, 79), indicating that the Lotus Sutra alone is the most fundamental Buddhist teaching.

*I*N Nichiren Daishonin's time, there were eight long-established schools of Buddhism in Japan: Tendai, Kusha, Jojitsu, Ritsu, Hosso, Sanron, Kegon and Shingon. In addition, there were two that had emerged relatively recently — the Pure Land (Jodo) and Zen schools. All of these, with the exception of the Tendai, were based on provisional sutras taught before the Lotus Sutra. Even the Tendai school, which once based itself solely on the Lotus Sutra, had turned its back on the sutra's true teachings after the death of Dengyo, the school's founder. The Tendai had done so by incorporating many teachings from the esoteric Shingon school and from the Pure Land school.

What happens if someone becomes attached to a teaching that is merely metaphorical, representing only a partial truth, and interprets it literally, believing it to be the whole truth? This may be compared to seeing a tiger's tail and mistaking it for the whole tiger. The tail alone looks harmless enough, but if you approach it carelessly, the whole tiger will turn on you and attack.

That is why, since establishing his teaching on April 28, 1253, Nichiren had been pointing out the errors in the teachings of the other schools.

In those days, the Pure Land school founded by Honen had spread most widely in Japan. This school was based on the three Pure Land sutras,[4] all provisional pre-Lotus Sutra teachings. Honen taught that this world is a defiled realm, and that all people should wholeheartedly invoke the Nembutsu — the practice of reciting the name of Amida Buddha (Namu-Amida-Butsu) — so that they could be reborn in Amida's Pure Land of Perfect Bliss in the western region of the universe. Honen also rejected the Lotus and all other sutras except the three Pure Land sutras.

However, Shakyamuni taught of Amida Buddha's Pure Land of Perfect Bliss and other Buddha lands throughout the universe only as expedients, as metaphors. He expounded on these realms only as a means to encourage those who were steeped in the suffering of this impure world. His true intent, however, was that this world of ours is fundamentally the Pure Land — that this strife-filled world is the Land of Eternally Tranquil Light. When people's hearts are impure, the land they dwell in is impure;

when their hearts are pure, they live in a Pure Land. A single thought can change this world from one of suffering into a Pure Land. This is what the Lotus Sutra teaches.

With its teaching of the impurity of this world and salvation lying await in some faraway realm, the Nembutsu or Pure Land school nurtured a sense of resignation and powerlessness in the people; it bred complacency and escapism. In addition, the times were chaotic, wracked by all manner of natural and human-made disasters. The Nembutsu philosophy contributed only to a pervading sense of imminent doom, adding further to feelings of dread and despair among the people.

Nichiren called the Pure Land chant "the melancholy drone of the Nembutsu" (*Gosho Zenshu*, p. 97), and his description was perfect: The sound of the weary chant only weakened the spirits of the already exhausted people.

*A*T Jisso-ji, Nichiren gave himself over totally to reading one sutra after another. His study of these texts clearly convinced him that the disasters and misfortune presently befalling Japan were caused by virtually the entire population turning its back on the Lotus Sutra, the Buddha's true teaching.

Beliefs have a great influence on our lives. For example, suppose we befriend someone we believe to be a good person, but who is actually disreputable. If we associate with that person, we, too, may be led down the path toward evil before we even realize what is happening.

This is all the more a problem where religion is concerned, because religion shapes the way people think and act at the most basic level. Belief in an erroneous religious teaching can cloud people's minds and make them fall victim to their desires — it can even rob people of their will to live. This naturally will affect society, which is a

product of human behavior, inviting conflict, confusion and stagnation. According to the principle of the oneness of life and its environment and the doctrine of a single life-moment possesses three thousand realms, disharmony in people's hearts and minds and disorder in society are one and inseparable. Such disharmony also affects the natural environment. Buddhism teaches, then, that the universe is essentially a single living entity and that human beings and the natural world, which includes our physical environment, are mutually dependent and interrelated.

Nichiren concluded that the only way for people to free themselves from suffering was to abandon all erroneous teachings and base their lives on those that are true and correct. Furthermore, from his reading of the sutras, there was every indication that two of the three calamities and seven disasters described in the scriptures that had not yet occurred — internal strife and invasion from abroad — would soon descend upon the country with a vengeance.

It occurred to Nichiren that priests of the other Buddhist schools must have read these sutras. Yet they had not succeeded in identifying in them the fundamental cause of the misfortune plaguing society. This only underscored the fact that they failed to rely on the sutras as they should have and had lost the spirit to directly confront, or seek a way to relieve, the people's sufferings.

The Tendai, Shingon, Kegon, Ritsu and other schools of established Buddhism merely contented themselves with being officially designated by the government to offer ceremonial prayers for the protection of the nation. And the newer schools, such as Zen and Pure Land Buddhism, cared only about gaining favor with leading members of the government. All of them strenuously avoided any discussion or debate on the validity of their teachings.

In other words, priests with fundamentally differing beliefs, whose most basic religious tenets were at odds, had come to overlook these and together latched on to the government as their means of support, drinking deeply from the well of official patronage. They had completely forgotten the true mission of religion: the salvation of the people.

The government, in exchange for the support it lent them, required these Buddhist schools to cooperate with its policies. As a result, government and religion had become inseparable.

NICHIREN wrote his treatise "Rissho Ankoku Ron" out of a desire to put an end to people's suffering. On July 16, 1260, he submitted the work to the retired regent, Hojo Tokiyori, still the most powerful figure in Japan then, through the offices of Yadoya Nyudo, a Kamakura government official who served Tokiyori. In 1246, when he was 20, Tokiyori had come to power as regent. He quickly fended off all opposition and consolidated the power of the Hojo clan. An innovative governor, he worked to root out corruption among the warrior class. He was also a practitioner of Zen Buddhism, and at the young age of 30 retired as regent, citing health reasons, to enter the Zen order and take up residence at Saimyo-ji, a temple of the Rinzai school.

Even though he was no longer officially regent, he remained as influential as before, though from behind the scenes. Moreover, ever since the Great Earthquake of 1257, Tokiyori had shown that he was seriously concerned about the natural disasters, famine and epidemics striking the land in recent years. He is said to have once lamented: "Is it the fault of the government? Is it because those who rule think only of personal gain? What error have we committed that has so angered both heaven and earth? What kind of offense could it be that the people must suffer so deeply?"

Nichiren had probably heard reports of Tokiyori's disquietude. He had also met and spoken with Tokiyori before presenting him with the "Rissho Ankoku Ron." What Nichiren had heard and seen no doubt contributed to his selecting Tokiyori as a fitting recipient of his formal remonstration with national authority.

This sorry state of society and the suffering of the people motivated Nichiren to compose the "Rissho Ankoku Ron," which begins:

Once there was a traveler who spoke these words in sorrow to his host:

In recent years, there are unusual disturbances in the heavens, strange occurrences on earth, famine and pestilence, all affecting every corner of the empire and spreading throughout the land. Oxen and horses lie dead in the streets, the bones of the stricken crowd the highways…. (MW-2 [2ND ED.], 3)

Such very real human suffering is the starting point of Buddhism, which takes as its goal relief from suffering.

In the "Rissho Ankoku Ron," Nichiren most frequently chose to write the words *land* or *nation* using a Chinese character formed of the pictograph for "the people" surrounded by a rectangular boundary. He did so in preference to more common Chinese characters for *land*, which have the pictograph for "sovereign" or a hand holding a lance symbolizing the protection of a territory or border (both similarly surrounded by a rectangular enclosure). Of the seventy-one times the words *land* or *nation* appear in the "Rissho Ankoku Ron," fifty-six of them, or about eighty percent, are written using the Chinese character formed of "the people" enclosed in a border. This symbolizes the importance that Nichiren gave to the people throughout his thought and writings.

I N the "Rissho Ankoku Ron," Nichiren adopts the form of a dialogue between a guest who laments the state of the world and a host who upholds Buddhism. This format illustrates that Buddhism is spread by inspiration and agreement born of personal dialogue founded on sound logic, and not through coercion or pressure.

Nichiren addressed his treatise of protest not so much to Tokiyori the powerful political figure as to Tokiyori the human being — a leader with sufferings and sorrows like everyone else — out of a sincere wish to teach him the genuine tenets of Buddhism. Nichiren hoped that this would enable Tokiyori to awaken to the correct path of humanism and begin to govern in a way that would be most beneficial for the people.

Nichiren never sought support or patronage from the government. For instance, after his pardon from exile on Sado, his prediction of impending foreign invasion seemed about to come true. Fearing imminent aggression by the Mongols, the government offered to build Nichiren a temple on the condition that he pray for the nation's protection and safety. Had he wanted to ingratiate himself with the political authorities, there would surely have been no better opportunity. But Nichiren refused the offer point-blank.

The "Rissho Ankoku Ron" contains the following exchange: The host declares that to bring order and tranquillity to society without further delay, it is vital to put an end to the slander of the Buddhist Law that fills the country. The guest then inquires whether this means condemning to death those priests and others who slander the Law and violate the prohibitions of the Buddha. The host responds by clarifying that ridding the world of those who slander the Law means simply to cease giving alms to wicked priests.[5]

Nichiren made this point to urge the government to cease its protection and patronage of Zen, Pure Land and other Buddhist schools and to sever the corrupt ties existing between government and religion. In contemporary terms, what Nichiren was talking about accords with the principle of separation of church and state. He rejected the idea that the fate of religion should be dependent upon the whims of the state. With this conviction, Nichiren strove to spread the True Law by examining the validity of each teaching through debate and dialogue among the different Buddhist schools.

When a given religious order seeks the patronage of the state, it is a clear sign of its degeneration.

Nichiren also warned in the "Rissho Ankoku Ron" that the two remaining calamities — internal strife and invasion from abroad — were bound to occur if erroneous Buddhist teachings were not rejected. This was not a mere prediction of impending catastrophe; it expressed the deep wisdom gleaned from contemplating the law of life as recorded in the scriptures. It was a caution based on his enormous compassion and sincere resolve to prevent any more suffering from being inflicted on the people.

NICHIREN expresses his conclusion in the following passage of the "Rissho Ankoku Ron": "Therefore you must quickly reform the tenets that you hold in your heart and embrace the one true vehicle, the single good doctrine [of the Lotus Sutra]" (MW-2 [2ND ED.], 40). What is the surest way to bring peace to the land, to transform a society that is weighed down with misfortune and suffering? Nichiren stresses that it begins with one person establishing the truth in his or her heart. The "one true vehicle, the single good doctrine" of which he speaks is the Lotus Sutra, the true Mahayana teaching that espouses life's supreme worth and dignity and instructs that all living beings are essentially Buddhas. When each individual awakens to and reveals his or her inherent Buddhahood in accord with this Mystic Law, the place that person lives becomes a shimmering Buddha land.

The goal of Nichiren's Buddhism is to create peace and prosperity in society by equipping individuals — the prime movers of society and shapers of the times — with the inner requisites to triumph in all endeavors. The "Rissho Ankoku Ron" reveals the underlying principle for achieving this. Because Buddhism regards all beings as Buddhas, it finds absolute dignity and limitless potential in each individual. These same ideals constitute the unshakable philosophical basis of democracy.

Moreover, as we bring forth our inherent Buddha nature, we develop compassion for others. "Embracing the one true vehicle, the single good doctrine [of the Lotus Sutra]" means, in one sense, abandoning all prejudiced and partial views of life and humanity and returning to a respect for the supreme dignity of life. It means doing away with egoism and living by the rule of compassion, basing ourselves on true humanism. Here we find the universal principle that provides the key to humankind's prosperity and peace on earth.

The "Rissho Ankoku Ron" was thus submitted, but Hojo Tokiyori ignored it. According to one account, when Tokiyori was about to read the treatise, a retainer told him that Nichiren was a proud and arrogant priest who disparaged others and sought only to establish his own school of Buddhism — this, he was told, was the sole motive behind the treatise. Tokiyori is said to have then decided not to read it. Whatever the actual circumstances may have been, it is clear that Tokiyori did not take Nichiren's message seriously. To make matters worse, officials close to Tokiyori twisted and reviled the content of Nichiren's work to the priests of the Pure Land and other Buddhist schools. The priests of Kamakura were already quite annoyed at Nichiren's efforts to point out errors in their teachings. Their anger reached a boiling point when they learned that Nichiren had dared to set down those criticisms in a treatise of protest to Tokiyori.

As a result, Nichiren's life was increasingly in peril.

NICHIREN was very much aware that if he presented the "Rissho Ankoku Ron" to Hojo Tokiyori, he would become the target of persecution. Yet, prepared for this eventuality, he went ahead and admonished the rulers of the land. It was an act arising from profound empathy for the people's suffering, which he felt was his very own.

Genuine empathy goes beyond simply sharing another's troubles and lamenting over them together — beyond mere words of sympathy and consolation. Those who truly empathize with others act with daring and strength to find ways to help people overcome their misery. Such individuals possess a fearlessness rooted in profound compassion, as well as unyielding faith and conviction.

On the evening of August 27, forty days after Nichiren submitted his "Rissho Ankoku Ron," his modest dwelling at Matsubagayatsu in Kamakura was attacked by a band of Nembutsu followers in what came to be known as the Matsubagayatsu Persecution.

Nichiren's prediction had come true. The deluge of persecutions that would assail him for the rest of his life had begun.

As he read the "Rissho Ankoku Ron," Shin'ichi Yamamoto was deeply moved. That year, 1961, had been marked by violent natural disasters and outbreaks of disease. At the end of May, Typhoon No. 4 was followed by a foehn, a warm dry wind, that affected parts of Hokkaido and the Tohoku region in the north of Japan, resulting in many fires. Then, with the onset of the rainy season, torrential downpours began on June 24 and continued for longer than a week. This wreaked enormous damage on many parts of Honshu, Japan's main island — especially the Ina area of Nagano Prefecture — and on the island of Shikoku. More than 350 people were reported dead or missing nationwide.

Polio, too, was rampant, and parents with young children were beset with fear and anxiety. The Soviet Union had developed a live polio vaccine, and talks had started

the previous year about its donating to Japan enough vaccine for 100 thousand children. But the Japanese government vetoed the plan.

Several factors were behind this decision: pressure by anti-Soviet elements in the Japanese government; the rigid stance of the bureaucracy, which used the national pharmaceutical law to obstruct the donation; and opposition by a segment of the pharmaceutical industry, which feared an imported vaccine would undermine sales of their own medications. National policy, political sentiment and profit by private industry were given precedence over the welfare of the Japanese people.

But voices demanding the vaccine for the purpose of saving children's lives grew louder and stronger, swelling into a national movement. Faced with the power of the people, the government finally, if reluctantly, decided to import enough live vaccine for 13 million children on a special emergency basis. In July, 3 million doses of polio vaccine from Canada and 10 million from the Soviet Union arrived in Japan.

O N the international scene, the Cold War was casting a dark shadow, and the acrid smoke of armed conflict rose here and there around the globe. In April, alarmed by activities of the newly installed communist regime in Cuba, the United States backed a military force of Cuban exiles in an attempted invasion of their homeland. The attack, known as the Bay of Pigs invasion, ended in failure. Though it was an exploit that had been planned by the previous administration, it brought international censure for the first time toward the new administration of President John F. Kennedy, who had been a hope for world peace.

On the other side of the globe, three factions were at war in Laos: rightists supported by the United States, centrists and leftists. Concrete negotiations for an end to the fighting and establishment of a coalition government got under way in May, but despite these efforts the fighting would continue for some time.

In Vietnam, divided at the 17th parallel into the Democratic Republic of Vietnam to the north and the Republic of Vietnam to the south, the standoff between the two sides grew more serious, in spite of the sincere wish of most Vietnamese people for a united country.

The United States, fearing the spread of communism in Asia, supported South Vietnam and was determined to eliminate communism from both the north and south. At the end of the previous year, America responded to the formation in South Vietnam of the National Front for the Liberation of Vietnam as if it were an invasion from the north and proceeded to increase its military support for the government of South Vietnam.

Against this turbulent background of world events, the first U.S.–Soviet summit during Kennedy's presidency was held in Vienna on June 3 and 4. The eyes of the world were on the leaders of both nations, and everyone hoped for an easing of East–West tensions. A passionate debate unfolded between the energetic, youthful Kennedy (44) and Nikita Khrushchev (69), the experienced and mature leader of the Soviet Union. But, partly due to Khrushchev's refusal to make any concessions on Berlin[6] and nuclear testing, the summit ended with pronounced differences remaining.

Shin'ichi was deeply concerned about these world-wide trends of instability. The word *land* in the principle "securing peace in the land through the propagation of the True Law" (*rissho ankoku*) is not limited to a single land or nation; it refers to the land of Jambudvipa that appears in the Buddhist scriptures. In today's terms, Jambudvipa means the entire world. To nurture and cultivate people's lives with a philosophy of humanism, in the pursuit of lasting peace and happiness, is what it means to implement the Daishonin's teaching of creating a peaceful society based on the tenets of his Buddhism. Herein lies the mission of the Soka Gakkai.

Shin'ichi decided that this was the message he needed to communicate at the summer training course.

T HE summer training course got under way with Shin'ichi's lecture on the "Rissho Ankoku Ron" as the central feature. Shin'ichi decided to base his lecture on the final section of the work, which begins: "The host said: You have clearly seen the sutras passages that I have cited, and yet you can ask a question like that!" (MW-2 [2ND ED.], 35).

Shin'ichi spoke with energy and enthusiasm before those who gathered in the Grand Lecture Hall of the head temple to hear his lecture: "The message of the 'Rissho Ankoku Ron,' simply put, is that each of us should accomplish a personal human revolution based on the principle of humanism and thus become key players in realizing social prosperity and world peace. It has been said that the Daishonin's lifetime teachings begin and end with the 'Rissho Ankoku Ron.'

"Nichiren Daishonin's purpose in writing this treatise was the salvation of the people, who were suffering pitifully under the onslaught of earthquakes and floods, famine and disease. The way to accomplish this, he decided, was to propagate the philosophy of life of Buddhism, a teaching of how to be truly human and achieve human revolution, the transformation in the very depths of people's lives. He was calling for a struggle to rid people's hearts and minds of evil and replace it with goodness; to open the eye of wisdom in their lives and transform their inner focus from self-centeredness to altruism, from destructiveness to creativity.

"Why did he choose this approach? Because people are the basis of everything. Plants flourish in fertile soil; if we cultivate the soil of human life, peace and culture will flourish magnificently there."

After giving a general outline of the "Rissho Ankoku Ron," Shin'ichi began to lecture on the text itself. He discussed the reason for the occurrence of the three calamities and seven disasters when he came to the passage from the Ninno Sutra that reads: "When a nation becomes disordered, it is the spirits which first show signs of rampancy. Because the spirits become rampant, all the people of the nation become disordered" (MW-2 [2ND ED.], 37).

"'Spirits' refers to functions that are of a metaphysical or intangible nature," he said. "In contemporary terms, thoughts and ideas might be said to fall into this category. In other words, when a country or a society becomes disordered, the first things to show signs of 'rampancy' are people's ideas and ways of thinking. Disorder and confusion in people's thoughts and ideas sap their vitality and distort their mental processes, which in turn cause chaos and disharmony in society.

"If people succumb to egoism, seeking only personal gain, pleasure and short-term gratification, society will naturally decline. To give an example, when the German people submitted to the insanity of Adolf Hitler's Nazism, the tragic results were Germany's invasion of Europe and the slaughter known as the Holocaust."

*S*HIN'ICHI Yamamoto continued lecturing, not even pausing to wipe the perspiration from his brow. "The cause of the social disorder and many tragic events we've been seeing lies in people being caught in a way of thinking that forgets to accord prime importance to the human being," he said.

"Since Japan signed the new security treaty with the United States last year, its people have grown disenchanted with and alienated from politics, and instead have turned their attention to economic prosperity. When they see policy dictated by partisan interests more than by what best serves the people, or legislation being railroaded through parliament by strong-arm tactics rather than being passed by a true democratic process, it's no wonder why people place little hope or trust in politics. Politicians are also responsible in that they have forgotten to work for people's happiness and welfare; they have forgotten that government exists for the people.

"If people lose interest in their government and are lax in overseeing it, though, the situation will only worsen. An economy indifferent to people's needs and well-being is a cruel thing. What will happen to society if all we care about are profit and economic growth? We may prosper materially, but our hearts will grow empty and desolate; we will destroy our environment, and, ultimately, we will suffer from it.

"Science, likewise, if it falls into a misguided belief in its own omnipotence, will become a force for harm, robbing us of our humanity and threatening our well-being.

"'Let us return to humanism!' — this, in contemporary terms, is what Nichiren Daishonin advocated in the 'Rissho Ankoku Ron.' His message is that every field of human endeavor — government, economics, science, education and art — must be put to the purpose of bringing happiness to humanity. This is the principle of creating a peaceful society based on the True Law."

Shin'ichi then came to the passage that reads, "If you care anything about your personal security, you should first of all pray for order and tranquillity throughout the four quarters of the land, should you not?" (MW-2 [2ND ED.], 38). The "four quarters" indicate that which lies to the east, west, north and south; in other words, representing all of society. Here Shin'ichi spoke of the social responsibility of a Buddhist:

"This passage means that if you are concerned at all for your personal security, you must first pray for the stability and peace of all society. This clearly expresses the attitude and posture we should have as Buddhists. People of genuine religious faith do not care only for their own comfort and safety; they are not content to confine themselves to their own private realm. To be truly human means working and praying to solve the problems that plague all people and to achieve peace and prosperity for society. There is no Buddhism apart from human society. A religion that divorces itself from society and only seeks serenity in the afterworld is already dead. It is not a religion in the true sense of the word — it is not a religion for the people. Yet such is the prevailing image of religion in Japan. This is because the government has rendered Japanese religion lifeless."

THE listeners' eyes glowed with seeking spirit. Shin'ichi continued: "The key to establishing peace and prosperity in our world, as expressed here, lies in the human heart — in people's prayer for order and tranquillity in society — and in each person establishing a solid self-identity through the process of human revolution.

"A person who prays for a peaceful and secure society and is considerate toward others will naturally become aware of the need to contribute to society, and will act on that awareness. The Soka Gakkai's goal is to realize the peaceful society described in the 'Rissho Ankoku Ron.' Our mission is to rid this world of every human affliction — war, poverty, starvation, disease and discrimination.

"With this goal in mind, then, what's important is what we do to actually achieve it. Without real effort, it's all just a fantasy, an abstraction. As a rule, when it comes to practical efforts, it is up to each person to decide and do what he or she thinks best and is capable of. But in some cases, the Soka Gakkai can establish separate institutions or organizations to promote peace and cultural exchange. Also, for example, to create a government that works in the interests of the people, we need to elect individuals of integrity while keeping a sharp eye on the activities of our government.

"But in each of these cases, the role of the Soka Gakkai will only be that of a mother organization that gives rise to these institutions or political candidates; it will be the responsibility of each institution or individual to take the initiative in developing their own activities and programs. The purpose of all these activities, however, is not to serve the Soka Gakkai organization — it is nothing so narrow; it is to achieve happiness for all people and peace in the world.

"It is only natural that opinions vary widely on social issues. There is no doubt we will have to feel our way through on many things. But we must base all our activities on our prayer for 'order and tranquillity throughout the four quarters of the land.' Our goal is to place people first, so that we each may lead a life of true humanity and savor a happy and joy-filled existence. Further, the spirit expressed in the 'Rissho Ankoku Ron,' and our wish as Soka Gakkai members, is to firmly infuse this philosophy in society and work to create an age of triumph for the human being."

Listening to Shin'ichi's lecture, the participants from around Japan awakened to their social responsibility as Buddhists. This inspired in them a deeper commitment to work for a peaceful society, and energized them toward fresh growth and advancement.

On August 30, the Headquarters Leaders Meeting was held at the Tokyo Gymnasium. There, it was announced that a phenomenal number of new households — 80,725 throughout Japan — had received the Gohonzon that month. It was a record-breaking achievement. In addition, a general chapter was established in Shikoku, and the Kanto region saw ten new general chapters, bringing the number there from five to fifteen general chapters overnight. The organization was growing by tremendous strides.

I N August, following the guidance tour of Asia by Headquarters representatives earlier that year, leaders were again dispatched by the Gakkai Headquarters to encourage and guide overseas members. Nine in all — including Soka Gakkai Vice General Director and

America General Chapter Chief Kiyoshi Jujo — were sent as three separate groups: one to the northern part of North America, another to the southern part of North America, and a third to South America. The trip lasted sixteen days, August 13 – 28.

Shin'ichi Yamamoto's lecture on the "Rissho Ankoku Ron" was a tremendous inspiration for the leaders heading overseas. The thought that they were setting out to build the foundation for world peace stirred a spirit of challenge in them.

At each stop, they gave their utmost to encouraging the local membership and helping them set up the organization. In the United States, chapters were established in San Francisco, Chicago and Washington, D.C., while twenty-three districts were formed around the country, including in New York.

In South America, five new districts were formed in Brazil and the first district was established in Paraguay. On their way from Brazil to Paraguay, the South American group flew from São Paulo to an airport near Iguaçú Falls. There, they boarded a jeep and drove a full day to the Argentine city of Posadas, before reaching an area in Paraguay called Chavez where many Japanese had settled.

Thirty-four Japanese families who belonged to the Soka Gakkai lived in Chavez. They had all come to South America to settle the land and pioneer the spread of Buddhism. Though they had no organization to speak of, they shared a passionate conviction and struggled earnestly together in their Buddhist practice.

Their faces flushed with excitement as they shared experiences of faith.

One member related that when he first moved to the area, the water was red with mud, unfit for drinking. He earnestly chanted daimoku to find a good source of potable water, and his prayers were rewarded. He uncovered a new spring that gave forth cool, fresh, clear water.

Living as they did in the wilderness, their houses were small and simply built, just shacks really. But each member was filled with energy and enthusiasm. They passed among themselves copies of the *Seikyo Shimbun* until the paper wore thin. They had been trying hard to share their faith with others, and their numbers were steadily increasing.

They resolved: "This is a fine land. The harvests are good here. We intend to transform this country into a garden of happiness." And now Paraguay had its first district.

The current of happiness and peace was spreading steadily and surely to the farthest corners of the globe.

*I*N September, unit-level discussion meetings were steadily gaining momentum, and experiences of members who were standing up with new commitment in faith as a result came pouring in a steady stream to the Gakkai Headquarters.

Shin'ichi spent most of September in Tokyo, except for a visit to the head temple on the 15th, followed by a trip to Kansai to encourage Osaka members affected by Typhoon No. 18 (also known as the second Muroto Typhoon). He needed the time to prepare for a twenty-day visit to Europe, with October 4 his scheduled departure date.

His main destinations were Copenhagen, Dusseldorf, West Berlin, Amsterdam, Paris, London, Madrid, Zurich, Vienna and Rome. The main purposes of the trip were to offer guidance to local members, purchase construction materials and fixtures for the Grand Reception Hall, and observe the state of religion in Europe.

It was the people of Germany Shin'ichi was most concerned about at this time. In the predawn hours of

August 13, 1961, the communist government of East Germany had built a more than forty-kilometer, barbwire wall along the border of East and West Berlin. Ever since the partition of the German state, the city of Berlin had existed as a forlorn and sundered atoll in the vast sea of the East German state. Berlin, too, had been divided into East and West. Yet despite this, until the wall appeared, people had been free to pass between the two sides.

An endless stream of refugees fleeing communist East Germany to the West via West Berlin, however, had prompted the East German government to physically divide the city with a wall, sealing off all access to the West. Most of the roads linking East and West Berlin were closed off with tanks and armored cars. Checkpoints were set up at those that remained open, and free passage between the two sides was no longer permitted. The subways, too, now ran only to the border.

From August 13 onward, the barbwire wall grew longer and more fortified day by day until finally a cruel and unyielding barrier of concrete and brick was firmly in place. The sudden closing of the passage between East and West Berlin split families, relatives and lovers. It was a small-scale model of the Cold War, in which people were oppressed and cast asunder by opposing ideologies.

With his visit to Europe imminent, Shin'ichi vowed that now was the time for a humanistic philosophy that would foster bonds that would spread widely among people and take root in the human heart. He would blaze his way toward securing peace in the world by establishing the correct principles of Buddhism — the way of *rissho ankoku*.

Shin'ichi was about to take flight into the clear blue skies of the twenty-first century on a monumental journey for peace.

"Rissho Ankoku" Notes:

1. Fukuzawa Yukichi, *An Outline of a Theory of Civilization*, trans. David A. Dilworth & G. Cameron Hurst (Tokyo: Sophia University, 1973), p. 146.

2. Ibid., p. 147.

3. Daijuku Sutra (Sutra of the Great Assembly): A collection of sutras said to have been preached by Shakyamuni to Buddhas and bodhisattvas. It contains references to the three calamities and predictions regarding the spread of Buddhism over the five consecutive 500-year periods following Shakyamuni's death.

4. Three Pure Land sutras: The basic sutras of the Jodo and Jodo Shin schools of Buddhism in Japan. They are the Muryoju Sutra (Sutra of the Buddha of Infinite Life), the Kammuryoju Sutra (Sutra of Meditation on the Buddha of Infinite Life) and the Amida Sutra (Sutra of Amida Buddha).

5. cf. MW-2 [2ND ED.], 34–35.

6. In 1961, despite protests by the West, Soviet-controlled East Germany began erecting barriers along the boundary dividing East and West Berlin to stem a growing tide of East Germans defecting to the West. These barriers were eventually replaced with the Berlin Wall, also in 1961, which stood until 1989 as an ominous symbol of the Cold War.

Great Light

THE ageless sun rises anew, calmly sending forth its golden rays. As an organization committed to the great Law of Buddhism, the Soka Gakkai is the sun for the entire world.

The sun's primordial brilliance dispels the darkness of mistrust and hatred, casting the bright light of peace upon the Earth. Even into the darkest valleys of misery and despair, it sheds the light of hope, transforming the human realm, which surges with suffering, into a beautiful flower garden of joy.

Nothing can stop the progress of the sun, which advances majestically on its own orbit, high above the black clouds of envy and jealousy.

From the window of the Europe-bound plane, Shin'ichi Yamamoto watched as the sun began its ascent into the sky.

Five hours earlier, at 10:30 P.M. on October 4, 1961, Shin'ichi and his party had left Tokyo's Haneda Airport. Now their plane was on its way to Anchorage, where it would stop briefly for refueling.

As the brilliant red sun made its appearance, the sea of clouds that spread out far below was dyed a soft pink, and the sky began to turn violet. As the sun rose higher, the entire sky looked like molten gold, solemn and majestic. From the great source, countless brilliant shafts of light ran in all directions. The sky became bluer by the second and the clouds, like pure white puffs of cotton, began to glimmer brightly.

As he took in this sight, Shin'ichi thought: "One sun illuminates the entire world. It is the same in the realm of kosen-rufu. A resolute stand by just one person can protect all others and break through the darkness of society, heralding a new dawn of justice. What matters is the presence of one earnest person, of one fervently committed individual.

"Moreover, there is a sun in everyone's heart. Those who embrace Nichiren Daishonin's Buddhism become suns that illuminate the way to happiness for their families and friends. The success of my visit to Europe hinges on how many sun-like people I can find and nurture."

The plane landed in Anchorage for refueling at 10:00 A.M. and, after an hour, took off for Copenhagen, the first destination on the group's itinerary. As they flew close to the North Pole, darkness fell outside the window. A shimmering moon illuminated the night sky with beautiful brilliance.

Shin'ichi put his thoughts and feelings into a poem:

At the North Pole,
The Great Heavenly Moon
Shines brightly,
Yearning for kosen-rufu
On the distant Earth.

*T*HE plane carrying Shin'ichi and his party arrived in Copenhagen just after 7:00 A.M. on October 5. The journey from Japan had taken seventeen hours. On their final approach, they saw a thick layer of clouds blanketing the Danish capital. But when they landed, they found that the clouds had dispersed and that the day was fair and pleasant.

Waiting to greet them was a Japanese man wearing a bow tie. Eiji Kawasaki, a Soka Gakkai member and medical doctor engaged in research at the renowned Collège de France in Paris, was to accompany Shin'ichi's party as their interpreter and guide on their tour of Europe.

Eiji Kawasaki was born in 1923 in what was then known as Takada City in Niigata Prefecture [now a part of Joetsu City]. Later his family moved to Tokyo, where he grew up and spent most of his years until junior high. He spent his senior high years in Mito City in Ibaraki Prefecture, after which he studied medicine at the Niigata Medical University (now the Medical Department of Niigata University). He stayed on as a graduate student to do further research and in due time received his Doctor of Medicine degree at 28.

He then embarked on research in endocrinology, specializing in thyroid hormones. He traveled to the United States, pursuing his research at Harvard University Hospital. Eventually, after returning to Japan and doing a short stint at the University of Tokyo Hospital, he was invited to become a vice director of a hospital in Beppu City in Oita

Prefecture, Kyushu, renowned for its successful treatment of thyroid-related diseases.

By that time, Kawasaki was already in his mid-30s. He began to think that it was time to settle down and get married. So he asked his younger sister, Emiko, if she knew of someone among her friends she could recommend. Unlike himself, Kawasaki's parents and sister were already Soka Gakkai members.

When Emiko heard her brother's desire to marry, she sincerely prayed that he would wed a member of the young women's division, hoping it might provide a wonderful opportunity for him to start practicing. She often spoke to him about faith in the Daishonin's Buddhism, but he had always been indifferent to the subject. He was neither particularly interested in nor biased against the Soka Gakkai; as far as he was concerned, any religion was fine. And yet, despite having achieved considerable success in his career, he was aware of an emptiness deep in his heart.

Emiko told her brother: "The girls I can recommend to you are all members of the young women's division. So if you like, why don't you go and speak with Mr. Shin'ichi Yamamoto, the general administrator of the Gakkai, who is responsible for the youth division, and ask him for his opinion?"

*E*IJI was hesitant about going to see a Soka Gakkai leader about something as personal as marriage. Nevertheless, one day while in Tokyo, he followed the advice of his sister, Emiko, and accompanied her to the Gakkai Headquarters where they called on Shin'ichi. That was in October 1959.

Shin'ichi greeted Kawasaki warmly: "So you're Emiko's brother? She's told me a lot about you. I'm more than happy to help you in any way I can."

After talking with the two for a while, Shin'ichi asked Kawasaki, "Do you have any real friends?"

Kawasaki thought for a moment. He had no one he could call a true friend.

"No, I don't," he answered. "There were a few who were all right in the beginning, but when my friendship no longer served their needs, they invariably took off."

"That may well be the way of the world," Shin'ichi said. "But as for me, I will remain your friend for as long as I live. I'll be praying for you to lead a successful life."

Their conversation was not long by any means, yet Kawasaki was deeply impressed by Shin'ichi's character. He had neither tried to ram religion down his throat, nor had he displayed the kind of preachy, holier-than-thou attitude common to so many religious leaders. His host had been polite and considerate, yet seemed to exude passion and energy. Though Shin'ichi was obviously a few years younger, Kawasaki felt he had been talking to an elder brother. As a result of their meeting, Kawasaki began to have a favorable impression of the Soka Gakkai.

Eventually, in January 1960, Kawasaki married a member of the young women's division his sister had introduced to him.

He joined the Soka Gakkai just before the wedding, but not with any real intention to practice. His attitude was noncommittal: His wife-to-be was a Gakkai member, and it didn't seem like such a bad religion, so why not join?

Kawasaki began his married life in Beppu. A short time later, however, he began to suffer severe abdominal pains. A colleague diagnosed this as appendicitis and Kawasaki immediately underwent surgery.

He was released from the hospital some ten days later, but that day again, he began to experience acute abdominal pain, making it impossible for him to sleep at night.

Kawasaki was readmitted to the hospital, but tests failed to reveal the cause of his ailment. A doctor prescribed morphine to ease the pain, but once it wore off, Kawasaki was in excruciating agony. His distress was so debilitating that he began giving himself morphine injections. The dosage gradually increased, until soon he could not endure the pain for even a moment without the drug.

AS Kawasaki lay sick in his hospital bed, he worried about attending an upcoming conference on thyroid medicine in London, where he was scheduled to deliver a paper. For him it was a precious opportunity to make the results of his research known to the world.

He became more frustrated and anxious as the days wore on, but his condition did not improve. The pain robbed him of sleep and his appetite, and he grew thinner day by day.

His wife, Yoshie, was extremely worried about his condition. One day, she made up her mind. As he lay in bed she told him, "You're forgetting something very important, you know."

"What's that?" he asked. "Something important? If you mean my medicine, I've been taking it every day, haven't I?"

"No, that's not it. I'm talking about faith. Since you don't know the cause of your pain, it seems to me that faith is your only alternative. It's said that no prayer to the Gohonzon goes unanswered, so don't you think you ought to start praying seriously?"

"What are you talking about?" Kawasaki replied with a strained smile. "I'm a doctor. I'm the one who knows best about illness. It's superstition to think you can cure an illness with faith."

"But there's a lot that medicine doesn't understand," his wife returned. "For instance, what about the suffering you're going through right now?"

That day, Yoshie stayed by her husband's bedside and began to chant daimoku earnestly.

"Please, don't do that!" Kawasaki implored. There he was, the hospital's vice-director, unable to treat his own abdominal pain — and having his wife pray at his bedside for a cure. It was a scene he wanted no one to witness. But Yoshie would not be deterred, and continued to chant vigorously. Strangely, Kawasaki's pain began to subside, and he had a good night's sleep.

The following day, Kawasaki asked his wife, "Would you mind staying here and chanting daimoku again today?"

"If my chanting helped you get a good night's rest, then I'm sure you'll sleep even better if you chant yourself," she said. "Why don't we chant together today?"

That night, they did precisely that, and Kawasaki slept soundly afterwards.

The next day, his face and eyes began to show signs of jaundice, symptoms that led his doctor to suspect he might be suffering from a gallstone. An X-ray soon confirmed the diagnosis: He had a large gallstone that would require immediate surgery to remove.

*E*IJI understood well his need for an operation. But he also knew that surgery would mean an extended hospital stay, ruling out any possibility of attending the medical conference in London, now only a short time away. He therefore asked his doctor to consider an alternative method of treatment, while fully aware that none of the options available at the time were as effective as surgery.

Now completely desperate, and at his wife's continued urging, Kawasaki finally decided to give Buddhist practice a serious try. He began to chant earnestly every day and soon showed marked signs of improvement: The color of his urine, which had turned coffee-brown due to the gallstone, gradually returned to normal. Finally, an X-ray taken shortly before his departure for London revealed that the gallstone had disappeared.

"So this is the power of faith!" he thought.

An ebullient Kawasaki went to London, where his presentation at the medical conference was so successful that it brought research invitations from several world-renowned universities and research institutes. Kawasaki had been longing to return to the research field.

In December 1960, Shin'ichi Yamamoto, who had become president of the Soka Gakkai the previous May, visited Oita Prefecture, still home to the Kawasakis, for the inaugural meeting of Oita Chapter. Shin'ichi had continued to take a keen interest in Eiji Kawasaki. When the latter visited Tokyo, Shin'ichi always tried to make time to see him. The two had met on several occasions. In Oita, Shin'ichi invited the doctor and his wife to the inn where he was staying.

Eiji Kawasaki informed President Yamamoto that he had received several offers from overseas research institutions and that for some time he had in fact been thinking of pursuing his research abroad. He was warmed by the Soka Gakkai president's genuine pleasure at this news.

Now, all that remained was for Kawasaki to decide in which country to pursue his research. But he vacillated over the decision.

While attending the Soka Gakkai summer training course in August 1961, a still undecided Kawasaki sought guidance on the matter from Shin'ichi. After talking things over together, Kawasaki finally settled on the Collège de France in Paris.

Shin'ichi congratulated Kawasaki on his new beginning. "I'm going to Europe, too, in October," he said. "I'd
be delighted if you could accompany me while I'm there."

Kawasaki was determined to do all in his power to
support Shin'ichi during his trip to Europe.

He arrived in Paris on September 24, ten days before
the Soka Gakkai president was scheduled to leave Japan.

*A*T the airport in Copenhagen, Shin'ichi greeted
Eiji Kawasaki with a firm handshake and warmly
thanked him for coming to meet them. He then
introduced Kawasaki to his traveling companions, Vice
General Director Kiyoshi Jujo and three young men's
division leaders, including the division chief, Shoichi
Tanida. The entire party boarded a bus for the city center.

Copenhagen was a beautiful city with a quiet, refined
atmosphere. Its many trees were cloaked in autumn col-
ors, and well-tended lawns could be seen everywhere.
Also conspicuous were the many cyclists gracefully
breezing up and down the streets.

Passing by a park, the visitors from Japan saw a row
of small, colorfully painted huts. These, they learned,
had been designed and built by children on a lot the
city provided expressly for this purpose. Shin'ichi felt he
was glimpsing an aspect of Denmark's unique educational system.

He recalled two individuals mentioned by Tsunesaburo Makiguchi in the preface to his book *The System of
Value-Creating Pedagogy*: N.F.S. Grundtvig (1783–1872),
the "father of the Danish renaissance," and his young successor, Kristen Kold (1816–70). Josei Toda, too, had often
talked to Shin'ichi about these two.

Grundtvig, one of Denmark's most respected peda-
gogues, was famous for founding Denmark's folk high

schools. He was also a poet, clergyman, expert in early Scandinavian literature and a political activist.

Grundtvig was born in 1783 in a small rural village in Zealand (the island on which Copenhagen is located). He was 6 when the French Revolution broke out. This was followed by the Napoleonic Wars, which engulfed Europe in the early nineteenth century and during which Denmark was defeated by England. As Danish fortunes declined, the foundation of its feudalistic system of absolute monarchy also began to crumble.

Grundtvig grew up in the midst of these tumultuous changes in his country. He hated authoritarianism and rigid formality and sought human freedom and independence. In his young adulthood, he began opposing the established power structure.

The young Grundtvig also had doubts about the worth of an education system based only on rote memorization. Many years later, in his treatise "Schools for Life" (1838), in which he set forth his ideas for education, he criticized these pedagogical methods as "dead schools" teaching "dead letters."

G RUNDTVIG had a strong dislike for the university-educated urban elite who despised the peasantry and thought little of folk culture. Deep in his heart, he felt that these ordinary people of simple means were the true Danes. He could not excuse the arrogance of those who looked down on them. He also turned a sharp, critical eye toward the church and clergy, which had grown corrupt and decadent, tyrannizing and demanding full obeisance from the common people.

Grundtvig demanded, "First, be a human being — then a clergyman!" His blatant criticism incurred the wrath of religious authorities and his writings were banned for more than ten years. His life was a series of persecutions, but he did not bend in his beliefs.

The groundswell of popular revolution sweeping Europe at the time also spread to Denmark. Seeing these changes and sensing the nature of the times, Grundtvig pondered what needed to be done to rebuild and revive his native land.

It was wrong for a small but powerful elite to dominate society and dictate the lives of the majority. If the people awakened to their rights and responsibilities, if they kept a close watch over those in politics, and if they had the power to speak their minds freely — then and only then would true democracy and a true revival of the country be possible. Grundtvig vowed to enable the people to be wise, courageous and eloquent.

To this end, he conceptualized the folk high schools (Folke Hoj Skolen), accessible to the general public and intended to bring higher education to the average person. In Denmark, higher education was then available only to a small handful — the sons of wealthy and privileged families.

At the folk high schools, Grundtvig conceived of a revolutionary new system of higher education where teachers and students lived together in a communal setting. Rather than the one-sided, authoritarian, knowledge-cramming approach, learning was allowed to take place in a free and unrestricted atmosphere of dialogue. Not only did this nurture wisdom for living and promote the acquisition of knowledge, it also cultivated the awareness that ordinary citizens are the principal players in society. The schools provided a "living education" where people shared in the process of learning and inspired one another.

The first folk high school based on Grundtvig's ideas was founded in 1844. Grundtvig's successor, Kristen Kold, played a key role in the school system's growth and establishment as a deeply rooted tradition in Danish society.

Kold, more than thirty years younger than Grundtvig, was a spirited and deeply committed educator.

KOLD became a teacher at a young age; but, unable to get used to an educational system based on rote memorization, he became depressed and discouraged. Then, by chance, he came across Grundtvig's ideas on education. The concept of folk high schools struck a resonant chord and the young Kold set to work to establish a school that would put it into practice. But not being a wealthy man, he soon ran out of funds. He went to seek help from Grundtvig. Though the latter had never met Kold before, he must have sensed an uncommon passion in the young man's request, for he readily agreed to assist him. As a result, Kold's first folk high school opened in 1851.

The two men exchanged views and opinions frankly and openly, working together for a shared ideal. Kold's school incorporated Grundtvig's view that women also have a right to education — it was the first in Denmark to open its doors to female students.

Many agreed with Grundtvig's philosophy and ideals, but it is said that only Kold took him as a mentor and applied his spirit and ideals in the practical realm of education. Always humbly dressed, Kold continued throughout his life to converse with youth, and with the common people. His warmth and dedication won him the nickname "Socrates in Peasant Clothing" and he was much loved by the people.

The 1860s saw the folk high schools' first rise to popularity. It was a bleak time for Denmark, after its defeat in the war against Prussia and Austria resulted in the loss of many of its territories. Determined to rebuild their nation through a policy of "recovering internally what has been lost externally," the Danes undertook the afforestation of Jutland, which had been largely a barren wasteland.

Similarly, the folk high schools served as "forests of education" for which Grundtvig had planted the seeds. They spread throughout Denmark, becoming a great force for nurturing able individuals who would take on the challenge of reconstructing their homeland. Most of those heading the newly founded folk high schools had themselves graduated from Kold's schools. Consequently, Grundtvig is known as the founder of the folk high schools, while Kold is known for having nurtured and developed them as an educational system.

TSUNESABURO Makiguchi stated in the preface to *The System of Value-Creating Pedagogy* that the publication of his book had been made possible only by the tireless efforts of his beloved disciple, Josei Toda. Makiguchi likened his own sense of gratitude to that which Grundtvig must have felt toward Kold, a disciple dedicated to bringing his teacher's vision to fruition. Makiguchi and Toda's ideas on education and schooling were very close to those of Grundtvig in that they were focused on building human character and enlightening ordinary people.

As he looked out the car window at the streets of Copenhagen, Shin'ichi Yamamoto thought that he, too, like Kold, must lose no time in establishing a network of schools based on the ideals of value-creating education entrusted to him by his predecessors Tsunesaburo Makiguchi and Josei Toda.

Soon, the party arrived at the hotel. Everyone was looking forward to getting some rest, but the reception desk clerk told them they could not check in until noon.

A glum Kiyoshi Jujo broke the news to Shin'ichi: "I'm sorry. I know how tired you must be, but they won't let us check in until this afternoon. I must say they're being very unsympathetic about this."

Shin'ichi smiled and tried to console Jujo: "The hotel has its rules, so it can't be helped. Let's see if we can leave our luggage here. Then we can have breakfast and go sightseeing around the city."

With this, Shin'ichi sent a telegram back to Japan reporting their safe arrival: "ARRIVED SAFELY IN COPENHAGEN. TAKE CARE IN MY ABSENCE. YAMAMOTO."

Shin'ichi had proposed a quick tour of the city so they could visit some of the major stores and see the kind of furnishings available. They hoped to make a number of purchases for the Grand Reception Hall during their stay. After visiting several furniture stores, the party toured various city sites: Copenhagen's Town Hall; a police station; a senior citizens' apartment complex; the Christians-borg Palace, said to be the site of Copenhagen's founding; the Amalienborg Royal Palace; and the statue of the Little Mermaid made famous by the tales of Hans Christian Andersen. On one street corner, they saw a model of Copenhagen as it looked in days gone by.

The countries of Scandinavia are known for their high level of social welfare. The apartments for the elderly they saw in Copenhagen were equipped with amenities far superior to anything available at similar facilities in Japan at the time.

A capital city is the face of a nation; its image reflects that country's culture and politics, and the hearts of its people.

As he made his way around Copenhagen, Shin'ichi silently chanted daimoku with an earnest prayer that in this city, too, Bodhisattvas of the Earth would emerge.

When they returned to the hotel at noon, they could at last check in to their rooms.

*I*N his hotel room, Shin'ichi immediately began writing letters to his fellow members in Japan. A short while later, the other leaders in the party came to his room. Someone informed him that Keizo Shioda, chief of the young men's division second corps of the Chugoku region in Japan, was in Copenhagen on business. He had just phoned asking if he might come by to see them.

Shioda worked as an engineer at Yahata Iron Manufacturing Plant in Hikari City, Yamaguchi Prefecture. He had gone to Paris with his plant manager to attend a steel industry conference, and had made a brief stopover in Copenhagen on his return trip to Japan.

"You mean he's managed to squeeze time from his busy travel schedule to go out of his way to meet me?" Shin'ichi asked. "Isn't his spirit wonderful?"

Shin'ichi had had hardly any time to relax since leaving Japan. Given his fatigued state, he really needed to get some rest. But it was far more important to him to meet with this young man and wholeheartedly encourage him.

"Let's all give Mr. Shioda a warm welcome!" Shin'ichi told the others.

But Kawasaki broke in, "Mr. Yamamoto, I think it would be better if you had a good rest before seeing people." As a doctor, he was worried about Shin'ichi's health.

"I appreciate your concern, but I'm fine," Shin'ichi said. "It's my mission to dedicate my life for the members and for kosen-rufu. The [Japanese] word for mission also means to use one's life. Without such a firm resolve, we cannot be Soka Gakkai leaders."

These words made a profound impression on Eiji Kawasaki. Though he respected Shin'ichi as Soka Gakkai president, being still new to faith he did not yet fully understand the Gakkai spirit nor appreciate the depth of Shin'ichi's consideration for the members. As a doctor, Kawasaki knew the meaning and joy of working for others. But when he asked himself whether he had really been thinking of others as he pursued his medical career, he wondered if he hadn't given greater priority to serving his own academic interests. Faced with Shin'ichi's selfless example, he could not help feeling ashamed.

"I've just thought of something," Shin'ichi then said. "I'd like to present Mr. Kawasaki with the Soka Gakkai's gold pin."

Shin'ichi took out a small pin from his briefcase and personally affixed it to the lapel of Kawasaki's suit.

"This is the pin worn by top Gakkai leaders," he explained. "I hope that you will strive in faith here in Europe with the same sense of awareness and commitment."

Kawasaki's eyes blurred with tears.

WHEN Keizo Shioda arrived a short time later, the group greeted him warmly.

"It's good to see you," Shin'ichi said. "We don't get much of a chance to meet in Japan, so I'm really glad we can do so here."

Shioda was usually so busy with work that he could not participate in activities as freely as he wished. "I'm very sorry for the concern I've caused you through my inability to attend meetings in Japan," he apologized.

"That's all right," Shin'ichi replied. "I understand how demanding your job is. You just have to make sure that in your heart you never become estranged from faith. It's also important, as you're doing right now, to meet me or one of your seniors in faith when you have some free time.

"I also have mountains of work to do and a limited time to do it. So I'm always careful not to waste even a second. For instance, just before you arrived, I was writing letters to members in Japan."

On the table, Shioda saw about twenty completed letters and postcards. A flame of courage arose in his heart.

He wasn't the only one who was busy, Shioda realized. President Yamamoto was far busier, yet he was struggling so hard. Shioda resolved that he, too, must challenge himself.

Shioda was not the only one impressed by Shin'ichi's actions. Eiji Kawasaki, too, was deeply moved by how the Soka Gakkai president was dedicating his life to encouraging the members.

Shin'ichi continued: "Life may seem long, Mr. Shioda, but it is actually very short. Our youth, especially, passes by in the twinkling of an eye.

"The Soka Gakkai is now looking toward the future, aiming for dynamic growth. The time has come to engage in an all-out struggle for kosen-rufu. The time is now. If you wait fifty years before deciding to really challenge yourself, you'll be unable to contribute anything of great consequence. The Daishonin writes, 'Do not spend this life in vain and regret it for ten thousand years to come' (MW-5, 173).

"I know you must be busy at work and under lots of pressure, but now is the time to act. Please put your creativity and imagination to work and find ways to make a contribution that you and no one else can. Through such efforts, you will not only forge inner strength and a fine character — you will amass eternal good fortune."

Sensing Shioda's seeking spirit, Shin'ichi had taken the liberty to speak to him frankly, hoping to inspire in him an even deeper conviction.

KEIZO Shioda accompanied Shin'ichi and his party on their shopping trip for furnishings for the Grand Reception Hall. They spent a great deal of time scrutinizing candlesticks, desks, chinaware and other items.

When they came upon a shop that had some beautiful ornamental plates on display, Shin'ichi went in and bought some.

"Are these souvenirs for people back home?" one of the group asked.

"Yes, they are," Shin'ichi said. "Shortly before she died, Mrs. Miyoko Shibayama of Kyushu told me that she had always dreamed of going to Europe to spread the Daishonin's Buddhism."

Miyoko Shibayama was the women's division chief of the Kyushu First General Chapter, who had died suddenly of a heart attack four months earlier.

"But she passed on before realizing that dream," Shin'ichi continued quietly. "I truly wish she could have accompanied us to Europe. Because she couldn't, I want to at least take back to her children some small mementos from the continent their mother so longed to visit.

"Many tend to forget the dead. But I can never forget the friends who have fought by my side and shared my trials and hardships — all the more so if they have left family behind. I shall always support and encourage those families warmly, as long as I live. I am always praying for their happiness. The Gakkai, after all, is a world of genuine sincerity and humanity."

One young man on the trip was Fumiaki Sugai, chief of the editorial division of the *Seikyo Graphic* and a reporter for the *Seikyo Shimbun*. As if it had just occurred to him, he asked Shin'ichi, "Is that why you held a youth division memorial service in September?"

On September 11, Shin'ichi had conducted a service for those who had died while still young in the course of the kosen-rufu movement, offering encouragement to their bereaved families.

"Yes, that is why," Shin'ichi answered. "They're our noble and precious comrades. We who dedicate our lives to kosen-rufu will always remain together throughout the three existences. Our friendship is everlasting, transcending life and death. We are an eternal family, linked by the Mystic Law.

"The bonds within the Soka Gakkai are strong precisely because they are based on this spirit. In today's world, only the Soka Gakkai can forge such genuine heart-to-heart bonds among people. Don't you think that one important challenge of the Seikyo Press, in addition to reporting on events and meetings, will be to convey and give expression to this beautiful realm of the heart in the Soka Gakkai?"

Sugai nodded in agreement.

*I*T was getting dark. Shin'ichi handed Keizo Shioda two of the plates he had just bought. "I would like to give one of these to you as a memento of our meeting today," he said, "and the other, I'd like to present to your plant manager who is traveling with you."

Shioda was surprised and humbled. "Thank you very much," he said, "for thinking not only of me but of my manager!"

Responsible for the Soka Gakkai, Shin'ichi wanted to show his gratitude to Shioda's boss, who was responsible for taking care of the young man at work.

After their shopping, Shin'ichi and his party said goodbye to Shioda in front of the hotel. That night, Shin'ichi was totally exhausted. During a meal with the others, he had to leave the table several times to get some air. He was not feeling well at all.

In his hotel room, Shin'ichi asked Eiji Kawasaki if it would be possible to have a vitamin injection to improve his strength. But, unfortunately, Kawasaki was carrying neither vitamins nor a syringe with him.

The next morning, they started early and spent a very hectic day. The group left for Düsseldorf, West Germany, the following morning. The flight took two hours.

The weather in Copenhagen had been fair, but as their plane neared Düsseldorf, clouds began to gather and thicken. Shin'ichi and the others started to worry about being unable to land at Düsseldorf Airport. They had heard it was not uncommon for flights to the area to be turned back because of bad weather.

But their plane eventually began its descent. The roads below glistened, apparently wet with rain. On landing, they saw the rain had stopped, and sunlight was streaming from between the clouds. Shin'ichi was thankful for the favorable weather.

Several people awaited them at the airport. The daughter of Kiyoshi Ozawa, a lawyer and friend of Josei Toda, had come to greet them with her husband. The couple lived in Germany, where the husband had been sent by his company. Another couple on hand to welcome them was a Japanese woman and her German husband, who lived in the West German city of Mannheim. She had joined the Soka Gakkai only three months earlier. Finally, there was Ichiro Karasawa, an employee of a Japanese electric company, who was in Düsseldorf on business.

WEST Germany was recovering spectacularly from its wartime devastation. Construction was taking place throughout Düsseldorf, and the people looked lively and positive. At a meeting of the Suiko-kai, Josei Toda once said: "Just look at the reconstruction of West Germany. Japan must learn from West Germany." Considering that it was only sixteen years since its defeat in the war, the country had made a remarkable recovery.

Shin'ichi invited Ichiro Karasawa and the couple from Mannheim to the hotel. Because the woman was the first Soka Gakkai member in Germany, Shin'ichi considered her role particularly important. He presented her with a special *fukusa*[1] and listened intently to everything she had to say. He encouraged her from the depths of his heart with the spirit of treasuring each encounter as one that might never come again.

"I know how isolated and lonely you must feel with no other members around," Shin'ichi said. "But now that you're practicing this Buddhism, you should take it as your personal mission to work toward kosen-rufu and steadily increase the number of members here, even by only one or two."

Shin'ichi continued to guide her with utmost sincerity. She had only joined the Soka Gakkai a short while before, but if she could stand up and take initiative, her efforts would pave the way to a promising future. Of course, even with the most sincere encouragement, it doesn't always happen that a person will rise to the challenge. It is actually quite rare for a person to be truly inspired and to develop as one might hope. Nevertheless, it is a leader's responsibility to maintain the conviction that each member is a Bodhisattva of the Earth and a person with great potential, and to spare nothing to encourage that person. Such consistent and repeated effort will lead to the development of truly capable people.

When their guests had departed, Shin'ichi and his party went out to have a look around town. Acting as their guide and interpreter was a middle-aged Japanese man, an employee of a Japanese firm living in West Germany, who had been introduced to them by a fellow member.

Düsseldorf, which spreads along the Rhine River, was the commercial center of the northwestern region of West Germany. Behind it lay the huge industrial area of the Ruhr.

The German poet Heinrich Heine was born in Düsseldorf, while composers Brahms, Schumann and Mendelssohn grew up there. The beautiful streets were lined with sycamores and horse chestnuts, adding to the city's distinctive cultural flavor. In the Marktplatz, the square beside the Town Hall, was a bronze statue of a man astride a horse.

The guide explained: "This is an early eighteenth-century statue of Johann Wilhelm, a feudal lord who once ruled this area. To the local people, he is known affectionately as 'Jan Wellem.'"

JOHANN Wilhelm ruled well and adopted excellent policies. He was an elector palatine — a leading secular prince of the Holy Roman Empire who was entitled to elect the emperor. Wilhelm built an opera house, supported court artists and musicians and promoted the arts. He also published regular newspapers and introduced street lighting to the region. It is said that the street lights he installed outnumbered those in Paris at the time.

Tradition has it that he cared so deeply about his subjects that he often went out among them, conversing happily while sharing drinks with them.

The bronze statue in the Marktplatz [completed in 1711] was commissioned by the elector himself who entrusted the task to Gabriel de Grupello, a famous sculptor of the time.

Looking at it, the guide said: "Let me tell you an interesting story about this statue: When it was about to be cast, there was not quite enough bronze. Hearing this, the townspeople went to their homes and brought back their own bronze utensils, which they gladly donated to complete the statue. They were all proud of Johann Wilhelm and loved him dearly.

"People were excited and pleased when the statue was completed. Seeing it standing there shining in the sun, many praised it. But some did not like the statue. These people had hoped to be commissioned to build the statue themselves and were jealous of Grupello's work. Envious and selfish, they began to find fault with the statue, saying things like, 'The horse doesn't look powerful enough,' 'The shape of Johann Wilhelm's nose isn't right,' and 'The boots are wrong.'

"Although most people could not really tell whether these criticisms were valid, they were made with such vehemence that praise for the statue stopped altogether.

"Grupello, with his apprentices, then built a wooden wall around the statue and disappeared inside, from where the sounds of hammering and planing began to emerge, giving the impression of a work in progress. A few weeks later, the wall was removed. This time, there was no criticism. Those who had berated the statue before, now joined the rest of the citizens in commending it.

"Wilhelm asked Grupello, 'Which part of the statue did you change?' Grupello replied, 'It is impossible to make changes to a bronze statue once it has been cast. It is as it was before. I am sure this will give you some idea of the motives of those who criticized it initially.'"

O N hearing this, Shin'ichi said: "That is a great story. When it comes to how society evaluates things, this is often the pattern. The Gakkai, too, has frequently been subjected to groundless, irrational criticism. Of course, this criticism has been spread deliberately by those who are jealous or afraid of the progress our organization has been making. When one segment of the media starts criticizing the Soka Gakkai, others tend to follow without attempting to check the validity of the stories. Even those who know the Gakkai well and think highly of it often dare not voice their support under such circumstances.

"One cannot accomplish anything of substance if swayed by such criticism, which is as capricious as smoke changing directions with the wind. I am convinced that the true worth of the Soka Gakkai will be appreciated in 100 or 200 years. History will prove this."

The party moved from the Marktplatz to the banks of the Rhine. There Shin'ichi gathered a few pebbles. To signify the worldwide propagation of the Daishonin's Buddhism, small stones from all parts of the world were to be buried in the concrete foundation of the main pillars of the Grand Reception Hall at the head temple. After gathering the pebbles, they stood by the riverside for a while.

One of the party, Akira Kuroki, a young men's division leader, asked Shin'ichi, "Doesn't looking at the Rhine remind you of the song 'Lorelei' by Heine?"[2]

Kuroki was a tan, strong, athletic young man — but he was also a man of letters, a graduate of English Literature from Waseda University with a good command of the English language.

Shin'ichi nodded and said: "Yes, it does. Although the setting for 'Lorelei' is further up the Rhine, the river certainly inspires a poetic feeling. I would like very much to visit the site of the Lorelei legend one day — although we don't have time on this occasion. Did you know, by the way, that during Hitler's rule, the songwriter of 'Lorelei' was listed as 'Anonymous'?"

Kuroki, astonished, said: "What! Such a famous song. Why was that?"

"Because Heine was of Jewish descent," Shin'ichi explained. "The Nazis banned everything related to the Jews or Judaism, including all Jewish achievements in literature and the arts. Of course, 'Lorelei' was too well known to be obliterated. Still they erased Heine's name from the work in an attempt to hide his achievement forever."

THE light of the setting sun shimmered on the Rhine's surface. Shin'ichi, looking serious, said emphatically: "Expunging the author's name from 'Lorelei' was just a tiny episode in the Nazis' persecution of the Jews. It is said some 6 million Jews were killed in Germany and in the regions invaded by the Nazis."

All listened intently, their expressions growing serious as the conversation turned unexpectedly to the Nazis' persecution of the Jews.

Hitler had maintained a seething hatred for the Jews from the beginning of his political career.

In 1919, in what is regarded as his first political statement, he wrote, "The ultimate aim of anti-Semitism must unalterably be the complete removal of the Jews."[3]

Also, in his autobiography *Mein Kampf* (My Struggle), he roundly condemned the Jewish people, saying: "We are facing the question [of the Jewish problem] without whose solution all other attempts at a German reawakening or resurrection are and remain absolutely senseless and impossible."[4]

Even as late as April 1945, when Germany's defeat was imminent, Hitler praised himself for the genocide: "National Socialism can justly claim the eternal gratitude of the people for having eliminated the Jew from Germany and Central Europe," he wrote.[5] Having killed several million innocent people in the hellish slaughter that was the Holocaust, he brazenly made such a statement with no sign of conscience or remorse.

Adolf Hitler was born in April 1889 in Austria, as a minor customs official's son. His father died when he was 13, and his mother when he was 18. He went to Vienna hoping to become an artist, but failed. To dodge military service, he emigrated to Munich in 1913 but later volunteered to serve in the German army with the outbreak of World War I. After the war, he joined the German Workers Party, a tiny reactionary political party in Munich.

Hitler proved a talented agitator, skillfully playing on the people's discontent, and he quickly rose to power in his party as he expanded its size and influence. He continued to strengthen his standing and influence in the party, soon renaming it the Nationalist Socialist German Workers Party (NSDAP, from which the term *Nazi* derived), and finally gained unchallenged authority as its leader.

*H*ITLER became chairman of the Nazi party in July 1921. A mere eleven and a half years later, on January 30, 1933, he was appointed chancellor of Germany, which marked the start of the Nazi regime.

A month after a fire engulfed the Reichstag, the parliament building in Berlin, the Nazis took advantage of people's fear and anxiety to lay the blame squarely on a communist plot. Widespread persecution of communists and other groups considered hostile to the Nazis commenced. By skillfully manipulating public opinion to convince the German people that the Nazis were the only force capable of dealing with this national crisis, the party won election to the Reichstag. They then promptly pressured the government into passing a bill that invested Hitler with total authority. Once in power, Hitler lost no time dissolving or banning all other political parties. In August of the following year, he was inaugurated as the *Führer*, or supreme commander, a position which combined the powers of chancellor and president. The Third Reich, the dark age of Hitler's dictatorship, began.

Shin'ichi related these details — the path by which Hitler had risen to power — briefly to the others.

Somewhat perplexed, Akira Kuroki asked: "Why did Germany permit Hitler's dictatorship? At the time, didn't the Germans have the Weimar Constitution, one of the world's most democratic constitutions?"

"Yes, they did," Shin'ichi answered. "That's a very important point." He then related the background of the constitution.

In the final stages of World War I, a revolution broke out in Germany, and Kaiser Wilhelm II was forced to flee the country. Following the collapse of imperial rule and the country's defeat, Germany entered a period of democratic government under the Weimar Constitution (it had been adopted at the city of Weimar). However, long years of feudalistic rule and little experience at being a modern democratic nation meant that the old patriarchal ways of feudal times remained deeply rooted in German society compared to the ideals embodied in the constitution. The people's hearts and minds, in other words, lagged behind the times as far as democracy was concerned.

Germany had also been ordered to pay huge war reparations under the terms of the Versailles Treaty. This put such a great strain on the country's economy that it triggered an economic crisis with crippling repercussions on the people's lives. The year 1923 saw the value of the German mark plummet disastrously. By August, it was an unbelievable 1.1 millionth of its prewar value. By October, it had dropped to a staggering one six-billionth of its original value. The situation was so wretched that a person had to work for two days to earn enough money just to buy a pound of butter. The economy's collapse caused great hardship and suffering.

A MID the dire distress inflicted on the nation by economic chaos, the conservative forces and the masses found an outlet for their grievances in directing their anger and criticism toward the Jews. At that time, the Jews comprised about one percent of Germany's total population, or a little over half a million.

Despite being forced to live a nomadic existence for many centuries, the Jewish people had always protected their own religious community. However, in a Christian society, Jews were regarded as different, alien — they were denied various rights taken for granted by the other citizens. They were discriminated against in almost every aspect of their lives: in the amount of taxes they had to pay, the occupations they could hold and their choice of marriage partners. They were also forced to live in areas separate from other citizens — ghettos outside the city walls.

Over the centuries, the attacks against the Jews were relentless. If an epidemic broke out somewhere, the Jews were accused of poisoning the wells and then slaughtered. Or someone spread the lie that infants were slain in Judaism as sacrificial offerings, and the Jews were again persecuted.

In the face of these unremitting attacks, the Jews could only murmur, "As the sea is deep, so is the suffering of the Jewish people."

It was only around the time of the French Revolution that Jews finally began to gain civil rights. But in Germany, which lagged behind other countries in the formation of a civil society, it was much later, toward the end of the nineteenth century, before the Jews managed to acquire basic civil rights. Even these were fragile, though. Anti-Semites regarded the religious-based community of the Jews as "a state within a state." Their sentiment was: Since the Jews were loyal only to their state within a state, they could not be loyal to a Christian state.

The German Jews were strongly united, yes, but they nevertheless strove with all their might to contribute to the country as German citizens.

The Nazis also propagandized that the Jews, who had been forced to scatter throughout the world, aspired to an international community that transcended the state and that they would unite with Jews wherever they were, thus posing a dangerous threat to the German nation.

Groundless rumors against the Jews were also started when the economy teetered on the brink of ruin, because some Jews were among the top financiers in the country. "The Jews started the war to make money," went the rumors. "The Germans are fighting on the battlefields while the Jews control society from behind the scenes and take a lion's share of the profit." However, more than 100 thousand Jews, some twenty percent of the total Jewish population in Germany then, had fought for Germany in World War I, and twelve thousand of them died in action.

*I*RRATIONAL resentment against the Jews was already running high in Germany when Hitler entered the political limelight.

He claimed that the Aryan people were superior to any other race on earth, with the Germans at the very summit. He called for scrapping the Treaty of Versailles, which he said made slaves of the Germans, and for territorial expansion to secure adequate living space (Lebensraum) for all Germans. At the same time, Hitler maintained that the Jews, whom he condemned as an inferior race whose intermarriage with Aryan people would destroy the purity of Aryan blood, were responsible for the decline of Germany, and he urged their complete expulsion.

Contrary to Hitler's assertions, however, there exist no such clearly defined racial groups as "Jews" or "Aryans."

Hitler's anti-Semitism was simply blatant ethnic discrimination with a political agenda.

Today, Israel's repatriation law defines a Jew as someone born of a Jewish mother or converted to Judaism. Jews are those who embrace a shared body of religious and cultural traditions based on Judaism.

But Hitler insisted that the Jews were not a religious community but a race, and he fabricated all sorts of lies about them. A typical example was that the Jews were trying to take over the German nation. According to Hitler, the Jewish religion was merely a cover for sinister political ambitions — so he was perfectly justified in cracking down on them to crush those ambitions. The Jews, Hitler maintained, were "parasites" who, without doing any work, made a huge profit through their financial power. They were "bloodsuckers" preying on the very lifeblood of the German people. Concerned only with worldly profit, he charged, the Jews single-mindedly sought money and power, and would stop at nothing toward that end. He told the Germans that the Jews were the cause of all their sufferings and unless they were expelled would surely devour Germany as parasites devour the host.

Hitler alleged that a dangerous situation had developed without the German people even being aware of it. Jews, he said, had crept into every field of society — politics, business, the civil service and academia — and were actually already in control behind the scenes. According to Hitler, the Weimar government and the Reichstag were simply pawns, instruments of the Jews.

These claims were nothing but malicious lies and outright fabrications. But their continued repetition amid the prevailing mood of anti-Semitism had a powerful effect on many, giving credence to the saying that "a lie repeated often enough becomes the truth in people's minds."

*H*ITLER had become a slave to the devilish lures of power; he aspired to rule not only all of Germany but all the world. Yet it was the Jews he accused of harboring such intent. This is a common ploy used by unscrupulous leaders wanting to eliminate those who stand in their way: accusing their enemy of what they themselves are guilty of.

But how do Hitler's allegations stand up to the facts?

During the fourteen years leading up to Hitler's rule, only five of the close to 400 cabinet members of the Weimar government, which Hitler had accused of being a Jewish puppet, were themselves Jews. And none remained in office for more than a short time. Thus, there was really no basis at all for the claim that Jews controlled the government.

It was true that some Jews wielded considerable influence in financial circles, but this had a basis in history. During the Middle Ages, Christians were forbidden to engage in money-lending as an occupation. As a consequence, this kind of work was relegated to the Jews who, at that time, were discriminated against in society and could not find other jobs. They had not purposefully entered the field of finance, nor had they any desire to rule society.

And it could not be denied that the Jews had produced many outstanding academicians and artists. Thirty-eight German nationals were counted among the Nobel Prize winners between the time of the award's creation and when Hitler came to power, of which eleven — nearly one-third — were Jews. Among them was Albert Einstein, the acclaimed physicist and originator of the theory of relativity.

This was the fruit of the Jewish tradition of valuing education. For the persecuted and expelled, a good level of education would ensure a livelihood wherever they might have to go. The Jewish people used the relentless

storm of hardships that buffeted them as the motivation to apply themselves, with tenacity and persistence, to learning and self-development.

This tradition of treasuring education was the soil from which a people of great ability emerged, and which enriched not only the lives of the Jewish people but also that of German society and, by extension, all humanity. Hitler's narrow-minded hatred of the Jews denied this spiritual legacy.

Furthermore, Hitler referred to a forged treatise called the Protocols of the Elders of Zion, which was purported by some to be a record of a Jewish conspiracy. Once the Protocols became widely promulgated, he used it to attack the Jews for plotting a "conspiracy to achieve world domination." Slurs made possible by the appearance of documents of mysterious or unknown origin — this is another common device employed by those in power to rationalize unjust oppression. Hitler even had the audacity to declare that the Jews' adamant disavowal of the Protocols was itself proof of the document's validity.

THE press, for the most part, functioned as Hitler's mouthpiece, producing a stream of sensationalist pieces intended to fan the flames of anti-Semitism. These articles were, of course, far removed from the truth.

There was even a macabre joke that circulated at the time attesting to the prevailing state of affairs: A Jewish man sits contentedly reading a Nazi newspaper. Another Jew comes along and inquires, "Why are you reading such a newspaper?" The man replies: "Because the Jewish newspapers only report on how the Jews are being persecuted. This newspaper says we're the richest people of all and that we now rule the world!"

Hitler connected everything he detested or abhorred with the Jews. Democracy, parliamentarianism, liberalism, internationalism and human rights, all of which granted people greater freedom and equality — in his eyes, these were nothing but "tools" devised by the Jews to subjugate the Aryan race.

But where exactly were these powerful Jewish rulers? Ultimately, they existed nowhere but in Hitler's mind. Nevertheless, his delusions, saturated with bigotry and prejudice, took on a mad, reckless momentum of their own. Thus the "Jewish problem" was fabricated and the expulsion of all Jews advocated as the "final solution," culminating in a plan for the mass extermination of the entire Jewish population of Europe in death camps such as Auschwitz.

It was utter madness, an abomination of unprecedented magnitude.

The physicist Albert Einstein opposed Hitler's regime and emigrated to America. In an incisive analysis of the workings of the oppressor's mind, he wrote:

> Hence the hatred of the Jews by those who have reason to shun popular enlightenment. More than anything else

in the world, they fear the influence of men of intellectual independence.... They see the Jews as a nonassimilable element that cannot be driven into uncritical acceptance of dogma, and that, therefore — as long as it exists at all — threatens their authority because of its insistence on popular enlightenment of the masses.[6]

As Einstein points out, despots fear nothing more than the people's enlightenment, knowing it means an end to having things their way. Consequently, those who wield authority will try to eliminate any religion or movement that aims to awaken the people and make them independent. This is a pattern that has remained unchanged through the ages.

*A*S soon as Hitler came to power, as if he had been awaiting the opportunity, he unleashed a torrent of violent persecutions upon the Jews. Naturally, these repressive attacks drew strong international condemnation, eventually leading to a boycott of German goods. The Nazis immediately declared the Jews responsible for this, and launched a boycott of Jewish goods and services within Germany as punishment. One after another, anti-Jewish bills were passed into law. To target the Jews and bring them to bay, the Nazis twisted reason, trampled on the country's democratic constitution and manufactured a spate of reprehensible legislation. In the first five years of the Nazi regime, more than a thousand such laws and regulations were passed.

The Nazis openly restricted the rights of Jewish people to live as German citizens — and even as normal human beings — depriving them of their freedom. They also aimed to strip the Jews of their wealth and destroy their financial power in Germany. In 1938, legislation made it obligatory for all Jews to register their assets and property. The Nazis then set about confiscating Jewish wealth and assets with systematic ruthlessness.

Who was actually preying on the lifeblood of the people? The answer was obvious.

The Nuremberg Laws of 1935 were among the most notorious pieces of anti-Jewish legislation to be introduced and were to have a decisive impact on the fate of Jews in Germany. Under these laws, all Jews were legally classified as members of a separate race subordinate to the German people; they were thus relegated to the status of second-class citizens and deprived of civil rights. The Nazi definition of a Jew at that time was someone with a grandparent who had espoused belief in Judaism. This clearly made a lie of the Nazi insistence that the Jews were a racial group. Ultimately, the Nazi persecution of the Jews involved legalized discrimination against German citizens who believed in a specific religion.

The assassination of a German diplomat by a Jewish youth in November 1938 triggered a huge wave of violence against the Jews throughout Germany. Under the cover of darkness, Jewish shops and synagogues were destroyed and nearly a hundred Jews killed. Another twenty to thirty thousand were arrested and sent off to concentration camps. Because of the amount of broken glass left in the wake of this storm of destruction against Jewish property, the incident came to be known as the Night of Broken Glass (Kristallnacht). It was thus far one of the worst pogroms to be perpetrated against the Jewish people.

All these events took place prior to September 1, 1939, when Germany sparked World War II with its sudden invasion of Poland.

*A*FTER describing Hitler's persecution of the Jews, Shin'ichi added firmly: "What we must not forget is that Hitler, while putting on the appearance of upholding democracy, cunningly inflamed and exploited public opinion to achieve his own ends. People swallowed the propaganda, failing to recognize the real nature of this dictator who epitomized the demonic side of authority. As a result, Germany's Weimar Constitution, which had been regarded as one of the world's most democratic, came to exist in name only. This subversion of democracy holds an important historical lesson."

Kiyoshi Jujo muttered indignantly, "Wasn't there any kind of resistance to these outrages?"

"Of course, some resisted," Shin'ichi said. "But by the time any serious opposition emerged, the Nazis had already grown into a monstrous force that controlled all of Germany. By then, it was too late to mount any meaningful opposition. Most of the German people stood by silently while the Nazis persecuted the Jews. They had little choice but to feign indifference. But by doing so, they effectively condoned the twisted Nazi logic.

"Mr. Makiguchi often said, 'To fail to do good has the same effect as committing evil.' To remain silent when faced with grave wrongdoing is, in effect, the same as participating in that wrong."

While Christian churches in Germany eventually launched strong resistance movements against the Nazis, when they first came into power, the churches, if anything, were cooperative.

Martin Niemöller[7] was a German Lutheran pastor who became a central leader in the anti-Nazi resistance movement. One German intellectual recalls the cleric's reaction to growing Nazi tyranny as follows:

He [Niemöller]…said that, when the Nazis attacked the Communists, he was a little uneasy, but, after all, he was not a Communist, and so he did nothing; and then they attacked the Socialists, and he was a little uneasier, but, still, he was not a Socialist, and he did nothing; and then the schools, the press, the Jews, and so on, and he was always uneasier, but still he did nothing. And then they attacked the Church, and he was a Churchman, and he did something — but then it was too late.[8]

Those who lived through this tragic period could feel with deep bitterness the truth of the following two proverbs: "Resist the beginnings" and "Consider the end."[9]

THE waters of the Rhine turned from a golden hue to deep purple and began to reflect the city lights. Shin'ichi continued, in a soft tone: "To the Jews who had been the targets of Nazi oppression from the very beginning, the true nature of the Nazis must have been crystal clear. To the average German, however, Nazi atrocities were like a fire burning on the opposite bank of a river — until sparks began to fall on their side, it seemed of little consequence. That kind of attitude and perception of events allowed the evil to escalate."

Shoichi Tanida appeared deeply affected by what he had heard, saying, "It seems to me that human beings are incapable of perceiving that persecutions of others may, in turn, also happen to them."

"That may be true," Shin'ichi concurred. "But as prejudice and animosity toward the Jews grew, so did the gap in perception and consciousness between the Jews and the average German about what was going on. This made it easier and more convenient for the Nazis to control the Jews and carry out their persecutions.

"In a sense, the problem lay in the consciousness of the people themselves. Lack of a shared awareness of the danger posed by tyrannical national authorities was one reason why that tyranny could take hold.

"One aim of the Soka Gakkai is to create a solid network of heartfelt understanding and awareness among ordinary people so that this will never happen again."

Nodding, Tanida said: "What you've just said touches on a very important issue, I feel. Though at the present Japan has a good constitution, founded on the ideals of peace and democracy, it is possible that it, too, could be trampled on and undermined in the future."

"Exactly," Shin'ichi said. "Even the Meiji Constitution of 1889 granted some degree of religious freedom, though with certain conditions attached. Why, then, did religious freedom disappear from Japan in recent history? The government insisted that Shinto was not a religion and put Shintoism under protection of the state, which meant it effectively made Shintoism the state religion. Eventually, through the repressive Peace Preservation Law, the government restricted the freedoms of speech and thought. And then, through the Religious Organizations Law, it established regulations controlling religion. Before the Japanese people were aware of it, they suddenly found that they had lost not only their religious freedom, but all freedom. It was like a small leak precipitated the destruction of a dam, and then the entire structure was swept away by its colossal waters.

"We cannot ignore the possibility of such a situation recurring in the future. Evil often tends at first to hide its ruthless nature, masquerading as goodness and justice. That's why we have to take a stand without delay when we become aware of injustice. This is something that we Japanese also must never forget."

A CHILLY wind blew across the Rhine after sunset as the group took a stroll along the riverbank. "Hitler's barbarism ultimately left millions of people dead and inestimable destruction in its wake," Shin'ichi observed. "My heart aches for all who lost their lives. But if the Jews — who experienced the most dreadful suffering of all — cannot win happiness, then where is there any justice in this world?"

Later that evening, the group dined at a riverfront restaurant. Shin'ichi asked their Japanese guide, who was scheduled to accompany them to Berlin the following day, about the situation there.

"Are you sure you want to go to Berlin, Mr. Yamamoto?" the man inquired with some urgency and a look of grave concern.

"Yes," Shin'ichi replied. "It's a main objective of my trip to Europe."

Leaning forward, the guide said: "Frankly, I wouldn't recommend it. It's too dangerous right now. There are reports almost daily in the papers about shooting incidents along the border of East and West Berlin. People trying to escape to the West are being shot by East German soldiers. The surrounding areas are also heavily guarded. Everything is strictly controlled. If you so much as take a picture without following police instructions, it can lead to serious consequences. I'd rather not take you to such a place. That's my honest feeling."

Shin'ichi smiled, but there was vehemence in his reply: "I understand your feelings and very much appreciate your concern. But, as a Buddhist, it is my duty to bring relief to the suffering and work to build lasting peace in this world. I want to stand before the Berlin Wall so that I may etch into my life the tragic reality of a divided Germany. I will pray with all my heart not only for the reunification of Germany, but for an end to the Cold War that now besets the world. With this spirit, I want to begin my journey, and the Soka Gakkai's journey, for peace. I know I'll be putting you to a lot of trouble, but I hope you will understand and accept my request." He then bowed deeply to the guide, who was surprised.

"I understand," the man said. "I'll take you there."

Looking around at the others, Shin'ichi said, "Tomorrow let's raise the curtain on a new phase in our struggle for world peace!"

A T 11:25 A.M. on October 8, the following day, the party left by plane from Düsseldorf for West Berlin. During the flight, Shin'ichi pondered the history that had led to the division of Germany and that of its former capital, Berlin.

After its defeat in World War II, Germany was placed under the control of the four Allied powers: the Soviet Union, the United States, Britain and France. The Soviet Union occupied the eastern zone, comprising almost half of Germany; Britain, the northwest zone; the United States, the southwest; and France, the central-western zone. Germany was thus divided under four separate administrations.

Berlin, the German capital, was also divided into four sections in much the same way as Germany itself. The eastern sector of the city was occupied by the Soviet Union, while the western half was divided into three parts and administered respectively, starting from the north, by France, Britain and the United States. However, a joint-control council, comprising military commanders from the four occupying powers, was responsible for administering matters that affected the whole of Berlin.

Since Berlin was located virtually in the center of the eastern German territory, the Soviets found themselves with an enclave governed by the three Western powers and occupied by those nations' troops in the Soviet zone. This further complicated the problems facing postwar Germany.

The Soviets were carrying out land reform in the German territory under their administration and nationalizing large companies in a transition toward communism. In the zones controlled by the three Western Allies, meanwhile, economic revival was in progress under the Marshall Plan, and a move to unify the zones was under way. These differences in occupation policy only served to deepen the rift between the eastern and western zones, accelerating Germany's move toward an East-West split. The paradigm of a world divided into rival Eastern and Western blocs was now mirrored exactly in the situation in Germany.

In March 1948, the United States, Britain and France, joined by the Benelux countries — Belgium, the Netherlands and Luxembourg — agreed to incorporate the western German territory as a full member of the Western bloc. The three western zones pursued a course of economic integration and, in June, issued a new German mark as their joint currency. The Soviet Union reacted with currency reforms in its own zone and then a blockade closing off all roads, railways and waterways leading from the western zones of Germany into Berlin through the Soviet-occupied eastern zone. This cut off major supply routes of food and other essential goods from the Western powers to West Berlin.

A DARK cloud of despair hung over West Berlin, where Cold War tensions between East and West now seemed on the verge of erupting into a "hot war." With all land access to Berlin severed by the Soviet blockade, the Western Allies initiated a massive airlift of food and essential supplies into West Berlin. Its blockade now rendered ineffectual, the Soviet Union eventually called it off, but this did not allay the West Berliners' fears.

The people earnestly wished to rebuild their homeland as a single unified Germany. But this was not to be the case.

In 1949, Germany was formally divided into the democratic Federal Republic of Germany (West Germany) and the socialist German Democratic Republic (East Germany). East Berlin became the capital of the latter.

However, it was still possible to travel with relative freedom between the eastern and western sectors of Berlin. Some residents of East Berlin worked in West Berlin, and vice versa.

For this reason, the Western Allies tended to view West Berlin as an important window through which to advertise liberal democracy to the citizens of the communist Eastern bloc. For the Soviet Union, however, this was an intolerable state of affairs. It had launched East Germany as a socialist state, yet here, smack in the middle of Soviet-controlled territory, was a showpiece of capitalist democracy and, worse yet, a base for Western troops.

In addition, people from East Germany were fleeing into the West in ever-increasing numbers. Between 2.5 and 3.5 million people left East Germany from 1949–61. Nearly half of these were people under age 25, which resulted in serious labor shortages in East Germany. Moreover, most of those who left did so via West Berlin, where they applied to a government agency for asylum and were flown into West Germany.

In November 1958, Soviet Premier Nikita Khrushchev thrust a proposal at the West calling for the four occupying powers of Berlin to relinquish control there and withdraw all military forces within six months, thus converting Berlin into a demilitarized free city. But the ultimate goal behind this, it was surmised, was to annex West Berlin to East Germany once the Allied powers stationed there had vacated.

I N June 1961, Soviet Premier Nikita Khrushchev and U.S. President John F. Kennedy met for a conference in Vienna. Here, again, Khrushchev demanded that Berlin be made into a free, demilitarized city. Fundamental differences in the two leaders' positions ultimately ensured that no progress was made on the Berlin issue.

In a speech he delivered on July 25, Kennedy called for maintaining the occupation rights of the three Western powers in Berlin and declared his intention to defend West Berlin from the threat of Soviet takeover at all costs. He declared that the zone had a significance far more important to the Western Allies than as merely a showcase for freedom and an escape route from East Germany's communist regime.

At a meeting in Moscow on August 3, a little more than a week later, the heads of the Warsaw Pact nations decided to close the border between East and West Berlin in the same manner they did their national borders. This opened the way for the construction of the Berlin Wall.

Beginning in the predawn hours of Sunday, August 13, 1961, and on into the early morning, scores of troops from the East German army and police gathered along the eastern side of the border between the two sectors of Berlin, arriving in a convoy of tanks, armored cars and trucks. Under the cover of darkness, they swiftly began erecting a barricade of barbwire along the boundary. They also blocked off the subway routes, railways and roads connecting East Berlin with the Western sectors.

East and West Berlin were now completely divided. Subway trains could run only as far as the border. Cars and pedestrians were allowed to cross at only thirteen locations where checkpoints had been established, including the Brandenburg Gate. East Germans or East Berliners wishing to enter West Berlin were now required to have a special visa from the East German government, while East Berliners were suddenly barred from working in the western sector.

West Berliners could still enter the eastern sector by presenting their identification card at the checkpoint, but West Germans not resident to West Berlin now had to obtain a visa from the East German government to enter, which if granted would be valid for only one day.

The worst, most fearsome tendency of authority had reared its ugly head. The arrogance, hypocrisy and extremism of totalitarian leadership was reigning supreme.

The Berliners were shocked, bewildered and outraged when they learned the border between the Soviet and western sectors had been sealed. Around five thousand West Berliners gathered in protest in front of the Brandenburg Gate, their outrage so intense that they had to be constrained by West Berlin police. An angry crowd also assembled in the streets on the eastern side of the border to stage a vocal protest, which resulted in many arrests.

RESIDENTS of Berlin who had long lived as neighbors now, in just one night, had an immovable wedge driven between them. State authority had savagely severed precious human bonds, as the wall suddenly separated friends, lovers and family members. Shin'ichi's heart ached to think of the suffering this forced division must have been causing the German people.

The fine weather at Düsseldorf Airport gave way to a heavy overcast as their plane approached East Germany.

To Shin'ichi, the clouds seemed to mirror the sorrow and heartache of the people of Berlin.

The plane landed at West Berlin's Tempelhof Airport shortly before 1:00 P.M. It was raining as they headed for their hotel. After meeting briefly to confirm their schedule, they went for a drive around the city.

The sky was dark. It was drizzling as they drove toward a shopping area known by Berliners as the Ku'-damm. It was bustling with life and energy as crowds of people happily shopped and browsed. A little further on, Shin'ichi and his party passed a neoclassical-style church, whose tower was partially shattered. It was the Kaiser Wilhelm Memorial Church, which had been damaged in the Allied bombing during World War II and was preserved in its present state as a reminder of the horror and destructiveness of war.

Soon the group came to a wide thoroughfare named June 17 Street, beyond which was a stone gate in the style of an ancient Greek temple. This was the Brandenburg Gate, which straddled the border between East and West Berlin.

Atop the gate, they could vaguely make out the back of a statue of the goddess of peace riding a Roman chariot driven by four horses. The Brandenburg Gate, which had been built as a gateway of peace at the end of the eighteenth century, had now become a symbol of Cold War division.

When they drove to within 500 or 600 yards of the gate, they came to a barrier in the road. They got out of their cars and stood in the street. A fine mist of drizzle swirled about them, though the sky was beginning to brighten. They were informed that pedestrians were not allowed to go beyond this point, but that foreign visitors were permitted to proceed to within 219 yards of the gate, providing they did so by car and remained inside their vehicles.

THERE was no peace here along the border. British armored vehicles mounted with machine guns roared up and down the road and West German police stood on duty at key places.

On the other side of the Brandenburg Gate, Shin'ichi and the others could make out the forms of East German soldiers. A tense atmosphere pervaded the area.

The sightseers who gathered there all kept their voices low and spoke to one another in whispers.

Shin'ichi and his colleagues decided to proceed by car as close to the gate as possible. On the left-hand side of the gate stood a monument marking the Soviet Union's victory in World War II, alongside which was displayed the first tank reportedly to have entered Berlin. That this monument to a Soviet victory should lie inside the territory of the Western camp only underscored the complexity of the city's partition. Also, in a grove of trees nearby were the tents of the British Army encampment.

As they drew nearer to the Brandenburg Gate, barriers and barbwire spread out all around them. The atmosphere was even more tense. From here, they could clearly see the forms of gun-toting East German soldiers on the other side of the gate. Their guide pointed to a sign on the road written in German and said: "That reads: 'Warning! You are now leaving West Berlin.'"

In the past, no residents of either side of the city would have given much thought to the sign as they made their way back and forth across the border. But now its warning of danger had become very real.

Shin'ichi wished that he could leave the car and stand right under the Brandenburg Gate. But that was not permitted. From the Brandenburg Gate, the party drove on directly to Bernauer Strasse, which was in the French-controlled district of West Berlin and ran along the edge of the border. The buildings on one side of the street belonged to East Berlin but the pavement area immediately in front of them belonged to West Berlin. The windows of these buildings' higher stories were as they had been before the partition, but the entrances and windows on the first and second floors had been closed up with bricks. In front of one such bricked-up doorway lay a huge bouquet of flowers.

Shin'ichi learned from their driver that an old woman had died there after jumping from a fourth-floor window in an attempt to escape to West Berlin. A hundred meters or so further on, they saw another bouquet of flowers lying on the road. Five or six people stood around it looking up at the buildings on the east side of Berlin.

THE driver stopped the car and told the passengers in German: "Several days ago, an East Berliner, attempting to escape, fought off the East German police on the roof of this building and jumped. The West Berlin police came quickly to assist him, but he was already dead. Since the wall was erected, incidents like this have been happening with distressing frequency.

"There was one woman who, when the guard's back was turned, passed her baby over the barbwire barrier into the hands of her husband who was in West Berlin. Though she is now separated from her husband and child and forced to remain in East Berlin, she is one of the more fortunate ones — at least she could get her child safely to the West unharmed.

"Another woman escaped from a third-floor window by climbing down a rope. When she reached the ground, her hands and feet were raw and bloodied, having been grazed by the walls of the house on the way down. And there was a man who badly sprained his ankle as he was fleeing. But both of them were lucky that they weren't shot dead.

"Look at the pillar on the corner — you can see a bullet hole there. People trying to flee into the West are being shot dead like animals."

Shin'ichi, listening to the driver through the interpreter, felt his own heart choke with sorrow.

The driver continued: "Granted, Germany lost the war, and we are a defeated nation, but Germans — families and relatives — should have the right to live together. We used to move freely within our country and live together happily...." Tears welled up in the driver's eyes.

"Do you have relatives in East Berlin?" Shin'ichi asked.

"I have an aunt there. She is now elderly. She is my favorite aunt," he said with emotion. The driver wiped the tears from his eyes, took a cigarette from his jacket pocket and lit it.

Shin'ichi and the others decided to get out and look around. As the driver had mentioned, a bullet hole, marked with white chalk, was clearly visible on the concrete pillar at the street corner.

A policeman standing nearby pointed it out to them.

As he gazed up at the bullet hole, Shin'ichi was seized by the feeling that he himself had been shot in the chest.

"How inhumane!" he murmured to himself.

*A*FTER walking a short distance, they came to a brick wall across which it was possible to see inside East Berlin. About twenty or thirty people had gathered there. Now and again, they waved. When Shin'ichi followed their gaze, he saw people at the windows of buildings in the distance. They must have been friends or relatives of those gathered. One instant those distant figures were waving back vigorously, and the next they had disappeared from sight. They probably feared being seen by East Berlin guards. If caught, they could be accused of signaling information to West Berlin.

The reality of the division made a deep impression on everyone in Shin'ichi's party. They were speechless.

At a border pass near Bernauer Strasse, they witnessed several West Berliners asking an East German policeman at a checkpoint to pass a message to an old woman standing alone beyond the boundary. The young policeman accepted their request and gave the old woman the message. Looking back, she nodded many times. Then, an East German soldier, who had been standing nearby and witnessing this exchange, went up to the old woman and ordered her to leave, shooing her away as if she were a dog. The West Berliners kept waving their hands and their umbrellas for a long while — until the old woman was no longer visible. It was a sad, heart-rending scene.

Shin'ichi and his party then traveled along the border by car. The brick and concrete wall continued endlessly. Here and there, people stood in front of it. The wall that blocked their path was only ten or twelve feet high; it could have been knocked down and removed quite easily. Yet this same wall was depriving them of their freedom, tearing apart human relationships, families and fellow citizens. How horrifying is the karma of human beings!

"For what are human beings born?" Shin'ichi cried silently, a powerful indignation burning inside him.

He thought: "People are denied the right to live together and to communicate with one another. Such activities are regarded as an offense. It is tantamount to ordering human beings not to be human. No one has that right.

"Yet the wall was built nevertheless — and built by none other than human beings. Though we may speak of an East–West conflict, ultimately it is the offspring of the

demonic nature of authority breeding in people's hearts. And this tragedy of division has assaulted not only Germany but also the Korean peninsula and Vietnam. And it doesn't stop there. The Holocaust and war in all its shapes and forms, as well as nuclear weapons — these are all products of the evil nature of power."

*S*HIN'ICHI vividly recalled the Declaration for the Abolition of Nuclear Weapons, which contained one of the most important tenets of Josei Toda's spiritual legacy.

"The spirit of that declaration," he reflected silently, "was to 'tear out the talons of the devilish nature latent in human life.' The only force that can conquer that evil is the power of the Buddha nature inherent in the life of each human being.

"The Buddha nature represents a wellspring of compassion; it is the driving force for the creation of peace, moving us from destruction to construction and from division to unity. Kosen-rufu can be called an undertaking that brings the sun of this Buddha nature to rise in people's hearts, dispelling the darkness of the devilish nature and forging unity among people."

Shin'ichi and his party drove back to the section of wall where they could gaze upon the Brandenburg Gate. Once more Shin'ichi got out of the car.

As the party stood taking in the sunset's magic, their driver, who had joined them outside, said with a smile: "When we have a beautiful sunset like this, we say that angels have come down from heaven."

The nearby steeples and buildings, the closed road and the Brandenburg Gate — all were bathed in the brilliant golden rays of the setting sun.

"Once the sun rises and the clouds lift," Shin'ichi mused silently, "everything becomes suffused with golden light. If the sun of life were to shine in people's hearts, the world would definitely be bathed in the light of peace, and a glorious rainbow of friendship would appear over humanity."

Looking up at the Brandenburg Gate, he said with firm conviction to his colleagues: "I am sure that in thirty years this Berlin Wall will no longer stand."

He was not merely making a prediction nor articulating wishful thinking. He uttered these words based on his unwavering confidence that the conscience, wisdom and courage of people dedicated to realizing peace would triumph. It was also an expression of his resolute determination to dedicate his life, even die if need be, for the cause of realizing world peace. Buddhism teaches that one's deep inner resolve can permeate the entire universe.

He vowed in his heart: "I will fight to see the end of this wall. I'll fight for peace. This struggle will entail igniting the same spark or commitment in others and pursuing dialogue to awaken people to their inner humanity. I will dedicate my life to this endeavor."

Shin'ichi faced the Brandenburg Gate and chanted daimoku three times, "Nam-myoho-renge-kyo...." Infused with his deep pledge and determination, his voice resounded in the sunset skies over Berlin.

Note: Passages from the Gosho, the writings of Nichiren Daishonin, are taken from the series *The Major Writings of Nichiren Daishonin*, published by NSIC in Tokyo. For reference purposes, we provide the volume and page number for quotations in the following form: (MW-x, xx). For example (MW-3, 202) would refer to *The Major Writings of Nichiren Daishonin*, volume 3, page 202.

Quotations from the Lotus Sutra are from: *The Lotus Sutra*, trans. Burton Watson (New York: Columbia University Press, 1993). Citations from this work will be given in the text and abbreviated as follows: LS followed by the chapter number, and then the page number. For example (LS2, 34) would refer to chapter 2 of *The Lotus Sutra*: "Expedient Means," page 34.

"Great Light" Notes:

1. *Fukusa*: Squares of cloth for wrapping precious items, such as prayer beads.

2. "Die Lorelei," a poem written by Heinrich Heine in 1824, has been set to music numerous times. The most famous version was written in 1838 by the German composer Friedrich Silcher. The Lorelei is a large echoing rock in the Rhine River near Sankt Goarshausen in the Rhineland–Palatinate, around which a legend was created by the German author Clemens Brentano in his novel *Godwi* (1801). According to this legend, which has become part of German folklore, a maiden threw herself into the river in despair over an unfaithful lover and was transformed into a siren whose song lures sailors to their deaths.

3. Translated from German: Werner Maser, *Hitler's Briefe und Notizen: Sein Weltbild in handschriftlichen Dokumenten* (Hitler's Letters and Notes: His Handwritten Records) (Düsseldorf: Econ Verlag GmbH, 1973), p. 225.

4. Adolf Hitler, *Mein Kampf*, trans. Ralph Manheim (London: Pimlico, 1992), p. 103.

5. *The testament of Adolf Hitler: the Hitler-Bormann documents, February – April 1945*, with an introduction by L.Craig Fraser (Los Angeles: World Service, 1978?), p. 81.

6. *Collier's: The National Weekly*, November 26, 1938.

7. Martin Niemöller (1892–1984): German theologian and pastor. In 1933, he formed the Pastors' Emergency League to combat interference in church affairs by the Nazi Party. He was arrested in 1937 and remained imprisoned in concentration camps until 1945.

8. Milton Mayer, *They Thought They Were Free: The Germans 1933–45* (Chicago: University of Chicago Press, 1955), p. 169.

9. Latin proverbs: *Principiis obsta* and *Finem respice*.